Rethinking Enterprise Software Selection

Stop buying square pegs for round holes

Chris Doig

Published by Wayferry, Inc.
2173 Salk Ave Suite 250
Carlsbad
CA 92008

www.wayferry.com
858.866.9780

ISBN: 978-1979055864

Front cover image credit: Iqoncept from Dreamstime.com

Contents

Then you will know the truth,
and the truth will set you free.

John 8:32

Dedication

For all of you who are tasked with selecting and implementing enterprise software. For all of you, who despite having the best of intentions when doing so, saw the project go horribly wrong anyway. This book is dedicated to you.

Thanks

So many people contributed to this book, and I am grateful to each and every one of them for the role they played.

My wife, Bev, was incredibly encouraging and supportive from start to finish. When the writing took much longer than expected she graciously dealt with having a missing spouse for months on end. As if that weren't enough, she contributed greatly to the content by drawing all the cartoons in this book.

Sean Nolan spent countless hours developing the Wayferry app. I am in awe of his ability to consistently turn functional requirements into code that did more than was expected.

Garrett Colbert provided tremendous encouragement and valuable feedback along the way. In fact, it was Garrett who ultimately got me to take the articles I had written for CIO.com and from them create this book.

And of course, you need editors; mine are Joan Wright and Sheryl Hodge. I thank them both for their contributions. Joan did an excellent job of the first round of editing and really helped get the text to flow properly. Sheryl was my editor at CIO.com when I began writing for them, so it is especially fitting and appreciated that she was a part of this project.

Introduction

In 2011, the Wall Street Journal reported Marc Andreessen as saying that "Software is eating the world." As the inventor of Mosaic, one of the first graphical browsers that led to the internet boom of the 1990s, Marc was well qualified to make this comment.

Six years later, his observation is more accurate than ever. For example, on a personal level, think of your GPS and camera being replaced by phone apps. At the office, think of phone systems and corporate data centers migrating to the cloud. At the company level, think of Borders Books being replaced by Amazon, Blockbuster by Netflix, and taxis by Uber.

So, if software really is eating the world, why do so many organizations get indigestion from major software acquisitions? Why do they usually take longer than planned, cost more than budgeted, disrupt business operations when going live, and seldom meet expectations? Why, when you dig a little, is there so much software buyer's remorse around? This book was written to answer these questions, and to give you the tools to make your next enterprise software purchase successful.

Who should read this book?

- CEOs. Particularly if your job or your company depends on the success of a major software purchase. The larger the purchase, the greater the risk, and the more value this book can provide (See the Finish Line story on page 8 and the FoxMeyer story on page 9).

- CFOs. Because you are responsible for the financial health of your organization. This book provides the tools to estimate the value and viability of a proposed software acquisition. It will help you identify those projects where the groundwork has not been done correctly, before it's too late. Major software purchases are significant investments; therefore it's imperative to discover there is an acceptable return on the investment (ROI) before the project gets underway.

Introduction

- Project sponsors, decision-makers, and line of business management responsible for revenue. You have the business needs for the new software, and have the biggest stake in the project's success.

- CTOs, CIOs, IT directors, and IT project managers who are responsible for providing resources and completing the project on time and within budget. Your reputation and career prospects are enhanced when your software acquisition projects are successful.

- Procurement or purchasing specialists. While you won't be doing much of the work described in this book, you do want to ensure your organization stays in control of the purchase. You should pay attention to purchasing software on page 255. In addition, the appendices contain information relevant to procuring the services of consultants.

- Software resellers can use this book under the following circumstances:

  o Enterprise software is complicated. When your customers don't know how to select software they won't purchase because they are rightly afraid of the consequences of a wrong decision. By following the process outlined in this book, your customers will develop the confidence to make the purchase. Chapter 5: Select Software for Value, Not Price on page 81 is a great place for these customers to start.

  o This book can help your customers avoid falling for the "latest shiny object", only to suffer from buyer's remorse because they bought the wrong software.

  o When you are competing with other vendors and want a fair shot at the business, having your customers follow the process outlined in the book helps them avoid falling under the spell of a good salesperson only to find the software doesn't meet their expectations.

  o If you refer your customer to a book like this you are perceived as acting in their interests rather than your own.

- Anybody who wants to learn more about selecting enterprise software. This book is a new way of looking at the software selection process, and the ideas presented here are sure to stimulate your thinking.

What you will learn

Most people totally underestimate what is involved in making a successful software purchase. City of San Diego CIO Johnathan Benkhe observes "the larger the organization the more chaotic the approach to selecting enterprise software."

A little internet research about enterprise software selection will turn up a lot of information. Unfortunately, much of the advice offered is too high-level to be useful, and some of it is simply wrong. This book will help you make successful software purchases by describing what to do, how to do it, and why it works. This is not academic theory; it is actionable advice, developed via multiple evaluations in the field. Understanding why it works is critical as it allows you to modify the process in order to meet your specific needs.

In this book, you will learn two critical things:

- How to select software that fits your needs like a "glove fits your hand."
- How to reduce implementation risks so the new software goes live on time, within budget and with minimal business disruption.

What more could you ask from your next enterprise software purchase?

How should you read this book?

This book can be read from start to end, which covers all the steps of the process. However, it is divided into sections that will allow you to go directly to the topic you seek information on at any time.

- To understand why so many organizations struggle with enterprise software purchases, start with Chapter 1: The Software Purchasing Problem on page 5, which opens by defining the problem of both outright and partial software acquisition failures. Chapter 2 on page 19 explains why selecting software is so difficult. Chapter 3 on page 39 highlights the risks faced when making major software purchases, and suggests mitigation strategies. *(Note: There is intentional repetition in the first four chapters in order to present certain information from different perspectives.)*

- If you are concerned with the business and financial value of a software purchase, start with Chapter 4: The Benefits of Best-Fit Software on page 73, which explains why it is worth making the effort to select best-fit software. Chapter 5: Select Software for Value, Not Price on page 81 describes how to estimate the ROI for a software purchase so that you can buy on value. You might also find Chapter 3: Software Selection Risks and Mitigation on page 39 helpful.

- If you are concerned with how a major software purchase should be aligned with organizational vision and strategy, start with Chapter 6: Software Strategy on page 106.

- If you are concerned with managing a software selection project, start with Chapter 7: Project Management on page 117. Chapter 8: Software Selection Toolbox on page 153 lists tools and resources invaluable in the selection process.

- If you want to jump right in and start with a software selection project, begin with Chapter 9: Requirements on page 165, and continue through to Chapter 12: Post Purchase. Chapter 13 on page 277 summarizes the entire selection process.

- If you are in procurement, you might want to start with Chapter 11: Selection and Purchase on page 242. Pay attention to Purchasing software on page 255, which lists some of the many contractual techniques vendors use to maximize revenue extraction from their customers. You might also want to read Chapter 5: Select Software for Value, Not Price on page 81.

- If you are a software reseller, Chapter 5: Select Software for Value, Not Price on page 81 is a great place for your customers to start. If your software will deliver outstanding value, you want your customer to know it because that helps you to close your sale. You can also point them to Chapter 6: Software Strategy on page 106, and especially to the section on the costs of not upgrading enterprise software on page 112.

Disclaimer

Nothing in this book is to be construed as legal advice.

Chapter 1.   The Software Purchasing Problem

According to some industry pundits, only about 10 percent of major software purchases meet expectations, while the remaining 90 percent experience some degree of failure. Why, after decades of purchasing software, does this still happen and what can be done about it?

We begin with several definitions. Then we examine the three kinds of pain that occur when these software purchases go wrong. This chapter concludes with a list of costs incurred when the new software does not fully meet expectations.

Major software purchases defined

A major software purchase is one that costs an organization a significant fraction of their annual revenue. Alternatively, the software will have a major monetary impact on the organization, for example allowing it to enter a lucrative new market.

Software success defined

A successful enterprise software purchase is defined as one that meets two goals:

- The selected software fits organizational needs like a "glove fits your hand." In other words the software fully meets the expectations of users and management.

- The implementation of the new software is on schedule, within budget, and it goes live with minimal disruption to the business.

If your new software meets the above two goals, you have hit the ball out of the park!

IT often views success as on time and on budget, but that is only part of the equation. The software must also meet the needs and expectations of the business. For example, a new CRM that was delivered on time and within budget would meet the IT department's standard for success. However, if it was rejected by the sales team it would ultimately be considered a failure.

Software failures defined

When a software implementation runs into trouble, purchasing organizations tend to blame anybody but themselves. However, the root cause of their buyer's remorse is invariably a poor evaluation and selection process.

While more egregious software failures are published, especially when they end up in court or involve public money, partial failures are far more common and much less visible. People do not like talking about what didn't work; however, denial will only lead to continued failures. It's important to recognize what went wrong so you can learn how to fix things going forward.

Partial software failures

Benign failures: The software takes longer to implement than planned but performs as expected in production.

- Implementation and other costs exceed the budget.
- The ROI on the new software is delayed.
- External deadlines may be missed, triggering financial penalties.
- Market opportunities may be missed, e.g. not being ready for holidays.

Moderate to severe failures: In addition to the above.

- Normal business operation is significantly disrupted when the software goes live, and there is a negative fiscal impact.
- Anticipated functionality is missing, meaning more work than expected.
- Cost savings do not materialize.
- The ROI is well below that used to justify the purchase.
- User and management expectations are not met.
- Employees may lose their jobs.

Complete software failures

Functional failures: The software goes into production, but is never a success. After struggling to use it for a few years, the decision is made to replace it.

Partial production: Some modules make it into production, but not all. A decision is made to abandon the software before it is fully deployed.

Never implemented: So many problems are encountered when implementing the new software that it never gets into production.

Ultimate fail: The failure of the new software causes a company to go bankrupt.

> *Porteous Fasteners imported and distributed construction and industrial fasteners in the U.S. and Canada. Founded in 1966 in the Los Angeles area, they grew to 16 locations and 250 employees. Porteous implemented a new warehouse management system and within about a year the company abruptly failed. Their assets were acquired by Brighton-Best International for pennies on the dollar.*

Software purchase pains

When a major software purchase does not meet expectations, it causes business and technical pains for an organization, and personal pains for the people involved.

Business pains

CEOs, CFOs, line of business management, and project sponsors are concerned about software purchasing pains because they directly affect the revenue and profits.

1. Implementation delays

The software implementation took much longer than scheduled and business plans had to be put on hold. In addition, there was the hidden cost of a delayed ROI.

2. Unexpected implementation costs

Because implementation took so much longer than planned, costs were much higher than budgeted.

3. Normal business disrupted upon going live

When the new software went live, it did not work as expected. This kind of disruption can have a severe impact on the business.

> *In January, 2016 Finish Line CEO Glenn Lyon said that business was severely disrupted by the implementation of a new warehouse and order management system. Finish Line had trouble filling online orders and replenishing stores that cost $32 million in lost sales in the previous quarter (about 8 percent of the company's revenue), and this caused an 11 percent drop in stock price. The poor software implementation cost CEO Glenn Lyon his job. In addition, a year later Finish Line was closing about 150 of its 617 retail stores.*
>
> *Finish Line had underestimated the challenge of the project, and especially the level of change management in moving from the old system to the new. There was inadequate training for associates and supervisors on the floor to help when ramping up the new system and too much trust was placed in the software vendor and the implementation consultants.*
>
> *(See: Supply Chain Digest article by Dan Gilmore, March 10, 2016)*

4. Unrealized cost savings

One reason for purchasing the new software was to cut costs, but after going live and allowing for things to settle down, costs did not decrease as expected.

5. Low ROI

The value of software is realized in the value of the benefits that flow from using that software. The ROI was estimated before making the purchase, but now that the software is in production it becomes clear the value of the benefits is far less than was expected.

6. Missed business opportunity

The new software was supposed to help the business "kick it up a notch," but it did not deliver. A strategic business opportunity was squandered.

7. Unmet expectations

There were lofty expectations of the new software, but after going live, these expectations have been unfulfilled.

8. Software failure

New software does not always perform as expected. For example, difficulties with the implementation may cause the software to be abandoned before going into production. Alternatively, the organization may struggle with the new software for a few years and then decide to replace it. Regardless of the circumstances, software failures are very expensive mistakes.

9. Business failure

The ultimate software failure is when a major software purchase drives a company into bankruptcy.

> *FoxMeyer Drugs was a $5 billion U.S. pharmaceuticals distributor. With razor thin margins, they wanted to use ERP software to increase operational efficiency. The project quickly ran into trouble. Although there was extensive executive support, support by warehouse employees was lacking because they feared the loss of their jobs. The project scope was too large in that it included both ERP and warehouse automation. There was a lack of experienced staff both inside Fox-Meyer and with Andersen Consulting, who was responsible for the implementation. Three years after purchasing the software, FoxMeyer filed for bankruptcy. The software purchase had caused the business to fail.*
>
> *(See The FoxMeyer Drugs' Bankruptcy: Was it a Failure of ERP? By Judy E Scott.)*

Technical pains

10. Unmet vendor promises

During the sale, vendors misrepresented their software or made promises they did not keep. After the purchase, little can be done.

> *NetSuite faced a lawsuit from a skin care product retailer that alleges an overzealous salesperson led them to buy software that utterly failed to meet their needs. SkinMedix had outgrown its website and shopping cart platform and was looking for a replacement that could manage both sales and back-office functions. Its existing system was managing an inventory of 3,000 products, but SkinMedix needed something that could eventually handle a 20,000-item inventory.*

> *It quickly became apparent that NetSuite's system was incapable of delivering as promised. NetSuite also failed to meet the deployment deadline, according to SkinMedix. Because the salesperson had misrepresented NetSuite's capabilities, SkinMedix had spent more than $250,000 on a "manifestly unusable" website, the lawsuit stated.*
>
> *(From an IT World article written by Chris Kanaracus)*

11. Poor functional fit

When an organization outgrows and replaces existing software, the new software is acquired for enhanced functionality. If there is a poor functional fit, that new software will not work as expected. Going live can seriously disrupt normal business operations.

> *Mega transportation company JB Hunt purchased the Mojo Route Optimization Software and Carrier Management System Software from MercuryGate. Two years after it was supposed to go live the software was still not in production. This prompted JB Hunt to file suit for $3.1 million because the software failed to meet the functionality agreed upon by the two parties. According to court documents, JB Hunt says the software "is virtually useless," save for 1 percent of its brokerage business. You have to wonder how JB Hunt selected the software in the first place.*
>
> *(www.overdriveonline.com/jb-hunt-hits-trucking-software-provider-with-3-1-million-lawsuit)*

12. Poor usability

Poor software usability causes multiple pains:

- It takes users longer than necessary to enter data. The workflow may be illogical, there may be unnecessary steps and screens, expected features may be missing, and tasks may take too many mouse clicks to complete.

- Data may not be captured. For example, salespeople struggling with a CRM system may skip some data entry because it is too much effort.

- There is an increase in data capture error rates because the user interface works against rather than for the user.

- Extracting useful information from the software may be so difficult that it is not done, leading to poor business decision making.

- There is an increase in user training costs.

In general, legacy software usability is inferior to modern, innovative software.

13. Unhappy users and a lack of buy-in

The new software does not perform as expected. Many tasks that were easily done with the old system are now more work. Most users have little interest in the new software, and some advocate returning to the old system. Other users simply refuse to use the new system at all, and when some of those users are in senior management, the entire project is at risk.

14. Inadequate vendor support

When seeking technical support after the purchase you discovered the vendor cannot provide the level of support that was expected.

15. Software bugs

When software is being implemented, there may be many more bugs than were expected. This problem can happen when a vendor added new features to entice the sale of the product, but those features were never tested or used by actual users/customers. It can also happen with smaller, innovative vendors who are pushing cutting-edge technology. Bugs slow down implementation, disrupt the business after going into production, or even prevent the software from going into production in the first place.

A major company in the entertainment field based in Maryland had almost 5,000 employees in the U.S. They were using Lotus Notes email and had a problem with file attachments causing mail files to grow by about 100 percent every 12 months. To decrease the need for new storage they purchased a software tool to de-duplicate file attachments. That tool reduced the growth of mail files to about 25 percent annually. Even though it was from a major vendor, the software was full of bugs. After trying to resolve these problems for a year, the software was still too buggy to release to general production. (At that point, a new CEO decided to switch the company to Microsoft Outlook and Exchange, so the problem went away.)

Personal pains

16. Personal reputation and career collateral damage

The new software promised so much yet delivered so little. This failure tarnishes the reputations and careers of all involved.

17. Impact on income

New software that fails to meet expectations can mean reduced bonuses and promotion denials. In extreme cases, you can lose your job.

> *Sports apparel company Finish Line experienced a software disaster when a new warehouse and order management system caused a $32 million drop in sales in one quarter. Both the CEO Glenn Lyon and Chief Supply Chain Officer Dan Marous found themselves without jobs because of this debacle.*

18. Loss of discretionary time

Problems caused by delays and disruption to normal business operations after the software goes live take time to resolve. Much of this time affects your personal life; you'll end up working overtime and weekends, and will likely have to cancel any planned vacation time.

19. Increased job stress

Implementation delays, excessive costs, business disruption, and unhappy users who do not hesitate to let you know how they feel. These all contribute to an increase in job stress for everybody involved with the new software.

The costs of poor software purchases

A successful software purchase is one that meets or exceeds the expectations for all parties involved. However, when the software experiences a partial or complete failure, many of the costs below can be incurred. Some of these costs are obvious, others not as much, and there may still be others not listed that apply to your specific situation. Like many other facets of business, doing the work up front reduces overall costs. If you take short cuts when purchasing software, you will pay the price later.

Chapter 1: The Software Purchasing Problem

1. Business disruption costs

Any major enterprise software change disrupts business to some extent while employees take time to learn the new system. A functional mismatch caused by selecting software that is not the best match for the needs amplifies this disruption cost.

2. Costs of delayed ROI

All major software purchases are made with the expectation of an ROI. When the implementation takes longer than expected, that ROI is delayed, which is a hidden cost. For example, if the software ROI was expected to be $1 million annually and implementation was delayed a year, that is a hidden cost of $1 million.

3. Replacement costs

The most obvious cost of a software selection failure comes from replacing that newly purchased software with another product. These costs can include early termination penalties if multi-year cloud or maintenance contracts were signed.

> *Mindful of "lessons learned" from the county's $30 million ERP failure, Marin County officials spent a further $1 million on consulting, and then negotiated a new software systems contract with Tyler Technologies for a total of $14 million. At the end of the day Marin County had spent about $45 million on software that cost $14 million to purchase and implement.*
>
> *(San Rafael Patch, Dec 12 2014: Marin County Green Lights $14 Million Software Agreement)*

4. Dual systems costs

When new software moves into production, the old system often runs in parallel for a short while. It may then be maintained for reference purposes, or decommissioned.

However, if the new system does not properly meet needs, the old system may stay in production until those problems are resolved. In addition to duplication of costs (admin, backups, disaster recovery, etc.), data must be entered into both systems and kept synchronized. The longer the systems run in parallel, the greater the costs.

5. Customization costs

Limitations of the new software can tempt companies to customize the code, especially if they did not select best-fit software. A problem with customizing (as opposed to configuring) is that customizations must be tested and possibly re-written every time the software is upgraded. Every upgrade cycle incurs customization costs, which accumulate during the life of the software and add to the total cost of ownership (TCO).

> *A major Silicon Valley computer hardware company had upgraded from MANMAN to Oracle ERP software. The company had a worldwide presence and tens of thousands of employees. To avoid retraining employees they spent millions of dollars customizing the new software to look and feel like the old.*
>
> *A few years later, they found they could not upgrade to the latest version of Oracle. They first had to spend even more money to undo those customizations, and only then could they upgrade. I worked for this company for a few years while this was going on, but was not involved with the Oracle project.*

6. Upgrade costs

Not entirely understanding their needs, an organization may select the wrong version of the software. After encountering problems, the decision may be made to upgrade to the next product level. With SaaS, this can mean paying for un-needed functionality just to get certain features. For software in the data center, this can mean a complete upgrade. In both cases, these are costs that could have been avoided by selecting the best-fit software option in the first place.

7. Third-party product costs

All software systems have a boundary and need to interface with other systems. It is common to extend core system functionality with third-party add-ons. For example, a company with an extensive field sales force could add an expense-management system to an ERP system. Third-party costs include the product itself, integration, maintenance, and admin costs, and can be substantial.

Problems include disruptions, for example, when there are data discrepancies and synchronization interruptions between the two systems. The organization may be forced to delay upgrades to the core software until a compatible version of a third-party product is available. Third-party vendors tend to be smaller, and there is the risk of them taking a long time to upgrade their product to be compatible with the latest version of the core software. There is also the risk of a small add-on vendor going out of business.

> *I was working for a San Diego-based life science startup in IT Management. We wanted to upgrade the core accounting system, but had to delay the project for more than a year while we waited for the latest version of an add-on product to that accounting system.*

8. Software selection and implementation costs

If the new system fails and the organization decides to restart the project, the software selection and implementation costs will be incurred twice. These costs are not trivial. For example, for purchased software the selection costs can be around 20 percent of the software license cost, while implementation costs can be in the range of 100 percent to 300 percent of the license cost. Costs vary significantly based on the type of software, for example ERP, CRM etc. and whether the software is in the cloud or purchased for the data center.

9. Retraining costs

Adequate end-user training is a critical part of rolling out new software, and economizing on training is a recipe for disaster. If the first product fails and new software is purchased, there are the direct costs for a second round of training. There is also the cost of training fatigue. Employees have too much to absorb, morale sinks and user errors increase.

10. Unsatisfied requirements costs

All major software purchases have some degree of compromise and some requirements that remain unsatisfied. The cost of unsatisfied requirements is the cost of doing that work external to the system. It can also be the cost of not doing that work, or doing it inadequately.

For example, suppose there is a report that the system is unable to generate, but it can be created manually with a data export and manipulation in Excel. If that report takes 4 hours to generate every month, and the fully loaded employee cost is $60/hour, the cost of not satisfying the requirements for that one report is almost $15,000 over five years.

When best-fit software is not selected the cost of all significant requirements that are not satisfied can be substantial. This hidden cost does not appear on income statements, but it is incurred every year the software is used.

11. Unknown requirements costs

Evaluating and selecting new enterprise software is a journey of discovery for an organization. Inadequate analysis leaves requirements undiscovered, which can lead to selecting the wrong software or an implementation that costs far more than budgeted.

Even if the best-fit software was selected "new" requirements found during the implementation cause delays and cost increases.

12. Time costs

There is a cost when support staff tries to develop ways to work around software limitations. Occasionally add-on products are required for missing features, which takes more time to evaluate, install and maintain. End users also waste time working around deficiencies. Most of these costs could have been avoided by selecting best-fit software in the first place.

13. People costs

Extra employees may be needed to overcome functional limitations of the new software. The new system may cause morale to drop while increasing recruitment costs.

A client of ours had bought two software systems to handle their manufacturing. One system managed production, while the other managed the financials. The two systems meant duplicated data entry, more data entry clerks, and they could never get the data in the two systems to agree with each other. In addition, they hired a small army of people to generate reports from the two systems, and all this work was manual. As the company grew, the limitations of this approach became more apparent, resulting in even more people being hired to "paper over the cracks." After four years of enduring this pain, they reached out to us, and we helped them find one ERP system that was a much closer match to their needs.

14. Opportunity costs

There is a hidden cost to selecting the wrong software. When employees spend time working around software deficiencies, this causes them to miss new business opportunities. For example, consider a CRM system that demands more work and decreases the time salespeople can spend with customers. The opportunity cost of the wrong CRM software comes from sales missed because the salespeople spend less time with their customers.

15. Customer perception costs

Customer perceptions of a company depend on the responses from that company when problems arise. If the wrong software increases response times, causes errors and results in unresolved problems, customers head for the competition. The loss of revenue from customers leaving directly attributable to the poor software choice is the perception cost of that software selection decision.

16. Legal fees

When a software project fails, customers may feel the vendor or system integrator misrepresented product capabilities, and take them to court. Legal fees are high, and success is by no means guaranteed.

Software vendors and implementation consultants have much more experience facing these situations than do their customers, and contracts are designed to protect the sellers. Meanwhile, customers tend to have little experience with software and implementation contracts and usually end up the loser in court.

17. Low ROI

Every major software purchase needs a justification. Part of this usually includes an analysis of the ROI. The CEO and CFO are usually the people most interested in this, and very often will approve a software purchase based on the ROI estimate. When the ROI does not materialize, it is a cost, or even a loss, that must be carried by the business.

Key lessons

Successful purchases of major software products are far more difficult to achieve than most people realize. When those purchases go wrong, they cause pains for everybody involved. Here are the key points from this chapter:

Chapter 1: The Software Purchasing Problem

- A major software purchase will be a significant financial investment for an organization or will have a major fiscal impact on that organization.

- Software purchasing success is meeting or exceeding the expectations of users and others involved with the purchase.

- Software purchasing failures happen when the new software does not meet expectations. There are several degrees of failure ranging from benign to complete.

- People do not like talking about their failures, which is why you do not hear about many of them. However, if you ask, people will often open up and tell you about their frustrations with the software.

- Software purchases that go wrong cause business, technical and personal pains. The personal pains are the ones that hurt the most.

- Poor software purchases incur many different costs. Some are obvious while others are not.

Chapter 2. Why Selecting Software is so Difficult

Organizations have been making major software purchases for decades, but despite the time and money spent, according to some industry pundits, fewer than 10 percent of these projects meet expectations. More than 90 percent fail in part or fail outright (See: Software failures defined on page 6). Why does this still happen with such depressing regularity?

> *Successful software purchases meet or exceed*
> *expectations, but failures do not.*

The short answer is that enterprise software selection is more difficult and more work than most people realize. Surprisingly, few organizations have a robust selection process. When selection projects run into difficulty or run out of time, shortcuts are taken and it's inevitably downhill from there.

The problem of software failures is like that of an iceberg. Like icebergs where you only see the small part above the water, the software failures you hear about are but a small fraction of all software failures. More egregious software failures are published, especially when they end up in court or involve public money. You might hear of a few failures from your professional network, but the vast majority of failures are never discussed. This is especially true when it comes to partial failures (See: Partial software failures on page 6), where the software does not meet expectations, but it is not bad enough to discard. This is precisely why so many industry professionals are unaware of how common the problem is, and contributes largely to why software selection is so challenging.

Software evaluation and selection projects have traditionally been the domain of the IT department, however, things are changing as the world migrates to the cloud. Most of what IT people know about evaluating software has been learned on the job. Major software purchases are infrequent and as a result it seems few organizations have considered software selection from a process improvement perspective. This is surprising, considering the magnitude of the impact a major software purchase can have on revenue and profit.

When software evaluation and selection projects are given to an IT department with no extra resources and people still have their normal responsibilities, is it any wonder that so few projects meet expectations? To make matters worse, many IT departments are populated with employees whose primary interest is in the technology itself. They have little appreciation for how much a major software purchase will ultimately affect the business.

In this chapter, we consider common reasons that make purchasing enterprise software so difficult. Being aware of possible problems before starting a project can help reduce the risk of failure with your next major software acquisition.

Why so little interest in evaluations?

When a major software acquisition does not meet expectations, it can make a significant dent in revenue and profitability. Despite knowing the risks, many organizations seem to have little interest in conducting thorough software evaluations. In this section, we consider why this happens, and why so many organizations take such disastrous shortcuts.

1. Overconfidence

Because you hear so little about software failures, many decision-makers falsely assume selecting software is not difficult, which leads to overconfidence. This problem is made worse when they mistakenly feel they know enough to dispense with an evaluation.

2. Underestimation

Most major software purchases involve thousands of requirements. Organizations completely underestimate the complexity and difficulty of the work in an evaluation and consequently do not budget the time and resources needed. When the selection project takes longer than expected, they take short cuts with the inevitable results.

3. Lack of time

Closely related to underestimations above, an organization does not budget adequate time when planning a selection project. Usually assumptions are too optimistic, for example, a midsized company will budget 3 months for an ERP evaluation and selection when they should, in reality, budget for at least 6 months. It is not only underestimating the work involved, it is also underestimating the delays, such as vendors taking weeks longer than expected to respond to a request for information (RFI) or a request for proposal (RFP). Software purchasers tend to forget they do not have control over everything involved in the purchase.

4. Overwhelmed

Selecting software is so much work, takes so much time, and is so difficult that some people become overwhelmed. Rather than get the job done properly they take their chances with shortcuts, and hope they will get away with it. That might work with smaller projects, but it seldom works with major, business critical software purchases like ERP.

5. Incompetence

Some people are simply professionally incompetent. How they managed to get the job they are in is anybody's guess, but they just do not appreciate how important a major software purchase can be to an organization.

6. Lack of skill

Major software purchases are infrequent, so organizations are unlikely to have employees who know how to evaluate software. Even if some employees have been through a few evaluations, how much did they manage to learn from the experience? Usually they go from selection straight into implementation without performing a project post-mortem to capture the lessons to be learned from the selection process.

7. The 5/8th job

Some people start software evaluation and selection projects with the best of intentions. However, once well underway they realize how much work is involved, at which point shortcuts become very attractive. Just like a builder who takes shortcuts when he under quotes on a construction project and has an unhappy client, the selected software will not meet expectations.

8. False economies

Some companies think an adequate evaluation and selection process is an unnecessary expense. This is a false economy because by skipping this step the implementation will take longer than necessary and cost more than expected. Benefits from the new software will be delayed, and if best-fit software was not selected, there is an ongoing hidden cost incurred every year the software is used.

9. Prioritization

The organization is aware of the pain caused by inadequate software, but delays starting the selection project until they are forced to. Then they want a decision made in a hurry and shortcuts are taken, especially in the requirements analysis phase.

Organizations do not realize that requirements development takes time and rushing will cause requirements to be missed. These requirements are then discovered during implementation where they cause delays, cost increases and business disruption when the software goes live.

10. Budget cycle

Sometimes decision-makers see the software selection project as part of the purchase, and do not want to start an evaluation because a major purchase is not in the budget. They do not realize the selection project is separate from the software purchase, and it takes months of work to evaluate enterprise software. The financial commitment of a major software purchase occurs only at the end of the evaluation and selection process, and usually will not affect the current budget.

11. Outsourced IT

Institutional process knowledge is lost when an organization outsources IT. In addition, outsourced IT is not privy to the inner workings of the organization and lacks the perspectives needed for software selection success. To make matters worse, outsourced IT rarely has the interest of the organization at heart, especially when they are working off-site.

12. Experience

Some people have experience with similar types of software, and assume they can select the new software with a minimum of effort. Perversely, this experience can cause the work in an evaluation to be underestimated. They may even decide an evaluation is not needed at all and just go ahead and buy the software. Then they find a big gap between expectations and reality.

13. Management edict

Executive management makes the purchase decision, and decides there is no need for an evaluation. This often happens when a new executive joins an organization and wants to use software that worked well at a previous company.

14. Inflated executive opinions

Despite not being an active part of the organization's daily operations, some executives tend to have an inflated opinion of their knowledge. They, unfortunately, often think they have more to contribute than those actually involved in the day-to-day operations. They do not realize that nobody can know every aspect of the business in the necessary detail, and a system for gathering and managing this information is needed.

15. Cognitive bias

Everybody has cognitive biases. It is part of being human and there is no way to avoid them. Biases can be a primary cause of selecting "less than optimum" enterprise software. A few of the more common biases encountered when evaluating and selecting software are listed below. (See Wikipedia for a more extensive list of cognitive biases: wikipedia.org/wiki/Cognitive_bias)

- Overconfidence effect: "I know the market for this kind of software."

- Confirmation bias: Seeking only confirming evidence.

- Bandwagon effect: Nobody ever got fired for selecting (insert favorite vendor name here).

- Anchoring bias: A tendency to be swayed by the first sales presentation.

- Dunning-Kruger effect: The tendency for unskilled individuals to overestimate their own skills, and the inability to recognize their own ineptitude.

Unfortunately, knowing you have biases does not free you from their effects. The best way to minimize the effects of bias is to use a data-driven and deterministic selection process (See: Process is the key to success on page 127).

16. Shiny object syndrome

Management makes the software selection decision based on the latest hot product, and refuses to evaluate alternatives. It is often a classic case of being "sold" by a capable salesperson. That is what they want, and that is what they will get. However, the new software seldom meets expectations and usually results in buyer's remorse.

17. Impatience

The decision-maker wants results quickly, and refuses to acknowledge the value of a thorough evaluation. Very often, the software most highly recommended by analysts is selected.

18. Undervalued employee input

All too often there are those executives that do not value the real-world experience of employees who know the business, and ignore their input. Employees, especially middle management with their intimate knowledge of daily operations, have a great deal to contribute to the software selection.

19. Lack of interest

While IT is tasked with the responsibility of selecting the software, the department is populated with people whose focus is on technology and not the business. As a result, they lack the insight, or interest, in ensuring the software meets business needs.

20. Do not care

Most people do care about their work and have a desire to do their jobs well. However, there are those who will only do just enough to get by because they simply do not care. Despite ultimately being incompetent, these people can be found in all levels of the organization because their one real skill is in building relationships (perhaps they should be in sales).

It might not be your money,
but it is your career and your reputation.

---

21. Immature selection process

While fast-growing companies are the exception, by their nature major software purchases are rare events for most companies. Employees have not repeated the software evaluation and selection cycle often enough to develop a mature software selection process, which stacks the odds against success.

> *A former consultant, now CIO at a large organization, told the story of a private company that manufactured electronics and wire harnesses for customers like automotive manufacturers and the military. They wanted a new content management system, and wanted it in a hurry. The company gathered an inadequate set of requirements, and then picked a commercial solution incorporating the company's intranet. Implementation was expected to take 3 months.*
>
> *The new software was given to IT along with guidance from the marketing and communications departments. As IT worked through it, they found serious limitations with core functionality. For example, while the system could manage text on a page very well, anything else like images was a problem. They worked with the vendor to resolve the issues, but it was slow going. He said, "We ended up slamming a square peg into a round hole to make it do what it was supposed to do." After about 9 months of struggling, IT suggested scrapping the project, but the business stakeholders felt they were very close. IT knew the "last mile" was going to be very difficult, but it was not their decision.*

The content management software took 15 months to implement, five times longer than expected, and the project went way over budget. User expectations were not met because the software was not well suited for what was needed. Recently, this former consultant spoke to a colleague still at the company who said that although the system didn't really meet their needs, the company was afraid to make any changes because it integrated to so many other business systems.

22. Unmanaged scope

Scope creep is defined as continually adding requirements while a project is in progress. If the scope grows too large, it can cause a project to fail. While this is a danger when developing software, it also happens when purchasing cloud or off-the-shelf software (See: How to minimize requirements scope creep on page 186).

23. Vendor controls selection

Without realizing it, some organizations allow vendors to wrest control of the selection process. You must be extremely careful here, because any evaluations controlled by a vendor will always be inadequate and will favor that vendor's products.

24. Analyst reports

Decision-makers can put far too much weight on software analyst reports from companies like Gartner, Forrester and so on. While they may be an excellent source of information at the start of a selection project, analyst reports should never be used for making the final decision because they are written from the perspective of the average purchaser, and do not factor in your specific needs or requirements. *You must do your own research.*

25. Not priming implementations

Most organizations purchasing software do not realize that the purpose of a selection project is to 1) select the software and 2) to gather critical information needed to prime the implementation team. If they realized how important the information collection part of the selection project was they would put a lot more effort into it.

Relying on committees to select software

Enterprise software is purchased to solve business problems, for example, the organization has outgrown existing software. While many organizations use committees to select software, real world experience shows that software selected this way frequently does not meet expectations. When it comes to selecting enterprise software, a committee based decision-making process is flawed for the following reasons:

1. Underestimating complexity

Committees lack the time, resources, tools, and methodologies to deal with the complexity of major software purchases.

2. Inadequate experience

A committee-based software selection assumes members understand organizational needs and have a good enough understanding of that software market. This is a false assumption for two reasons:

- A few committee members can never have the detailed experience needed to understand all software requirements.

- Committee members have their normal jobs; they are not software specialists. They may have some experience with a few products, but a lack of time prevents them from gaining a wider knowledge.

3. Unchallenged assumptions

When making a major software purchase, most organizations need "out-of-the-box thinking," i.e. perspectives from outside the organization that can challenge the unstated assumptions employees do not realize they have. Committee members invariably come from inside the organization and are not likely to challenge such assumptions.

4. Underestimating time required

The selection project for some enterprise software purchases entails hundreds or even thousands of hours of work. Even though much of the work will be delegated, committee members are never prepared for the amount of time needed from them.

5. Inadequate requirements discovery

Committee decisions that take the shortcut of substituting experience for the requirements discovery process will fail because enterprise software always has too many requirements.

6. Inadequate implementation estimates

Software selected by a committee lacks the analysis needed for an accurate implementation estimate. Implementations take longer and cost more than expected which is a common occurrence with software like ERP.

7. Implementation delays and cost increases

When a committee substitutes experience for analysis, "new" requirements are discovered during implementation. Dealing with them takes time and increases costs. Some people call this scope creep, but it is not. Those requirements should have been found in the requirements analysis phase.

8. Voting process logically flawed

Using a committee to select software only masks an inadequate decision-making process. When there is a vote or consensus, there is no logical path between the requirements and the software selected, and the correctness of that decision can never be verified.

Compare this to a deterministic selection decision driven by a gap analysis. There is a logical path between the organization's requirements and the software selected. The selection decision can be verified from the requirements using a traceability matrix.

9. General committee decision-making problems

Examples of general decision-making problems that software selection committees can suffer from are:

- **Strong leadership** that can lead to authority deference.

- **Weak leadership** that can lead to one person dominating the selection process.

- **Groupthink** is where a desire for group conformity leads to flawed decision making.

- **Group decision fatigue** where the selection project seems to drag on forever. Committee members just want to make the decision and move on.

The main advantage for using committees is that if things go wrong, there is no one person to pin the blame on! That may well explain their popularity.

Work done in the wrong order

Some tasks in the software acquisition process are very often done in the wrong sequence. When this happens, it delays the production rollout of the new software, and it can even cause the wrong software to be selected.

Starting a selection with demos

Not knowing any better, many organizations start a software selection project by reaching out to vendors and requesting demos. This is how software was selected in the last century, and is the wrong way to proceed for the following reasons:

- While the high-level requirements may be known, at the start of a project there is little idea of the details. There are also unknown requirements that must be discovered. Usually the major software products meet the high-level requirements; the difference is in how the detailed requirements are met.

- The demo will be optimized to sell the software, and will emphasize the latest and the greatest. To be more useful to the purchasing organization, the demo should focus on the buyer's showstopper requirements.

- The demo gives vendors an opportunity to pull senior executives and decision-makers into their "reality distortion field" and infect people with the "shiny object syndrome." Vendors take the opportunity to seize control of the sale, which is done so well that buyers do not even see it coming until after the deal is closed.

- Demos can waste a lot of time, especially when there are too many. When selection projects start with demos there is seldom a structured process to collect feedback, and after several demos, users are too confused to provide useful feedback.

There is always the risk of demonstrating products that are missing showstopper features. When these omissions are found, the demo is cut short and everybody's time has been wasted.

There is also the risk of products that could be a better fit being overlooked simply because they are not market leaders. Bear in mind that challengers usually provide significantly greater value than market leaders because they must. This is called the Avis principle; see page 55.

When demos should be held

Demos should be held near the end of the selection project, after all the research has been done. The gap analysis measures how well potential software products meet the requirements. The gap analysis is used to make the selection decision, and the demo then confirms that decision (See: Software demos on page 243).

The gap analysis makes the software selection,
and the demo confirms that decision.

Process analysis and optimization

As organizations mature, work processes are developed. These processes grow when issues are discovered and new steps are added to prevent recurrence. These processes prove to be surprisingly durable, and can survive new software, new management, reorganizations, and even a company being acquired. The problem, however, is that process steps can survive long after the reasons for their existence are past. They have become steps that add no business value.

When a decision is made to purchase new enterprise software, it is an opportunity to analyze and optimize business processes. Should this analysis and optimization be done before gathering requirements, or should it be done as part of the implementation?

Many people would say that requirements are tied to processes, so you must at least analyze the existing processes to gather those requirements. That is certainly true if you are developing software, but in most situations when new software is purchased, starting with a detailed process analysis is counterproductive for the following reasons:

- There is not much point in buying new software only to replicate inefficient existing processes. When new software is purchased, it is an opportunity to improve business processes. This means current processes are only a guide to requirements.

- If it has been more than 10 years since the last purchase, new software may have solved many existing process problems. Processes in the new software may have been optimized, may be better than existing processes and the new software may even include processes not previously considered that turn out to be very useful in practice. Trying to fix existing process problems before the purchase would be a waste of time.

- If business processes are analyzed and optimized before the software is purchased, you are operating in a vacuum. However, if this business process re-engineering is done after the purchase, the new software provides the framework for optimizing processes.

- The software vendor's best practices may reduce the need for much of the analysis and optimization work. Using those best practices and configuring the software for use is more efficient than analyzing and optimizing existing processes before the purchase.

Time spent optimizing business processes before selecting new software only delays the final production rollout of that software. That time is better spent on a more thorough requirements analysis, which can even result in selecting different software that is a better functional fit. Once the requirements are specified in enough detail you can decide if a potential software product can handle those processes.

Another perspective: Requirements gathering can start with the needs and work towards the software, or start with the software and work towards the needs. Process analysis starts with the needs, which is a very 20th century approach to selecting software. A better approach is to start with potential products and work towards the needs, which is reverse engineering features back into requirements (See: Reverse engineering on page 177). Regardless, you are limited to the products currently on the market to satisfy the needs you've identified.

Leaving requirements discovery to implementation

One of the biggest causes of delays and corresponding cost overruns with major software purchases is discovering "new" requirements during implementation. Those requirements should have been found during the requirements analysis phase.

First, there are meetings to weigh the newly discovered requirements. Then the implementation team attempts to satisfy them with system configuration, developing code, business process re-engineering, or purchasing extra software modules or third-party products. All this extra work takes time, and discovering too many "new" requirements are what causes those nightmare implementation projects that take much longer to complete than planned.

When implementation schedules are breached, management may decide to leave certain parts of the implementation for later. Shortcuts like these can cause major disruption to normal business operations when the organization attempts to take the new software live.

When it comes to selecting software, developing the requirements is usually around 50 percent of the total work in a selection project, but may be more. It takes a lot of work to complete a thorough requirements analysis, and many organizations are tempted to take shortcuts. However, one way or another you will do that work. If those requirements are not found in the upfront analysis, they are found during the implementation or when going live. And when found later in the process, they take even more work, time and money to resolve.

When there is an inadequate requirements analysis, project schedules slip, costs are higher than expected, and there is greater disruption to normal business than necessary when going live. To make matters worse, and inadequate requirements analysis can even result in the wrong software being selected.

Why users can't articulate their requirements

While every software selection should start with user interviews because this builds rapport, most users only know the pain points of their existing software. Users focus on their jobs, and software is a tool to get that job done. They know what doesn't work well, what takes too many steps, and everything that makes their work life more difficult. However, the context of their jobs prevents them from articulating requirements too far removed from their current pains.

They may be working extra hours to overcome the limitations of current software and do not have time to look at alternatives. Few users are aware of what is on the market and how it could make their lives easier. Users also tend to specify the ability to replicate existing processes as requirements when those processes may be far from optimized.

Sometimes a user will have worked at several companies over the course of a few years, and will know the software those companies use. Given the rate of change in the software market, experience that is more than three years old is likely to be of limited value. Also, because a certain software product worked well at another company does not mean it will work well at their current company.

If a company has outgrown its existing software and users have only a high-level idea of requirements, how do they find the requirements to select new software? How do they find requirements they do not know they need? Too many missed requirements can mean software that does not meet expectations, and that leads to all sorts of pains for the organization.

Why capturing requirements is so difficult

When purchasing enterprise software, most project failures can be traced back to inadequate requirements. Why don't users supply all the requirements when asked? Why is gathering requirements so difficult, and what can be done to improve the situation?

1. Relying on users

Some consultants contend that users are the only legitimate source of requirements, but this is simply not true. Most users know only their pain points and not much else. When an organization relies on users for requirements, they are guaranteed to miss many.

2. Work underestimation

Suppose an organization has decided to replace a major software system. The first item on the selection project plan often looks something like "gather requirements." These two words can contain 50 percent or more of the work when selecting software.

Most people grossly underestimate the amount of work involved when gathering requirements. They take shortcuts in the rush to complete projects, and that means requirements are missed, which causes most of the problems with enterprise software purchases.

3. Missed requirements

Requirements can be missed for many reasons, e.g. they are unknown, there is not enough time to gather them, relying on users etc. When requirements are missed during the analysis phase of the project, they have significant consequences:

- Missed requirements may result in the wrong software being selected, which means the expected ROI will not be realized.

- When "new" requirements are found while implementing the software, dealing with them takes time and increases the cost of the implementation project.

- When "new" requirements are found while taking the software live, they cause disruption to normal business operations.

- Occasionally, missed requirements will cause outright failure, leading to the project being abandoned.

4. Analysis paralysis

Analysis paralysis can happen when the decision-makers do not have confidence in the process for identifying and selecting the software. They keep going back to the requirements, looking at the problem from different angles, and wondering what they have missed. They are afraid of making a mistake that can damage their company and their careers. Rather than commit, they keep extending the requirements analysis.

Warning signs and symptoms

No chapter on the difficulties of selecting software would be complete without listing common warning signs of impending problems.

1. Inadequate executive interest

Without exception, every major software purchase will hit problems. Sometimes an executive will sponsor a project by making the budget available, but then refuses to do any more to help when problems arise. A lack of executive interest means that when this happens, the political power to overcome those problems is missing, and that can cause the project to fail.

2. No ROI analysis

If there is no ROI analysis, a project of marginal value might get started, especially when there are enthusiastic backers in the organization. However, when the business environment gets tough, the project is one of the first to be cut because there is little value in completing it (See: Software ROI on page 98).

3. Lack of resources

Dumping the software selection project on employees and expecting them to do their normal jobs as well is a sure recipe for failure. In addition, there is usually no incentive for those employees to prioritize software selection tasks.

4. Relying on users for requirements

Users know their current processes and pain points, but few users know much more than this. Users are not specialists in software requirements; they have their normal jobs to do. User input is very important, but relying largely on users for gathering requirements will only guarantee that a great many will be missed.

5. Tight deadlines

An organization with a mature software selection process might pull off a major software rollout with a tight deadline, but forget it if there is an immature software selection process (See: A mature software selection process on page 130).

6. Subjective decisions

Objective data for making selection decisions are available if you are prepared to do the work to get it, but subjective software selection is a sure recipe for failure.

7. Using vendors for selection

Do not ask a barber if you need a haircut. Anybody who has an interest in the outcome will find a way to justify the selection to favor that interest.

8. Narrow focus

If one department is making a decision that will affect many other departments, the software selected may work very well for that department, but may be a significant mismatch for others, such as finance selecting a new ERP system without input from the rest of the business.

9. Delayed implementations

Significant "new" requirements found during implementation cause project delays. This is a symptom of an inadequate requirements analysis, and when this happens, there is likely to be significant business disruption when going live (See: Why requirements are important on page 168).

10. Using the wrong tools

A symptom of an immature software selection process is using tools like a spreadsheet or MS Access for an ERP selection. These tools do not scale up to handle the thousands of requirements in these evaluations, and lead to shortcuts being taken (See: Chapter 8: Software Selection Toolbox on page 153).

11. Immature selection process

There is an immature software evaluation and selection process, and that is not realized. One symptom of immaturity is a lack of process documentation (See: A mature software selection process on page 130).

Key lessons

Major software purchases can have a huge effect on revenue and profitability, but many organizations find it very difficult to select software that meets expectations. Here is a recap of the reasons why this happens.

- Despite the substantial amounts of money involved, both in the TCO and the effect the software can have on revenue and profitability, many organizations have surprisingly little interest in software selection projects. We factor this in when we consider why the people involved behave as they do.

- Software for major purchases is often selected by committees. Experience shows this seldom results in the new software meeting organizational expectations.

- If a software product receives complimentary reviews from analysts, for example it is a leader in the Gartner Magic Quadrant; many organizations feel that is good enough for them. Again, experience shows selecting software based on analyst reviews usually leads to expectations not being met.

- The root cause of most software purchase failures is an inadequate requirements analysis. Rather than doing process analysis up front, an organization should spend that time on a more thorough requirements analysis.

- We list a number of warning signs and symptoms that a major software purchase is about to run into serious problems.

Chapter 3.   Software Selection Risks and Mitigation

Buying enterprise software can be a risky proposition for an organization. Having an idea of the risks faced when making major software purchases can help develop risk mitigation strategies.

What they really needed

What they thought they needed

How they documented the requirements

How the sales person sold it

What they actually bought

What was eventually delivered

How it performed in production

What the users thought of it

Companies usually seek a return on enterprise software investments. All too often, that planned ROI does not materialize because the best-fit software was not selected. Even when best-fit software was selected, the selection project was not structured to minimize implementation risks.

No book on software evaluation and selection would be complete without a chapter examining the risks these projects pose, along with risk mitigation strategies. We examine common software selection risks, along with suggestions to mitigate those risks.

- Where applicable, there is a cross reference to detailed strategies for dealing with a risk.

- This is not an exhaustive list of risks and you may well find others.

- Some information from Chapters 1 and 2 is repeated, but here it is from the perspective of risks.

Organizational risks

1. Political interference

This happens when some executive forces a software selection decision instead of following the selection process. Some reasons for political interference are:

- Newly hired executives who want to make their mark.

- Existing relationships an executive has with salespeople from previous companies.

- Previous experience with the software was good, and some executive thinks that experience can be repeated at their new company.

- The executive has been "sold" on the software and is convinced beyond reason that it is the right choice.

- Bribes that can take the form of cash, but that is usually too blatant. More common are "incentives to purchase" like holiday trips that "just happen" to be available or "favors" like jobs for family members.

Risk mitigation

The defense against political interference is process: a comprehensive data-driven evaluation that shows where the favored solution is weak compared to the best-fit software. Of course, this relies on the case being made persuasively, but at least there is the data to back up the claims.

2. Inadequate executive sponsorship

All major software purchases need adequate executive sponsorship to help overcome the inevitable issues that will occur during the project. Without this, a project faces serious risks.

Risk mitigation

Use the evaluation and selection project to test executive management interest in the new software. Propose using external consultants for the project. If no executive sponsor will fund the selection project, the new software is not seen as important to the business, and the project can be stopped before it starts.

3. IT lacks business experience

What would you get if you asked a building contractor to design the interior of an upmarket home? You can be certain that an interior designer would do a far better job of the décor than a building contractor would.

Because it is their domain, IT is often tasked with selecting software. However, IT is more like the building contractor than the interior designer. While IT takes care of essential tasks like keeping systems operating, archiving data, security, backups, disaster recovery and IT projects, they seldom have the business focus needed to select functionally adequate software.

Risk mitigation

Have IT analysts become experts in specific business functional areas. These people on the IT payroll have been seconded to a business unit, and they will understand both the business needs and the IT needs.

> *From Abe Lietz, former CIO at Curves Jenny Craig: For years, the best business analyst teams have touted themselves as knowing how to ask questions and what to listen for. However, gathering business requirements is more than hiring good analysts who can ask the right questions. Rather, business analysis has matured into relationship management where analysts have a much deeper rapport with the business.*
>
> *It starts by building relationships with business units. For example, as marketing thinks through their next promotional season or develops a brand strategy, an analyst from IT who has a deep understanding of marketing should have a seat at their table. That person is there to listen, provide thought leadership, and*

contribute to the dialog. The goal is for the chief marketing officer to feel entirely comfortable making them part of their staff meetings. When the time for a new marketing solution arrives, that analyst knows what both the business and IT need. They ask the questions that never get asked. For those IT people in the business units, that is a full-time job.

4. The business lacks software selection experience

Unless they have been intimately involved with previous software selection projects, most business people have little idea of what is involved. If a business user is driving a selection project, particularly if they are not senior management, they often focus only on their immediate requirements. They can end up outgrowing the chosen software quickly and usually fail to take care of IT requirements like integration and security.

An HR manager at a large life science startup had a need for a system to manage employees. Without involving IT, she bought a subscription to a cloud HRIS. This product satisfied her immediate needs, but some of the things she did not consider were security, audit trails, backups and disaster recovery. Another limitation was the inability to integrate with payroll.

Risk mitigation

When it comes to software selection, the business must understand the larger picture and not just their immediate needs (See: The power of vision on page 106). Employing former IT people with application experience in a business capacity can help.

The problem of employees putting cloud purchases on corporate cards, using consumer software for confidential information etc. is called shadow IT. One potential solution is to require all software purchases that involve corporate data follow a standard software evaluation and selection process.

While an organization can have policies in place to prevent shadow IT, they may not be effective. It is a people rather than a technical problem, and it is up to IT to find a way of working with the users to avoid the problem in the first place.

5. Relying on procurement

The nature of business demands that procurement spend most of their energy on more commodity type purchases. Commodity products have few requirements, and are where procurement teams use their negotiating skills to deliver value to the organization.

Enterprise software is at the opposite end of the scale, usually with many thousands of requirements. This complexity is often unfamiliar territory to procurement departments, who may try to treat enterprise software as a commodity purchase. They may also lack experience when negotiating cloud contracts or software licenses (See: Software contract risks on page 255 for risks specific to software contracts).

Risk mitigation

Have a well-defined software evaluation and selection process in place with procurement roles properly described. For example, procurement would add value by performing due diligence on software or implementation vendors. Also, educate procurement departments on the intricacies of purchasing software.

6. Underestimating system importance

There is the temptation to dismiss back-office systems as non-critical. However, if new systems like payroll, invoicing, accounts receivable have problems, you will find out about them soon enough!

Risk mitigation

The solution is a thorough requirements analysis with system users weighing requirements for importance to the organization.

Project management risks

7. Immature evaluation and selection process

While fast-growing companies are the exception, by their nature major software purchases are rare events for most companies. Employees have not repeated the software evaluation and selection cycle often enough to develop a mature software selection process, which stacks the odds against success.

Risk mitigation

Take the steps necessary to mature the software selection process (See: A mature software selection process on page 130).

8. Overconfidence

Overconfidence is a major contributor to software selection failures. It causes a blind spot, trapping people in their areas of experience and expertise. Even if you have implemented several different systems, you know only those systems, and you know only the most recent system well. The rapid pace of software innovation and the number of requirements involved makes it impossible to select best-fit software without using a comprehensive selection process.

The core of the overconfidence problem is people not appreciating the complexity of selecting best-fit software, and of not understanding the business consequences of a poor choice. When this happens, the opportunity to maximize the value returned by that software is missed.

> *From Wikipedia: The overconfidence effect is a well-established bias in which a person's subjective confidence in his or her judgments is reliably greater than the objective accuracy of those judgments, especially when confidence is high. Overconfidence is one example of a poor calibration of subjective probabilities. Throughout research literature, overconfidence has been defined in three ways:*
>
> *1. Overestimation of one's actual performance*
> *2. Over-placement of one's performance relative to others*
> *3. Expressing unwarranted certainty in the accuracy of one's beliefs*

Unfortunately, some people only learn if they personally experience a significant loss. When these people cause software selection failures and their employer pays for their mistakes, they learn little and remain overconfident. They only learn when the loss is personal, e.g. the software failure causes them to be demoted or to lose their job. Since many software failures are partial rather than complete (See: Software failures defined on page 6), the problem is often not recognized by the organization and the personal loss seldom happens. These people then repeat their mistakes with the next major software purchase.

Risk mitigation

Realize that you will not know the right system when you see it, and that judgment can be swayed by your existing knowledge, persuasive salespeople, and so on. Use a data-driven software selection process to select the best software for your needs.

9. Underestimating work

Enterprise software is complicated, with thousands of requirements that need to be satisfied. Ensuring a good match with organizational needs takes time and effort, and the magnitude of the software selection task is often severely underestimated.

When requirements are missed in the initial analysis phase, they are discovered during implementation, where dealing with them takes time. Discovering too many "new" requirements causes schedules to slip and corresponding cost increases. When schedules slip too far, some items are left for "Phase 2" of the project, which will disrupt normal business operations when going live.

Risk mitigation

Allow adequate time for the selection project, especially for developing a comprehensive list of requirements (See: Chapter 9: Requirements on page 165).

10. Taking shortcuts

By the time the people involved realize how much work is involved with the software selection, they have usually committed deadlines to the business. To meet those deadlines, they are tempted to take shortcuts in the selection process, which paves the way to failure.

Risk mitigation

Allow adequate time for the selection project so that you are not forced into taking shortcuts. It is always better to start a selection earlier rather than later.

11. Complexity

Enterprise software is complex, with thousands of features. The value of the software flows directly from how well those features satisfy your organization's requirements. The complexity is caused by the sheer number of requirements and the depth of detail needed. To appreciate the magnitude of that complexity, consider that with larger software products like ERP there are consultants whose entire careers are devoted to just one module of that software, for example supply chain or production planning.

Familiarity breeds contempt: IT professionals understand software, but can fail to appreciate how complex large products like ERP really are. This complexity can be well beyond the capacity of any one person.

Risk mitigation

Use a data-driven selection process (See: Process is the key to success on page 127). Use the right tools to manage the complexity of substantial numbers of requirements (See: Chapter 8: Software Selection Toolbox on page 153).

12. Limited project resources

Many companies run their IT departments at full utilization, or even just over. A major software purchase is significant work, and the employees involved with the software selection still have their regular responsibilities. An IT team running at full utilization would be seriously overcommitted with selecting new software, which would increase the selection project risk.

Risk mitigation

Ensure adequate project resources are available. Employees who will play a large part in the software selection project need to have their work in other areas scaled down.

If adequate resources are not available, outsource the selection project to independent consultants (See: Appendix A: Selecting Software Selection Consultants on page 283).

13. Analysis paralysis

Analysis paralysis occurs when the only decision made is to continue the requirements analysis. Major software purchases involve large sums of money, and decision-makers want to feel in control of the purchase process. When they do not feel in control, they stop moving forward and continue the analysis.

A primary cause of this is a lack of confidence in the selection methodology, especially with unknown requirements. Decision-makers are afraid of a software selection failure and do their best to delay making a purchase decision until they feel in control.

Risk mitigation

The solution is a mature software evaluation and selection methodology that keeps the process moving forward (See: A mature software selection process on page 130).

14. Time pressure

With software evaluation and selection projects, there is an inverse relationship between time and risk. The amount of work in these projects is often underestimated, and occasionally there is an accelerated timescale. This can be a management decision, a regulatory deadline, or some other reason. Whatever the reason, selecting enterprise software in a hurry leads to serious problems and potential software failures.

Provided a mature evaluation and selection process (see page 130) is being followed, the more time spent evaluating and selecting the software, the less the project risk. Of course, there is a limit here: a time will come when spending more time on the evaluation and selection will not reduce risk. The point is to avoid rushing the project and taking shortcuts that significantly increase risks.

Risk mitigation

Outsource software selection projects to consultants. If the consultants already have libraries of requirements, this will further speed up the project (See: The role of the software selection expert on page 118 and Appendix A: Selecting Software Selection Consultants on page 283).

Be prepared, and remember that initial estimates for the duration of a selection project are likely to be low. It is better to start a project early when there is time to avoid the risks caused by rushed work and shortcuts taken.

15. Project scope not actively managed

While major software acquisitions can be seen by some users as an opportunity to fulfill wish lists, all purchases involve some degree of compromise. No one enterprise software system does everything, but sometimes organizations want it to do too much.

The scope of the problem they want one software system to solve is too broad. There is a danger of buying software that does everything but is not particularly good at anything. This occurs when no products being considered have an adequate fit score on the gap analysis.

Risk mitigation

Control scope creep by keeping users focused on weighting requirements, rather than asking them, "Is that all?" Reduce the scope of the requirements by eliminating certain areas of functionality. Those areas can be handled by complimentary software products (See: Scope check on page 231).

16. Following wrong industry advice

The web is replete with advice on how to select software. Often this advice is at too high a level, and does not contain enough information to be useful. Usually it is lists of tasks without any explanation of what those tasks are supposed to achieve, and of how and why they work. The advice may be well intentioned, but all too often it is completely wrong.

Risk mitigation

Use a mature software selection process (See: A mature software selection process on page 130).

17. Process optimization before software selection

When writing software, it is common sense to optimize business processes before coding them. However, when purchasing software, it is best to leave process optimization to the implementation phase of the project. All that is needed is to ensure the new software can properly handle existing and potential future processes.

Risk mitigation

Leave process analysis and optimization to where it belongs, in the implementation stage of the project (See: Process analysis and optimization on page 31).

18. Not building user buy-in early enough

One of the most easily avoidable mistakes organizations make with a major software purchase is leaving user buy-in until the implementation phase. When this happens, users feel the software is being pushed on them without their input. Some may be indifferent to the new software; others may actively push against it and refuse to use it. Disinterested or passive-aggressive users can put an enterprise software rollout in serious jeopardy.

> *Commitment to the new software from both top management and lower-level employees is essential. At FoxMeyer, although senior management commitment to the new software was high, there was a definite morale problem among warehouse employees. This was not surprising, since the project's Pinnacle warehouse automation integrated with SAP R/3 ERP threatened their jobs. With the closing of three warehouses, the transition to the first automated warehouse was a disaster. Disgruntled workers damaged inventory, orders were not filled, and mistakes occurred as the new system struggled with the volume of transactions. $34 million worth of inventory was lost.*
>
> *(zimmer.csufresno.edu/~sasanr/Teaching-Material/MIS/ERP/FoxMeyer.pdf)*

Risk mitigation

The time to create and nurture user buy-in is during the software evaluation and selection process. Inviting as many users as practical to the requirements weighting meetings is a vital part of building user buy-in. If buy-in is left to the implementation phase, it is too late and there is a serious risk of users rejecting the new software.

In addition, management needs to commit to retraining users for new jobs that are more fulfilling, and avoid laying people off because the new software has reduced the need for employees (See: Creating and nurturing user buy-in on page 122 and Weight requirements for importance on page 201).

Requirements risks

There are many reasons why major software purchases fail, but one of the most common is that of an inadequate requirements analysis. People unfamiliar with requirements gathering techniques grossly underestimate the amount of work involved. In addition, few people realize the requirements analysis process should be designed to collect critical information that will be used by the software implementation team.

Requirements are to software selection as foundations are to buildings. We all know what happens to buildings with inadequate foundations, and the result is the same for software selection. The requirements are the standard against which software is evaluated using a gap analysis. If that standard is deficient, is it any wonder that the purchased software does not meet expectations?

The requirements analysis must go into enough detail, and the devil is always in the details. You will eventually get into that detail anyway, whether it is in the selection, the implementation or when going live. However, the earlier the requirements are discovered, the lower the cost of satisfying them (See: Selection project costs on page 140 and How to write good requirements on page 187).

An implementation project that starts with a comprehensive list of all significant requirements, and those requirements are written to be implementable enables the project manager to develop a realistic implementation plan. When no significant new requirements are discovered, the implementation is on schedule and within budget. Requirements that include who wants them, why they are wanted and how important they are, help implementation consultants get their work done faster.

Enterprise software usually has thousands of requirements and it can take months to develop a comprehensive list (See: Selection project duration on page 137). If this preparatory work is inadequate, the entire software acquisition project is at risk. If you think this is too much work, just think of how much work a failed software project entails, and what it can do to your career and your company! See: Software purchase pains on page 7 and Chapter 9: Requirements on page 165.

19. Poorly written requirements

Too often requirements are badly named, written at too high a level, are ambiguous, have poor or missing descriptions that lack context, and do not include examples.

While vendors can quite reasonably claim to meet such requirements, the way the requirement is written does not reflect the real needs of the organization, which can lead to the wrong software being selected. Also, the requirement does not have the information needed for the implementation. Too many badly written requirements lead to delays, unexpected costs and business disruption when going live.

Risk mitigation

Requirements need to be well written, including detailed descriptions and examples so they can be properly understood in context (See: How to write good requirements on page 187).

20. Requirements that are missed

If the initial analysis misses significant requirements, there is a risk of purchasing the wrong software. When this happens, the missing functionality is discovered during implementation or when going live in production, *but at that point contracts have been signed and it is too late to do anything about it.*

Even if best-fit software was selected, lack of sufficient requirement detail is a large cause of software implementation problems because "new" requirements will be discovered during implementation. Too many new requirements lead to delays, unexpected costs and business disruption when going live.

> *A client of ours had developed some ERP requirements already, and one of them was: "Monitor and manage material shortages." We pointed out that this requirement was not broken down into enough detail, and gave them examples of questions that needed to be answered:*
>
> - *How do you want shortages monitored? Email, pop-ups, dashboards?*
> - *What is the escalation when a shortage problem is not solved?*
> - *How much notice of shortages is wanted?*
> - *Different notice periods for different categories of items?*
> - *How do you handle parts on order but not yet delivered?*
> - *What happens when vendors don't keep promised deliveries?*
> - *Do you want to test part availability before committing orders?*
> - *How do you want provisional part holds to be implemented?*
>
> *This was all we could fit on one PowerPoint slide, and that high-level requirement would still deliver many more detailed requirements.*

Risk mitigation

The requirements analysis must be broad enough to capture all requirements. The greater the level of detailed requirements the lower the overall project risk. The way to develop such requirement detail is to use the process of reverse engineering (See: Reverse engineering on page 177).

21. Un-implementable requirements

Typically, un-implementable requirements are written at too high a level. For example, the requirement was that mobile devices could be used to complete forms and sign them, but the requirement was written as, "Has mobile device app."

Risk mitigation

Verify that all requirements on the evaluation can be implemented (See: Implementable requirements on page 197).

22. Unknown requirements

Unknown requirements are those that the buying organization is not aware they have. When selecting software, these unknown requirements can cause a project to fail. Typically, they are found during software implementation or when pushing the software live. Dealing with these newly found requirements takes time, costs money and they disrupt normal business operations when the software goes into production.

> *To quote Donald Rumsfeld: There are known knowns; there are things we know we know. We also know there are known unknowns; that is to say we know there are some things we do not know. But there are also unknown unknowns – the ones we don't know we don't know... (Wikipedia)*

Risk mitigation

Use the process of reverse engineering requirements from the features of potential products. Done in enough detail, this will discover all significant requirements, even unknown ones (See: Reverse engineering on page 177).

23. Unstated requirements

The purchasing organization has requirements, but does not state them. For example, these could be requirements that are assumed to be met, or the organization had not done the work needed to discover those requirements.

When buyers claim the vendor misrepresented the software, you may find that claim is based on requirements that were assumed and not documented. This is another example of how an inadequate requirements analysis will cause problems.

Risk mitigation

Vendors cannot be held accountable for not meeting unstated requirements. It is the responsibility of the buyer to do the work of documenting all requirements. Use the process of reverse engineering requirements from the features of potential products. Done in enough detail, this will discover all significant requirements, even unknown ones (See: Reverse engineering on page 177).

24. Relying on users to supply requirements

Some consultants say that users are the only source of requirements, but that is not true. The source of requirements does not matter; what does matter is how important they are to the users.

Users know requirements related to their pain points very well, but seldom know much beyond that (See: Why users can't articulate their requirements on page 33). If users were involved in a software selection project at a previous company, they may have a broader view of requirements, but this is still limited, and the process will be slow because users struggle to articulate requirements. The chief benefit of involving users in the requirements phase is that it helps build rapport and buy-in to the new software.

Risk mitigation

While many people think requirements are discovered by wringing them out of users, there are several other methods for capturing them (See: Sources of requirements on page 174).

25. Requirements supplied by vendors

When evaluating software for a major purchase, vendors might supply lists of requirements if asked. As mentioned above, the source of requirements is unimportant. Bear in mind that requirements supplied by vendors will usually be arranged to show their product in the best light, and they will seldom provide requirements that their product does not meet.

Risk mitigation

If several vendors provide requirements, the deficiencies of those supplied by any one vendor may be remedied by requirements supplied by other vendors. Take all the requirements you can get from vendors because they can save time.

26. Duplicate requirements

When gathering requirements from multiple sources duplications are inevitable. If too many of these duplicated requirements are left in the evaluation, they cause excess work. However, they are not easy to remove because different wording has been used to express the same requirement in different ways.

Risk mitigation

Use a software selection tool designed to manage requirements. When related requirements are collected in groups, duplicates are easier to see and remove. In addition, the tool should allow one requirement to appear in multiple groups (See: One requirement in multiple groups on page 200 and How to de-duplicate requirements on page 201).

27. Not weighting requirements

Some RFPs list requirements and then have a column for *yes* or *no*. There is no concept of weighting a requirement for importance to the organization. Requirements should be weighted because:

- In the absence of weights, all requirements must be treated equally. This is never accurate because some requirements are always more important than others.

- Weights are used when calculating product fit scores. Without weights, fit scores are less accurate.

- Weighting requirements allows all requirements that are less than "important" to be excluded from the evaluation. This reduces the work that vendors must put in when responding to an RFI or RFP and therefore increases the likelihood of a vendor response.

- When requirements are weighted as "no interest" and the reason is captured, there is an audit trail showing why that requirement was deemed of no interest.

- Weights are used by implementation consultants. If questions arise about implementing a requirement and it is weighted as a "showstopper", consultants put a lot more effort into ensuring they understand exactly how to implement that requirement. If it were rated as "nice to have", they would put in far less effort. This keeps implementation effort focused on the requirements that really matter to the organization.

- Buy-in is created and nurtured when users see their needs being taken into account (See: Creating and nurturing user buy-in on page 122).

Risk mitigation

Have appropriate users weight requirements for importance to them. For each requirement capture who wants it, why they want it and how important it is to them (See: Weight requirements for importance on page 201).

Selection risks

28. Selecting the market leader

Market leaders in a software category are usually considered a "safe" choice, for example, "Nobody has been fired for buying [insert vendor name here]." However, because a product is the market leader does not mean it is the best-fit for an organization's needs. Often a company challenging the market leader can provide greater value.

> *For years, Avis car rental had challenged market leader Hertz without success or profitability. Then they ran commercials along the lines: "We try harder because we have to. We are only No 2." This campaign was an instant hit for Avis, who, for the first time in a decade, were profitable the year after launching it.*

Software companies challenging market leaders provide more value because they must. Without that extra value, they can never successfully mount a challenge. We call this the Avis principle.

Be aware that there are always some people in an organization who want the "safe choice," but they seldom realize that if a thorough requirements analysis was not done deciding on the safe choice can be very dangerous indeed.

Risk mitigation

Do not take a shortcut and assume that market-leading software is the best-fit for your organization. Rather, make a software selection based on a gap analysis (See: The gap analysis on page 218).

29. Following the competition

Some companies falsely assume that the software used by a competitor will be adequate for their needs. However, without inside information, they have little idea of how well that software works for that competitor. For all they know, the competitor could be looking for a replacement.

Even if the competitor successfully uses the software, a project may fail because employees do not have the necessary skills with that software. Also, there may be enough differences between the two companies so the software used by the competitor is not the best-fit for the company looking to acquire new software.

Risk mitigation

Do not assume software that is being used by the competition will work well for your company. Rather, select software based on a gap analysis (See: The gap analysis on page 218).

30. Relying on previous experience

Sometimes people assume that because software worked well at a previous company it will work well for their new employer. However, there usually are enough differences between the old and new employers to invalidate this assumption. A problem occurs when the person is senior enough to force a purchasing decision, and often occurs when a new executive joins the organization.

> *An established pharmaceutical company in San Diego hired a new HR executive. This person had used the SAP HR module at his previous company, and wanted to implement that software for his new employer. Unfortunately, the new company was an Oracle shop. This executive was senior enough to force the project through, but it was such a disaster that it cost him his job.*

Risk mitigation

Do not assume software that worked well for a previous company will work well for your new company. Rather, select software based on a gap analysis (See: The gap analysis on page 218).

31. Falling for the latest and greatest

People can fall in love with the latest software trend or fad, which is known as suffering from "shiny object syndrome." These trends go through a predictable cycle of hyper-inflated expectations, disappointment when those expectations are not met, and finally realistic expectations. When decision-makers fall for the latest fad, you can be sure that expectations will not be met.

Risk mitigation

Use a comprehensive gap analysis to *measure* how well potential software products, including the latest and greatest, meet your specific requirements. Select the software based on the fit score (See: The gap analysis on page 218).

32. Selecting immature technology

If the software or vendor is new, there are always elevated risks of things not working as promised, for example missing, incomplete or buggy features. If you are making a major software purchase, you need to consider very carefully whether your organization can accept these risks.

Risk mitigation

A way to uncover such risky products is to search LinkedIn profiles and the job boards for references to that software. If few people mention the software, that is a sure sign of low market penetration, and that is something to be avoided in most enterprise situations.

33. Selecting end-of-life software

End-of-life software can be defined as software where significant new features are no longer being released. Software can move into an end-of-life when:

- When a vendor buys a competitor to acquire their customers rather than their technology, the software can go into end-of-life mode. The acquired product is milked for revenue, but development ceases.

- A change in the vendor marketing strategy can leave orphaned products. New development ceases, and only security updates are released.

Risk mitigation

End-of-life software should be avoided unless there is an exceptionally good fit with your requirements. It can be difficult to predict end-of-life, but some indicators are:

- When you examine the software release history, no significant new features have been introduced over the last 12 months. Note that security updates do not count as significant new features.

- If the software has been on the market a long time, for example more than 10 or 15 years, you need to examine the recent release history.

- Has the software recently been acquired by a larger vendor? If there was a takeover, were large numbers of development employees laid off?

- Look at the language the software is written in and the platform it runs on. For example, would you buy an enterprise product written in COBOL, FORTRAN, Lisp, Basic, or Lotus Notes today, even if it was a great fit with your needs? Are other vendors in that market category using that language or platform?

34. Using software vendors for selection

Asking software vendors to help select software is like asking the fox to guard the henhouse or asking a barber if you need a haircut. You cannot rely on them to help select software because there is such a huge conflict of interest. Unless there is an obvious poor fit between the needs and the software, the vendor will always recommend their software. That can lead to software being bought that is not the best fit for the needs. Be especially careful with reseller vendors who claim to be unbiased because they represent more than one software company.

Risk mitigation

Select software based on the gap analysis (See: The gap analysis on page 218).

35. Using implementation consultants for selection

Consulting companies make their money by selling consulting hours. They specialize in the largest and most popular applications because that allows them to get the greatest number of billing hours from their resources. They will not recommend software that they do not support because they cannot make any money out of it, which is why they cannot help you identify the software that best meets your needs.

No consultant that undertakes software selection and implementation projects will be satisfied with only a selection project from a client. They will select the software they implement. They will also use an initial selection project to find other projects within the organization. The strategy is called "Penetrate and Radiate." It all comes down to maximizing margins and billing hours. For a fuller treatment of this problem see Enterprise Software Selection by Shaun Snapp: Chapter 4: How to use consulting advice on software selection.

Risk mitigation

Select software based on the gap analysis (See: The gap analysis on page 218). If you need help with software selection, avoid a conflict of interest by using consultants who do not implement software (See: The role of the software selection expert on page 118 and Appendix A: Selecting Software Selection Consultants on page 283).

36. Relying on reviews or analyst reports

Analysts like Gartner, Forrester etc. produce comprehensive analytical reviews of software in a sector. For example, software that is featured in the top right corner of the Gartner Magic Quadrant is considered the best, and enterprise software selections are sometimes based on that analysis.

The danger is that reviews and analyst reports are written for an audience of many, and not for your organization's specific needs. In addition, relying on analyst reports instead of undertaking a software selection means that you are not capturing critical information needed by the implementation team.

Risk mitigation

Reviews are a suitable place to start with product research, but if you base an enterprise software purchase decision on them, the software will not meet expectations. For an in-depth look at using reviews, read: The place of product reviews and analyst reports on page 161.

37. Using the demo to make a selection decision

Too many organizations still make enterprise software purchase decisions based on demos, but that is a very 20th century approach. In those days, a demo was one of the few ways to learn about the software, whereas today the internet is a rich source of product information. Using the demo as the primary input for a software selection decision is a big mistake for the following reasons:

- The demo shows off the absolute best features of the software only. Even if the demo follows your script, there is never enough time to go into the details, and the devil is always in the details.

- The demo is done by expert salespeople who are skilled at creating a "reality distortion field," which is swaying the audience to believe their product is the best choice. Executive decision-makers unfamiliar with detailed requirements are particularly vulnerable here.

Risk mitigation

In the twenty-first century, buyers should be far more informed than previously, and make software selection decisions using a gap analysis. The purpose of the demo is to:

- Confirm the gap analysis decision.
- Nurture buy-in by having users participate in the demo.

The only time the demo is used to make a selection decision is when the fit score from the gap analysis is similar for the top two or three of the products being demonstrated (See: Software demos on page 243).

38. Purchasing on price instead of value

Some organizations base their software selection decision on the initial price of the software, but neglect to examine the TCO (See: Estimating the TCO for enterprise software on page 91). Invariably this means the best-fit software was not selected, resulting in a partial or complete project failure (See: Software failures defined on page 6).

Risk mitigation

Do not be seduced by the software with the lowest up-front price. Select the software that has the greatest value for your organization (See: Chapter 5: Select Software for Value, Not Price on page 81).

39. Not accurately measuring functional fit

Imagine you are relocating to a new town in an unfamiliar part of the country. You research houses based on internet listings, and neighborhoods with Google street view. Then you buy a house without ever looking at it in person. There is an excellent chance you will have overpaid, and that you will not be happy with your new home.

That process is similar to how some organizations select software. They do a very high-level fit analysis, and find that several software products appear to meet their needs. Often the final choice is made by the demo, especially if one of the sales teams is very persuasive. Then, when the implementation begins, the problems start to appear.

Risk mitigation

Use a comprehensive gap analysis to *measure* how well potential software products meet your specific requirements (See: The gap analysis on page 218). Also, verify that the scope of your requirements is matched by the products you are considering (See: Scope check on page 231).

40. Using spreadsheets for the gap analysis

Many people use spreadsheets for collecting requirements and doing the gap analysis. While they might work well to get the project started, spreadsheets are too manual and do not scale up to handle the large numbers of requirements in an enterprise software selection (See: Spreadsheet limitations on page 158).

Risk mitigation

Use a tool designed to manage requirements and do the gap analysis (See: Chapter 8: Software Selection Toolbox on page 153).

41. Software bugs

All software has bugs, but some software products have many more bugs than others do. Usually newer products tend to have more bugs, but sometimes vendors add features to existing products purely for marketing and sales purposes. These features have never actually been used by a customer and will have an excessive number of bugs, even though the rest of the software is acceptable. If these features are important to your organization, you need to do some research.

Risk mitigation

The primary way to find out how buggy software is in practice is to ask other users. One of the best ways to find users is to search for LinkedIn profiles that contain the product name. If the user profiles look suitable, reach out and ask the profile owner if they would be prepared to answer questions about the software. You will be surprised how helpful some people can be.

Regarding buggy new features, you can examine the software release history. If those new features are important to you, ask the vendor for reference clients who use those new features.

42. Relying on committees to select software

While many business decisions are made by committees, selecting software for a major purchase should not be one of them. The general idea behind a committee is to benefit from the combined experience of all members, but in actual practice this does not work well when selecting software.

Risk mitigation

Instead of making selection decisions by committee, use a mature selection process (See: Relying on committees to select software on page 27 and Process is the key to success on page 127).

Vendor risks

43. Skipping software vendor due diligence

When buying from companies like Microsoft, IBM or Oracle there is insignificant risk of their going out of business. Unfortunately, larger vendors are seldom hotbeds of innovation. If you want more innovative software, you may need to consider smaller vendors or startups. However, that option comes with the risk that these companies may not be what they appear.

Risk mitigation

Undertake software vendor due diligence. This is an area where procurement departments can be valuable (See: Software vendor due diligence on page 228).

44. Skipping implementation vendor due diligence

With larger software vendors like Oracle, SAP, Microsoft etc., implementation is usually done by specialist third-party consultants. Smaller software vendors often have their own teams to implement their software. In both cases it is critical to perform due diligence on the party that will be implementing the software.

Risk mitigation

Undertake implementation vendor due diligence. This is an area where procurement departments can prove very valuable (See: Implementation vendor due diligence on page 222).

45. Trusting vendors

When software requirements are unclear, ambiguous, incomplete, or lack enough detail, software vendors make assumptions in their favor. Couple this with the natural enthusiasm of salespeople, and there may be a large gap between what buyers think the software can do and what it does. Sales teams are skilled at making software look like just what is needed. Buyers must remember that sales teams are selling day in and day out and know their craft. They are also highly incentivized for closing the deal, which means that their interests are not aligned with those of their customers.

> *Kentwool signed a contract with NetSuite for an ERP system that would tie the company's operations into a single platform. NetSuite had claimed they could handle Kentwool's manufacturing needs, and Kentwool had relied on their pledges when signing the contract. However, the software failed in critical areas and Kentwool took NetSuite to court.*
>
> *The Kentwool complaint stated that "order approvals, an integral part of the purchase order and procurement functions of the software, were easily thwarted by simply entering transactions for a low dollar amount and then amending the order to amounts in excess of the approval limits selected by Kentwool," NetSuite had already cost Kentwool 30 percent more than the original estimate, and when Kentwool tried to get the problems resolved, NetSuite wanted even more money and another 8 months for implementation.*
>
> *(Article by Chris Kanaracus. See: pcworld.com/article/2451980)*

Kentwool had relied on NetSuite's promises, but vendors sometimes misrepresent themselves during the sale. Also, if a company does not do their homework and specify their requirements in enough detail, they really don't have any leverage when the software doesn't meet those unspecified details.

Implementation vendors base project estimates on information supplied by the customer. When that information is incomplete, the project always takes longer than planned. One of the biggest causes of slipping implementation schedules is discovering "new" requirements that should have been found during the requirements analysis phase (See: Unknown requirements on page 270).

Risk mitigation

It is the duty of buyers to be skeptical, and not just believe vendor assurances. A thorough requirements analysis (See: Chapter 9: Requirements on page 165) followed by a gap analysis (page 218) is the best defense against purchasing the wrong software.

A thorough requirements analysis means no significant "new" requirements are found during implementation, which means projects are completed on time, within budget and go live with a minimum of business disruption.

46. Future features

Certain features may be desired, but they may be missing from the software. When asked, the salesperson promises they are on the development roadmap, and should be in production "very soon."

Risk mitigation

Even with the best of intentions, the vendor's priorities can change. Don't make a selection decision where key features are promised in a future release. The best way to factor in future features is to give them a low rating appraisal weight in the gap analysis (See: The product rating appraisal list on page 212).

47. Not auditing vendor responses

Vendors responding to RFIs or RFPs have been known to claim that their software meets certain requirements when it does not.

Risk mitigation

It is the duty of the buyer to verify that the software performs as expected before signing the contract. Sometimes the vendor's misrepresentation of the software may be exposed in the demo because it is so blatant. However, it is more common to discover misrepresentation when auditing the RFI or RFP response. If the vendor passes the audit you can be reasonably sure the software will perform as expected. Of course, this assumes there is an adequate set of requirements against which to audit (See: Audit and validate on page 247).

48. New in industry

Software vendors are always on the lookout for new industries into which they can expand. However, sometimes the next industry they target may be too big a jump from their current market, and this entails significant risks for their early customers in that new market.

> *A process manufacturing ERP vendor wanted to move into pharmaceutical manufacturing in the U.S. market. Their ERP product does not include financials and must interface to a separate accounting system. One of their first pharmaceutical customers struggled with this dual ERP and accounting combination for 4 years before giving up and contacting us for help with selecting a new ERP system.*

Risk mitigation

You do not want to take the risk of being among the first customers in a new industry for a vendor. Ensure that the software vendor has several customers in the same industry as yours, which are of comparable size to you, and check those references (See: Appendix C: Questions for Software References on page 294).

Software contract risks

For risks specific to software contracts read, Software contract risks on page 255.

Implementation contract risks

This section covers contract risks that apply when implementing software in both the cloud and the data center.

49. Lack of implementation contract experience

Implementation vendors have spent years refining their contracts to transfer project risk to the customer. Their goal is to be paid for the hours worked, take no responsibility for the outcome, and maximize the hours. They are very happy when the schedule slips because they make more money at negligible risk to themselves.

> *A failed SAP implementation: Bridgestone filed a civil lawsuit against IBM claiming that IBM had committed fraud, misrepresented itself, violated the Tennessee Consumer Protection act, was grossly negligent, and breached its contracts with Bridgestone. According to Bridgestone, IBM was insisting that it was just there to work by the hour, do only what it was told, and collect over $78 mil-*

> *lion in hourly fees, bearing no responsibility for the damages to Bridgestone caused by IBM's material breach of fundamental common law and contractual duties attached to its services.*
> *(upperedge.com/ibm/bridgestone-vs-ibm-bridgestone-wins-round-one-and-increases-the-pressure-on-ibm)*

Risk mitigation

Pay special attention to where contractual risk lies. Pay for outcomes, not work done or goals met. It is irrelevant if some aspect of the application has been implemented when it does not work for the customer. For example, do not make payment contingent on implementation goals; make it contingent upon passing user acceptance tests.

You should be able to negotiate a fixed-price contract. Although the total amount will be higher than the cost based on the projected hours, some of the risk will have been transferred to the implementation vendor. If your requirements analysis is thorough and you primed the implementation for success, no significant "new" requirements will be found during implementation. There will be no need for change orders that increase costs (See: Prime implementations for success on page 270).

For larger software implementations involving millions of dollars, it is well worth hiring a consultant who specializes in negotiating software implementation contracts because they will know how to ensure risk allocation is factored in.

50. Allowing consultants to learn on your dime

Many implementation vendors woo customers by parading their best experts before the sale. However, once contracts are signed, those experts are nowhere to be seen. Instead, you get lower-level staff, and even junior consultants who are developing their expertise at your expense.

Risk mitigation

If you can negotiate a fixed-price contract, the vendor's interests will be aligned with yours. They will have every incentive to complete the work early to maximize their profit. There is no incentive to use cheap labor by training junior consultants.

If you cannot negotiate a fixed-price contract, you need to prevent the vendor from training junior consultants on your dime by specifying in the contract who will do the work, and who might replace them if they are unavailable through illness etc. Again, it is worth hiring a consultant who specializes in negotiating software implementation contracts.

Implementation risks

In this section, we look at implementation risks that can be minimized by undertaking a comprehensive evaluation and selection. Other implementation risks, for example data conversion and testing, training, etc. are not considered.

51. Inadequate implementation estimates

With fixed-bid implementations, vendors may understate costs to win the bid. They expect to find many "new" requirements, and will use change orders to increase their project revenue.

Risk mitigation

A thorough requirements analysis means no significant new requirements are found during implementation. Vendors have the information needed to provide an accurate implementation cost. There are none to very few change orders to increase costs (See: Chapter 9: Requirements on page 165).

Another risk mitigation method is for the contract to be written with two schedules. Schedule A could list everything that is in scope and is included in the contract. Schedule B could list everything that is out of scope, and must be vetted by the vendor for accuracy. The caveat is if something is not listed on Schedule B, it is automatically assumed to be included on Schedule A at no additional cost. (See: *Lost clauses: What to look for in IT agreements* by Phil Downe published on purchasingb2b.ca)

52. Not priming the implementation for success

Many organizations fail to structure the evaluation and selection project to collect information critical for a successful implementation. They don't prime the implementation for success.

Risk mitigation

Structure the software evaluation and selection to collect the information needed for a successful implementation:

- Use reverse engineering to discover all significant requirements. When no significant new requirements are found during implementation, the project stays on schedule (See: Reverse engineering on page 177).

- When weighting requirements for importance, record who wants each requirement, why they want it and how important it is to them. This information is used by the implementation consultants (See: Weight requirements for importance on page 201).

- Export the winning product information in a format that includes all requirements with their importance weights, and how well the winning product meets those requirements. Then pass this information over to the implementation project manager (See: Prime implementations for success on page 270).

53. Business disruption

Discovering too many missed requirements exerts pressure on implementation project schedules. Dealing with these "new" requirements may be left for later to keep the project on schedule. When the software goes into production this functional mismatch can seriously disrupt normal business operations.

Risk mitigation

Since an enterprise software deployment will disrupt business, it is wise to examine the risks and have mitigation strategies in place. For example, adequate training of users is critical. Key to minimizing business disruption is a thorough requirements analysis, which means no significant new requirements are found during implementation (See: Chapter 9: Requirements on page 165).

54. Noncompliance risks

Selecting the right vendor means minimizing the risks of vendor noncompliance, which can put your business at risk. For example, in the case of cloud software, vendor security and IT governance should not compromise your business. Current vendor compliance with appropriate certifications like SSAE 16, ISO 27001, FINRA, HIPAA, 21 CFR Part 11 and so on will minimize these risks.

Risk mitigation

Check recent audits of the vendor to verify these comply with appropriate standards or certifications. If the vendor claims a current certification, or passed an audit, but in fact said certifications have expired, that is a red flag.

55. Progress payments

Vendors like to be paid for work done, for example modules implemented. However, this is meaningless from the customer's perspective. Software implementations must deliver business outcomes, not just meet milestones.

> *Buckley Powder, a Colorado company offering explosives and other products for mining and construction firms, entered into an agreement with Infor to install its SX.e software. The work was to take no longer than 6 months, but after 18 months had passed with no working system in place, Buckley filed suit against Infor. Buckley had paid Infor more than $185,000 and was seeking the return of that money as well as interest, attorney's fees and other costs.*
>
> *(Infor hit with lawsuit over alleged software project failure by Chris Kanaracus: pcworld.com/article/2044493)*

Risk mitigation

Structure contracts to pay for business outcomes rather than work done or milestones met. For example, while the implementation can meet the milestone of creating a vendor order, can the system handle the entire order workflow down to the goods arriving and becoming part of the inventory? Again, while the implementation may meet the milestone of being able to create an invoice, can the system be used to deliver the product or service and invoice the customer?

56. Changing project scope

Once implementation starts, various parties may want to change the project's scope. If these changes are allowed to proceed, they will delay project schedules and increase costs. They can even cause the entire project to fail.

Risk mitigation

The scope problem is minimized with a thorough requirements analysis. Because the software is being purchased rather than being developed, the decision has been made to limit requirements to those that can be satisfied by the features of potential products on the market. Reverse engineering requirements from the features of those products can capture all significant requirements (See: Reverse engineering on page 177). When this is followed by employees weighting requirements for importance, their focus remains on what is possible with the software, which minimizes scope creep (See: How to minimize requirements scope creep on page 186).

In addition, a thorough requirements analysis takes time, and that gives employees time to think through the scope of the project. This is a good reason for starting a selection project earlier rather than later (See: Selection project duration on page 137). When these changes are fleshed out in the requirements analysis phase, the cost of accommodating them is always much lower than when changes are made to the implementation project.

Sometimes changes in scope are unavoidable. An effective way to manage these can be to defer them to a later phase of work, so the original implementation project stays on schedule.

57. Expectations not actively managed

A major software purchase can be greatly anticipated by management and employees, but salespeople and enthusiastic internal supporters can easily over-inflate expectations. All major software purchases involve some degree of compromise, and if expectations are not actively managed, in their disappointment employees can reject the new software.

Risk mitigation

All major software purchases involve some degree of compromise. It is vital that the compromise be communicated to management and users before making the purchase. Remind users that the evaluation of the selected product defines and documents their expectations.

For example, if the best-fit software product was purchased and it does A to Z, but does not do X, they cannot later complain the software doesn't do X. That was a compromise that was accepted when making the purchase. Recap that the decision was based on a data-driven analysis and not subjective opinion. Refer users to a heat analysis so they can see that all other products were even bigger compromises (See: Use a heat map to manage requirements scope on page 234).

In addition, it is crucial that the software selection decision is seen as a data-driven process that factored in all input, made the best selection for the organization and minimized compromises.

Personal risks

58. Risks to your job, income and career

When major software purchases go wrong you can be at risk of losing bonuses, a promotion or even being fired. A failed enterprise software project can tarnish your reputation and affect your next job (See: Personal pains on page 12).

Risk mitigation

In all cases, personal risks are reduced with a mature software evaluation and selection project (See: A mature software selection process on page 130), and priming the implementation for success (See page 270).

Key lessons

Software selection risks are part of the overall risk faced when making an enterprise software purchase. However, selecting best-fit software and priming the implementation for success significantly reduces overall project risks.

- The recurring mitigation theme through these risks is that a comprehensive requirements analysis followed by a software selection based on the product gap analysis is the best way to minimize software selection risks.

- Use a software evaluation and selection project to test that there is sufficient interest from executive sponsors.

- Manage expectations and build user buy-in right from the project start.

- Project management risks such as overconfidence, underestimating complexity and not managing project scope are a real threat to success.

- Ensure due diligence is performed on both software vendors and implementation vendors. Pay attention to vested interests; you can hardly expect a vendor who sells or implements software to give you impartial advice. Everything they tell you is designed to get you to purchase their product or services.

- When it comes to contracts, if you are spending millions of dollars for the software or for the implementation, it pays to hire a consultant who specializes in negotiating these types of contracts.

- Structure the evaluation and selection to collect information to be used by the implementation consultants. There is no need for them to repeat this work because it only delays implementation and increases costs.

Chapter 4.   The Benefits of Best-Fit Software

If you picked stocks based on what friends tell you or from miscellaneous articles on the internet, you would be gambling because you had not done your homework. Over the long run, this kind of investment strategy would lose money. On the other hand, if you researched multiple companies and selected stocks that closely matched your strategy and risk tolerance, you would be investing in a portfolio capable of realizing your needs.

The same applies when selecting enterprise software. While you might buy a car for the pure pleasure of owning it, few organizations buy enterprise software for that reason. The software is bought to realize the benefits that are expected to flow from using that product. There are four categories of benefits:

1. Increases in revenue, profit, growth, efficiency...

2. Reductions in costs, time, complaints, complexity...

3. Improvements to productivity, quality, reliability...

4. Creation of strategy, alignments, new products...

For the detailed list check out, Hard benefits on page 86.

Best-fit software defined

Best-fit software is the software with the most valuable benefits. Expressed in:

- Monetary terms: the best-fit software is the software that generates the greatest ROI when compared to other software products.

- Functional terms: the best-fit software is the software that best meets the expectations of the users.

- Numerical terms: best-fit software is the software with the highest fit score.

Note: the fit score is a measurement of how well the software meets requirements, where 100 percent means that every requirement is fully met (See: Actual and fit scores on page 214).

Identifying best-fit software implies:

- The creation of a comprehensive list of requirements that fully describes the needs of the purchasing organization.

- Weighting those requirements for importance to the purchasing organization.

- Measuring how well potential software products meet those requirements, and expressing this as the fit score.

No software is perfect, and all have some degree of compromise. Best-fit does not mean perfect; it means the *best of the available potential software products.*

The payoff from a rigorous software selection

Something I learned early in my career: "When the brains don't do the work, it's the hands and feet that do." If you are making a major software purchase that will be used for 5-10 or more years and the TCO runs into multiple millions of dollars, it makes sense to make the effort to identify and purchase the best-fit software for your specific needs.

The key to maximizing success lies in the preparation. Rigorous software evaluations are many months of challenging work, and the payback only comes once the new software is in production. However, you can be rewarded with exceptional returns because that software is precisely matched to your organizational needs. The value that flows from using best-fit software is "the gift that keeps on giving," and it continues for as long as that software is used.

> *A client wanted to improve the efficiency of a call center they used to recruit volunteers for clinical trials. From a call center perspective, recruiting trial volunteers is like sales, but there were extra requirements related to complying with FDA and HIPAA rules. Metrics are extremely important to call centers. Before the project started, the head of the call center said she wanted at least a 20 percent improvement in metrics, but was hoping they could get closer to 50 percent.*

Chapter 4: The Benefits of Best-Fit Software

We helped select the software, and about a month after going live, I asked her how it was going. With a big smile, she replied that they had experienced a 300 percent improvement in metrics! This achievement happened because the process described in this book was used to find the software best matched to their specific needs. This is a great example because call center metrics directly measure how much the new software improved operations, and that improvement can be easily translated into dollar values.

It is possible to select best-fit software by experience or even sheer luck. If you have a good idea of the software you want, is it worth undertaking a rigorous evaluation and selection? Examine the list of benefits below before answering that question.

1. Discover unknown requirements

When starting a software selection project, organizations have a high-level idea of their needs. They know some requirements, there are requirements they know they don't know, but most critical are unknown requirements. These are "unknown unknowns" and they can sometimes be significant. A rigorous requirements analysis will discover and document these unknown requirements (See: Reverse engineering on page 177).

2. Avoid analysis paralysis

Analysis paralysis occurs when there is little confidence in the decision making process and the consequences of a wrong decision are so high the decision-maker is afraid to move forward. Following a well-defined data-driven software evaluation and selection process as described in this book can provide that confidence and keep the process moving forward. The gap analysis objectively measures how well the proposed new software meets requirements, allowing a rational selection decision to be made.

3. Create and nurture user buy-in

If users resist the new software, the project is in serious trouble. This can happen when employees are afraid the new software could cost them their jobs. The best time to create and nurture end-user buy-in is to involve users in the selection process as described in: Creating and nurturing user buy-in on page 122.

4. Test executive sponsorship

Without exception, every major software purchase will run into some difficulties during implementation and strong executive support may be necessary to overcome them. How can you verify this support exists before purchasing the software? One way is to undertake a software selection project. If there is no executive support for a rigorous evaluation and selection it means those executives are not seeing enough value in the project. You will have exposed a serious risk early on, which can allow the project to be halted before too much has been spent in terms of time, money and resources.

5. Set expectations

No product is perfect, and all software purchases involve some compromise. When users know those compromises before the purchase is made, and they see that the best-fit software has the fewest compromises overall, their expectations are aligned with what the software delivers. There is no buyer's remorse.

> *A client had asked us to help select clinical trials management software. On the evaluation, the fit score of the top product was not as high as we would have liked, but that product was the best compromise for their specific needs. The IT Director responsible for the implementation said that whenever he wondered why they chose that software, he returned to the evaluation and saw it was indeed the best choice for them. All other products were even bigger compromises. The evaluation had set his expectations.*

6. Set a realistic scope

It is tempting to buy software that appears to meet all your needs, but the question is how well does it meet those needs? You want to avoid buying software that can do everything but is not particularly good at anything.

Measuring how well multiple products meet your specific requirements allows you to make a data-driven decision about what requirements should be in and out of scope. For example, if no software has a high enough fit score you may want to:

- Reduce the scope of the project by eliminating certain groups of requirements

- Consider two (or more) complementary software products

- Change the products you are considering

You need to adjust the scope of your requirements before making the purchasing decision. After contracts are signed, it is too late to make any changes (See: Scope check on page 231).

7. Gap Analysis

The gap analysis *measures* how well different software products meet your specific requirements. Even in the same industry, every organization's needs are a little different. Although a product may be popular in your industry, it may not be the best-fit for your company. Likewise, you may find the software being pushed internally is not the product that best meets your needs.

With a gap analysis, you *measure* how well the software will meet your specific needs *before making the purchase*. Selecting the software most closely aligned with your company's needs can provide an edge in the market.

8. Buy on value

The value of software flows from the benefits of using that software, and those benefits come from meeting your requirements. Using the gap analysis to measure how well competing software products meet your requirements allows you to buy on value, and avoid the trap of buying on price. You can also verify if an internally favored product really does deliver on value or if other software is better (See: Chapter 5: Select Software for Value, Not Price on page 81).

9. Vendor due diligence

Vendor due diligence is not an afterthought. It is where implementation risks are reduced by formally evaluating vendors and their implementation partners. Note that where partners will be implementing the software as opposed to the software vendors themselves, it is those partners who will respond to your RFI and perform the demo. For that reason, you need to perform due diligence on implementation vendors before inviting them to respond to an RFI.

For more on due diligence see: Implementation vendor due diligence on page 222 and Software vendor due diligence on page 228.

10. Negotiation strength when purchasing

The gap analysis measures how well each potential product meets your organizational requirements. When the selected software is one of several products with very similar fit scores, you know any of those products could be purchased. This knowledge gives you an advantage when negotiating with the software vendor (See: Purchasing software on page 255).

11. Prime implementation for success

The evaluation should be designed to capture critical information that will be used by the implementation team. Exporting the winning evaluation and supplying that information to the project manager primes the implementation for success (See: Prime implementations for success on page 270).

- The evaluation contains all significant requirements so the project manager can accurately plan the implementation project schedule (See: Implementation handover on page 272).

- To maximize the effectiveness of implementation consultants, requirements should be well written, without ambiguity and include examples (See: How to write good requirements on page 187).

- Requirements should include the names of people who want them, why they are wanted, and how important they are to them. Implementation consultants know whom to reach out to when questions arise (See: How to weight requirements for importance on page 203).

Priming the team with this information reduces risks, and helps keep the implementation project on schedule and within budget.

12. Reduced implementation costs

Whether it is done during requirements analysis, implementation or even early production, eventually all requirements will be discovered. The difference is that the earlier they are found, the less they cost to satisfy.

One of the biggest causes of delays and corresponding cost overruns with major software purchases is discovering "new" requirements during implementation when they should have been found during the requirements analysis phase. It takes time and money to deal with these requirements. Discovering too many "new" requirements is what causes an implementation project to turn into a nightmare that takes months or years longer than planned (See: Reverse engineering on page 177).

13. User acceptance testing

One of the last steps when implementing enterprise software is that of user acceptance testing. Although this book doesn't cover implementation, a thorough and comprehensive requirements analysis will provide the basis for developing user acceptance tests.

14. Demonstrate impartial selection

There could be several reasons why you need to prove the software selection was impartial. For example, you may be asked by compliance auditors, there may be allegations of bribery, or for reasons beyond your control, the project did not work out as expected. These painful situations can be put to rest by showing the software choice was based on an objective and data-driven selection process. In addition, an impartial solution helps nurture user buy-in and ownership (See: Creating and nurturing user buy-in on page 122).

15. Traceability

Sometimes the board, regulatory bodies, taxpayers, etc. may question why a specific software product was purchased. A data-driven decision provides full traceability from the product selection all the way back to the requirements, who wants them and why they were wanted.

16. Unanticipated future events

Suppose you went through the work of selecting the best-fit software. Then the vendor was bought and the product discontinued, the vendor went bankrupt, a cloud vendor closed down or something similar happened. While you cannot predict the future, you would be ready to find a replacement at short notice.

All the information needed is in the original evaluation, along with alternative products. If some time has passed, you may want to update the evaluation or add new products that have since appeared, but most of the work is done. Selecting a replacement product would be but a fraction of the work from the original selection, and the problem software could be rapidly replaced.

17. Develop business direction

Today, while software is an engine that drives business, organizations have become constrained by that same software. Replacing it can open new avenues of business previously unavailable due to limitations of the old system. When an organization decides to replace their software, they start with a view of their problems framed in terms of their experience. Their challenge is to "think outside the box" and avoid missing the opportunities opened up by the new software.

When it comes to selecting enterprise software, one of the best ways to "think outside the box" is to use potential products to expand the understanding of what is available. We call this process reverse engineering, and it involves examining product features and then rewriting them as requirements (See: Reverse engineering on page 177). It's like doing software development backwards.

As the organization examines the features of potential products, they can see new possibilities. For example, a feature set from the new software can suggest a whole line of business that was not practical previously. After identifying those possibilities, they can be evaluated and factored into business plans.

Key lessons

A formal software evaluation and selection project is significant work and will take months to complete. However, this upfront work has numerous benefits. Ultimately, it reduces the risks associated with software purchases, minimizing the pain and maximizing the gain.

- Significant requirements not discovered in the analysis phase of the project can result in money being wasted and business opportunities lost.

- The key to making successful software purchases is selecting the software that provides the most valuable benefits and minimizes compromises.

- A selection project designed to capture critical information that will be used by the implementation team reduces risks. It primes that implementation project for success.

Chapter 5.   Select Software for Value, Not Price

Among other things, the corporate procurement process usually focuses on achieving the best purchase price for items. While this may be the right approach when buying commodity items, when it comes to buying enterprise software it is completely wrong. A far better approach is to select software based on the value returned. To paraphrase Benjamin Franklin, "The bitterness of poor functional fit remains long after the sweetness of a low price is forgotten."

> *When I was a kid, my mother was a very successful realtor. She had the saying that "only the rich can afford cheap carpets." By this, she meant that if you bought cheap carpets they would not last. They would have to be replaced and you would end up spending more than you would have spent if you had bought quality carpeting the first time around.*

We start this chapter with an explanation of why it is worth buying software on value rather than price. We consider two methods for estimating the value of a software purchase. Then we describe how to estimate the TCO of that software. We bring the value and TCO together by showing how to estimate the ROI for a software project and individual software products. We conclude by considering when undertaking a full software evaluation is worthwhile.

Software investment costs and returns are considered over a period of five years for the following reasons:

- Successfully implemented major software purchases typically stay in use for at least five years, and often much longer.

- At about five years, the TCO for data center software and cloud software are about the same.

Why value matters

The value of enterprise software comes from realizing the benefits that flow from using that software, i.e. from the ability of the software to meet an organization's specific requirements. When that value can be estimated and expressed in dollars, it is called a hard benefit. For example:

> Suppose an insurance company spends $1 million per year on labor to process a specific type of claim. If the company introduced new software that processes those claims more efficiently and reduced labor costs by 20 percent, then the gross value of that benefit is worth $200,000 per year to the company.

The above is a very simple example, but it shows that the value returned by the benefits of using software can be estimated in hard dollars.

Before a major software purchase is made, the ROI (i.e. the value) of the software project should be estimated. Only if there is sufficient ROI in that project should you proceed. Once requirements are finalized and potential software products are evaluated against those requirements, the ROI of individual software products can be estimated. This ROI is determined by each product price, TCO and by how well those products satisfy the requirements.

Why the odds are stacked against software buyers

Enterprise software buyer's remorse is more widespread than realized, but because people don't like talking about their disappointments you seldom find out about them unless they appear on the web or surface in your network. This is especially true when it comes to partial software failures (see page 6) where the new software fails to meet expectations.

Without sufficient software purchasing experience, organizations have little idea of the difficulties and pains they face when making a major software purchase.

It's not a level playing field!

Major software purchases are infrequent events for organizations, but vendor sales teams work on nothing else. They wine and dine customers and stroke unsuspecting egos. They know how to control evaluations, and the less preparatory work the buyer does, the more control of the sale is abdicated to the vendor. If buyers knew how skilled software sales teams were, they would be far more cautious, especially when they discover that vendors are experts at extracting revenue from their customers.

The four costs of poor software purchasing

With inadequately prepared buyers and the odds stacked in favor of vendors, it is no wonder that enterprise software costs more than budgeted and seldom meets expectations. The arrows in the chart below show where the costs of poor software purchasing are incurred (bullet point numbers correspond to callouts):

1. The extra costs of an implementation taking longer than planned.

2. The value of software is realized in the value of the benefits of using that software. When an implementation is delayed, the value from those benefits is also delayed. That is the hidden cost of a delayed ROI.

3. The cost of disruption to normal business operations when going live.

4. The hidden cost of not meeting expectations. This ongoing cost is incurred every year the software is used.

While these two hidden costs do not appear on income statements, they are very real. You could think of them as "lost opportunity" costs. Showing how a mature selection process can avoid these four costs is part of the aim of this book.

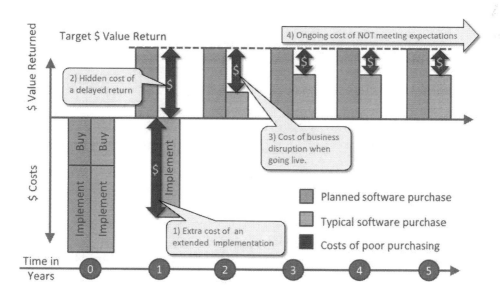

Figure 1: The four costs of poor software purchasing

A Californian County has three departments: The Assessor's office that deter-mines property valuation, the Controller's office that determines property and location taxes like water tax, school tax etc., and the Treasurer's office that manages tax collection.

The County is still using three legacy COBOL programs running on a mainframe, and wanted to use one platform to manage these three functions. The software went out to bid. When the County demanded the winning bidder's financial statements be made public, the winner refused the project because they were a private company. The second choice said they could do the project in two years because so much of it was Commercial-Off-The-Shelf software [COTS]. They are now four years into this two-year project and hope to have it completed in an-other two years.

This was a fixed bid contract. Since the county had specified over 7,000 require-ments there have been few change orders to raise costs. Even so, when the soft-ware eventually goes live the County will have missed at least 4 years of ROI, and that would be a substantial hidden cost.

Purchase price value estimate

The quick way to estimate the value that will flow from using software is based on how much an organization is prepared to pay for that software. When using this method to estimate value, the conservative approach is to use the software with the highest price that would be considered for purchasing. All other things being equal, if software with a lower price was eventually selected, the value re-turned would be higher.

Since the software has not yet been selected, it could be in the cloud or the data center, so this section contains an example of each. Note that these are rough estimates. Actual numbers will vary depending on the type of software being considered.

For every $1 spent on the software, it *must* return at least $1 in value; or there is no point in making the purchase. However, any commercial corporation is going to want a return on their investment. For round figures, assume that over a five-year period the software should return at least $2 in value for every $1 invested. (Government and nonprofits may use different numbers for returns, but the con-cept remains the same.) There are already many assumptions in this estimate, and factoring in net present value (NPV) would just make things unnecessarily complicated, thus it is not used.

It is an unfortunate fact that not all of these projects succeed. To factor in project risk, make the simplifying assumption that 80 percent of these projects will fully meet expectations while 20 percent will fail outright. We divide the $2 by 80 percent to get $2.50. Thus, for every dollar spent on the software you want a return of $2.50 over 5 years, or 250 percent.

For purchased software

For every dollar spent on software licenses for a major purchase, you can estimate spending another $2 on implementation and $1 on software maintenance over five years, i.e. a total of $4. Multiply this by the 250 percent above to get $10. Thus, for every $1 spent on software licenses, you desire the software to return at least $10 worth of value over five years.

Applying this rule of thumb, if you feel that spending $600,000 on software licenses is reasonable, you are expecting the software purchase to return $6 million worth of benefits over five years.

For software in the cloud

Cloud software usually costs significantly less to implement than purchased software because there are no hardware and system installation expenses. For every dollar spent on annual seat costs, you can estimate spending about $1.50 on implementation and another $4 on annual seat costs for the next four years, i.e. a total of $6.50. Multiply this by the 250 percent above to get $16. Thus, for every $1 spent on annual seat licenses, you desire the software to return at least $16 worth of value over five years.

Applying this rule of thumb, if you feel that spending $375,000 per year on cloud software is reasonable (i.e. about $31,000 per month), then you are expecting that software to return $6 million worth of benefits over five years.

Using the purchase price value estimate

The value of software is in the value of the benefits that flow from using that software. If the value of the expected benefits will be less than the purchase price value estimate, it does not make business sense to proceed with the purchase.

For example, suppose new cloud software being considered would cost about $500,000 to implement and $360,000 per year in seat costs. That is a cost of $2.3 million over 5 years. If the savings from using the new software were $1.2 million per year it would be worth proceeding with the project. However, if those savings were only $600,000 you should not proceed because there is insufficient value, especially when factoring in project risk.

The purchase price value estimate returns the lower limit of the value of the benefits that should flow from using the software. However, the value returned may be significantly higher. To discover if that value exists, use the risk adjusted benefits value estimate.

Benefits value estimate

The *Purchase Price Value Estimate* is inherently subjective. If you feel purchasing the software is worth the price quoted, you are making a subjective estimate of the value of that software. You might feel the software is well priced or even expensive, but it is still a subjective judgment. For a more objective estimate of the value of the software, additional work is needed in the form of the risk adjusted benefits value estimate. (The risk-adjusted value method is based on the work of David A Fields. For a more in-depth treatment of the subject, see his book: The Executive's Guide to Consultants published on Amazon.)

Discover value

Normally enterprise software per se has no value to an organization; the value comes from the benefits that flow from using the software. Start by considering all usage outcomes as potential sources of value and combine them to estimate the gross value of the software purchase being considered.

Hard benefits

The first step in determining value is to determine the benefits that flow from the desired outcomes. These are called hard benefits because a dollar value for the benefit can be estimated. Using *Table 1: Sources of hard benefits* below, for each outcome that applies to this software project, estimate the dollar benefit that will accrue once the software is operational. Then sum all the benefits to estimate the total value of the hard benefits.

Increases to:	Reductions in:	Improvements in:	Creation of:
Revenue	Time	Reporting	Strategy
Profit	Effort	Capabilities	Alignment
Growth	Cost	Processes	Systems
Value of offerings	Risk	Information	Transformation
Retention	Defects	Quality	New processes
ROI, ROA	Complaints	Reputation	New business
Efficiency	Complexity	Reliability	New products
Flexibility	Conflict	Usability	New services
Visibility	Attrition	Productivity	Inspiration
Equity	Administration	Motivation	
	Infrastructure	Service	
	Training required		

Table 1: Sources of hard benefits

While all outcomes on the table should be considered (and you may even add a few), not all will apply to any specific project. Occasionally most of the value flows from a few or even just one outcome.

> *A local government authority had tax collection software that was no longer supported, and needed replacing. In addition, repairing obsolete hardware like dot matrix printers that failed was becoming increasingly difficult. They were afraid the system might become unusable at some time in the future and prevent the county from collecting taxes owed. In this case, most of the value of this project involved the taxes that would be lost in the event of a failure. Other benefits of new software were secondary.*

For a partial expansion of this list, check out: The costs of not upgrading enterprise software on page 112.

Underestimation errors

As you consider the items in the above table, watch out for value underestimation errors. Keep asking yourself, "Is that all?" You may uncover more areas of value than originally anticipated.

Multiplier effect

Here you look for anything that multiplies the value of the benefits. Where else will this software project have an impact? Look for core benefits, parallel benefits, related benefits and similar benefits. You want hard benefits estimates for each department (or division, location, etc.) that will be affected by the new software, and add them to the total. Again, keep asking yourself, "What other areas of the organization will benefit from this software and what will those benefits be worth?"

For example, if you were considering a new help desk application for IT support (the core benefits), could you also use the same software for facilities support or customer support? These would be parallel benefits. You may also find the new software allows better forecasting of support needs, which can lead to savings. Likewise, better reporting and dashboards may reduce management time. Those would be related and similar benefits respectively. After uncovering all the multiplier benefits, you might find the total value of the software project is substantially increased.

Total hard benefits = sum of hard benefits + sum of multiplier benefits

Operational life

For any investment, the time over which the investment generates returns must be considered. Software starts generating a return after implementation is complete; it is in production and is delivering value in the form of benefits. These benefits continue until the software is retired. That time is called the operational life of the software. For major software purchases, an operational life of five years is often used for the following reasons:

- If an organization is making a major software purchase, they usually intend on using that software for at least five years.

- As a rule of thumb, at five years the cost of cloud software is about the same as the cost of hosting software in the data center.

You can select an operational life shorter or longer than five years. If you do, use the software implementation period as a guide. Software that can be implemented quickly is more likely to be replaced sooner than software that takes a long time to implement. The reason is that a shorter implementation has less work, cost, and typically has less business disruption. All of that makes it easier to move to a different product if needs change, or to a better product if one appears on the market. For example:

- For software with an implementation of 1 to 3 months, you might use an operational life of three years.

- For a major software purchase like ERP where implementation is a year, you might use an operational life of 10 years.

Whatever operational life you select, remember the operational life starts after the software has been implemented and it is being used. Use the formula below:

Gross value of hard benefits = total value of hard benefits x operational life

Soft Benefits

While you cannot put a monetary value to the soft benefits of a project, they are nevertheless real and worth considering. Examples of soft benefits are:

- **Recognition**: A major software purchase that meets or exceeds expectations usually gets recognition from the organization for the sponsor, leaders and participants.

- **Awards and rewards**: Recognition following several successful projects leads to things like awards, bonuses, salary increases and promotions.

- **Authority and stature:** When you consistently select and implement software that meets or exceeds organizational expectations, you become an authority because you have proven you can deliver.

- **Increased budgets:** When executives see your major software purchases consistently delivering the expected ROI, their trust in you grows. This can result in increased budgets and greater responsibility.

- **Pride and job satisfaction:** There is the pride of a job well done, and the tremendous satisfaction that comes from purchasing and implementing software that fully meets expectations.

- **Reduced stress:** When new software meets expectations, there is none of the stress that occurs when things go wrong.

- **Increased discretionary time:** Implementations completed on schedule and software that works as expected leaves time for other things. In addition, there is little need to work late or over weekends.

Reduce the value

In the *Discover the value* section, we estimated the gross value of hard benefits for the software purchase. In the interests of being conservative and realistic, we now reduce that gross value.

The egocentricity error

When enterprise software is bought, you are buying the benefits that flow from using that software. This is usually done in the context of a larger project, for example improving operational efficiency, launching new customer services etc.

The egocentricity error occurs when you overestimate the value that a specific software implementation will contribute to the overall project value. Ask yourself what else is required to achieve the overall value, and then use your judgment to reduce the contribution the software makes. For example, the software itself may contribute only 75 percent of the project's value. The other value may come from elsewhere, for example from hiring new employees.

Risk-adjusted value

Every enterprise software project has some risk of failing or achieving only a fraction of the expected ROI. The last step in estimating the risk-adjusted value of the project is to account for that risk.

The simplest way to estimate the risk is to make a judgment call, for example to estimate there is a 75 percent chance that the project will generate the planned ROI. You would then multiply by 75 percent to get the risk-adjusted value. While there are other ways to estimate software failure risk, given all the assumptions already made, they are seldom worth the complexity involved.

Risk-adjusted value = gross value x egocentricity x project risk

Although there are many assumptions involved, the risk adjusted value estimate is a relatively objective measure of the value the software purchase should provide to the organization.

Estimating the TCO for enterprise software

The TCO for enterprise software is the sum of all direct and indirect costs incurred by that software. It is a critical part of the ROI calculation, but is often ignored or woefully underestimated. Software and implementation vendors who will benefit from a favorable TCO are *always* biased. For example, cloud vendors tend to show favorable TCOs when compared to COTS software. Estimating the TCO is the responsibility of the purchaser, and not of any vendor. These TCO estimates do require domain expertise.

In this section, we look at the lifetime costs incurred by the three main types of enterprise software, namely:

1. Cloud software, for example Salesforce, Workday or NetSuite.

2. COTS typically runs in an on-premises or hosted data center.

3. Custom software that is developed by an organization for their own use.

There are variations like a hybrid between off-the-shelf and cloud, or open source. There is also the case of custom software in the cloud, for example written on a platform like Salesforce's PaaS product. Although they are commercial products, FinancialForce and Rootstock ERP are written on Salesforce PaaS, and they illustrate the idea. We will not specifically cover these software variations, but they will incur many of the costs listed below. The purpose of this section is to list common costs to help build a realistic TCO estimate for the proposed software.

The TCO is usually different for each software option. To estimate the TCO, consider the items listed in the *Table 2: TCO items to be considered* below. Estimate the cost of each item in the acquisition, operation, and retirement costs sections. Add these individual costs together to get the TCO, the total cost of ownership for that option.

TCO = acquisition costs + (operational costs * operational life) + retirement costs

Note that the TCO can be estimated for existing systems or proposed new systems. For example, you could compare the TCO of an existing system with that of a potential replacement system.

Notes on the table below:

- The X signifies a cost usually applied for that line item. The amount of that cost may differ between the three columns.

- While this table lists the more common costs, be alert for others specific to your situation.

Table 2: TCO items to be considered

TCO Description	Cloud	COTS	Custom

Acquisition costs

These are the costs incurred when getting new software into production.

TCO Description	Cloud	COTS	Custom
Software selection: Every major software purchase incurs software selection costs, which are not trivial. There is the cost of time spent developing requirements, in product research, in meetings and demos. In addition, there may be the cost of hiring software selection consultants particularly when employees cannot spare enough time for the project.	X	X	-
Software licenses: User licenses plus system or server licenses. There are several types of user licenses, but the most popular are named users and simultaneous users. User licenses are sometimes called seats.	X	X	-
Hardware: The cost of servers and storage to run the software, and other costs like hardware for backup and disaster recovery.	-	X	X
Finance costs: Only applies if the software purchase was financed.	-	X	-

TCO Description	Cloud	COTS	Custom
Implementation: The cost of setup, configuration, user acceptance testing, etc. so the software is ready for use in production.	X	X	X
Development: The cost of developing custom software (Note: we are not listing detailed development costs because this book is focused on selecting software for purchase).	-	-	X
Data migration: The cost of moving data from the old to the new system, including data format changes. Sometimes this is not economically viable, so the old system might be archived in a read-only mode.	X	X	X
Initial training: The cost of training employees to use the software. Note that in addition to end-users, help desk and system admin employees must also be trained. Remember to include the fully loaded cost of employees while being trained in the cost because they cannot do their normal work.	X	X	X
External system interface costs: No enterprise system operates in isolation, and they all require interfaces to one or more other systems.	X	X	X
Customization: This is the cost of modifying app source code to meet specific needs (Best avoided because it causes problems when upgrading to new versions of the app).	-	X	-
Documentation: The cost of documenting the system configuration, creating user documentation etc.	X	X	X

TCO Description	Cloud	COTS	Custom

Operational costs

Also called application ownership costs, these are all the regular, ongoing direct and indirect costs associated with using an application. These costs apply every year for as long as the system remains in production.

	Cloud	COTS	Custom
User licenses: As the number of users grows, new licenses or subscriptions must be purchased (assuming cost is based on the number of users). • For COTS software, if the number of users decreases, there are no refunds. • For cloud software, licenses usually require an annual contract. If the number of users increases, this cost increases. If the number of users decreases, this cost may decrease, but usually only when the contract is renewed.	X	X	-
Inactive licenses: You may need to keep all user licenses on the system to preserve audit trails, but you certainly do not want to pay full user costs for inactive user licenses. The software contract should allow inactive user licenses at no cost, but this is not always the case.	X	-	-
Software maintenance: Ensures you are entitled to get all patches, upgrades, and new versions of the software. Typically, this costs 18 percent to 24 percent of the total software purchase price per year.	-	X	-
Patches: The cost of applying security and bug-fix patches. Remember to factor in testing the patches and the risk-adjusted cost of business downtime if the patches cause the system to fail.	-	X	-
Periodic upgrades: The cost of upgrading the software to a new release or latest version. Typically, this happens every 3 to 5 years. Upgrades can be large, expensive, and time-consuming projects, and can be a real risk to the business. Remember to factor in the risk-adjusted cost of business downtime if the upgrade causes the system to fail.	-	X	-

TCO Description	Cloud	COTS	Custom
Enhancements: The development cost of providing new functionality, for example, when the business environment changes or new regulations come into effect. Remember to include things like documentation and project management costs.	-	-	X
Bugs: The business cost of bugs, and the cost of fixing those bugs.	-	-	X
Testing: The cost of testing new releases of an application or a new release of custom software. Remember to factor in the risk-adjusted cost of business downtime if the new code causes the system to fail.	-	X	X
Change management: The cost of managing changes to the system configuration and related documentation. If the software was custom, the cost of managing changes to that software.	X	X	X
Fully loaded staff costs: Analyst and developer salaries, overheads, and management of those staff. Remember to factor in things like recruiting costs. Note that although all three types of software usually use analysts and developers, those costs are much higher for custom software.	X	X	X
Documentation: The cost of maintaining configuration, interface, and user documentation for the system.	X	X	X
Usability: Software that is difficult to use requires more training, and takes more time and support to achieve results. In addition, this software always costs more to maintain.	X	X	X
Ongoing training: New users come from company growth and employee turnover. In addition, when cloud vendors push enhancements some training may be required. Training costs are also incurred when replacing support staff.	X	X	X
User and admin support: The cost of help desk, system admins and any analysts or developers who will be supporting the system. Use the fully loaded employee cost, and factor in the costs of managing them.	X	X	X

TCO Description	Cloud	COTS	Custom
Disaster recovery and high availability: This ranges from backups through to hot failovers and includes regular testing. Hot failover can be very expensive to implement for off-the-shelf or custom software. With cloud products, it is often part of the standard offering, except for smaller vendors. There is an additional cost for cloud products, namely being able to recover if the cloud vendor goes bankrupt.	-	X	X
Bandwidth costs: Software in cloud, VoIP, video conferencing etc. all require bandwidth. These days bandwidth is not much of an issue, but like power and cooling costs for a data center, these costs can mount up. In addition, some systems have outbound bandwidth fees.	X	-	-
Data center: The costs of running the software in your data center like power, cooling and floor or rack space. This should also include indirect costs like security, data center maintenance, management of the data center and so on. If you are using a hosted data center, it is the monthly cost of running the hardware used by that software.	-	X	X
Downtime: The risk adjusted cost to the business for when the software is unavailable. • Custom software is seldom tested as well as cloud or COTS, and is therefore likely to have more downtime. • COTS software is more likely to go down than cloud software because cloud vendors invest in things like hot failover.	X	X	X
Depreciation: Writing off the capital cost of the software and the hardware it runs on.	-	X	X
Hardware replacement: Hardware like servers, storage, backup systems etc. usually needs to be replaced about every five years or so.	-	X	X
Security: The costs of keeping an application secure, especially if the application is visible outside of the firewall.	-	X	X

TCO Description	Cloud	COTS	Custom
Lost user productivity: Usually caused by a poor user interface or bugs, this happens when users should be able to perform a task with the software, but need support to complete that task.	X	X	X
Customer costs: Cost incurred because the software is not a good fit with the organization, for example: The software is difficult to use, so employees are constantly making order errors. It also takes employees longer to respond to customers than they should.	X	X	X
Opportunity costs of downtime: The cost of lost business when the system is down. Customers cannot place orders and turn to competitors instead. This can even result in those customers moving permanently to a competitor.	X	X	X
Compliance costs: Cost incurred by staying in compliance with regulations, plus the cost of auditing that compliance and remediating any issues discovered.	X	X	X
Security: The cost of ongoing security auditing, testing, and remediation.	X	X	X
Interfaces: Where the application needs to exchange data with other applications, there is a cost to maintaining that interface. If any of the applications are in the cloud, there may be data quantity related charges.	X	X	X
Reporting: Costs where data from multiple applications must be normalized and merged. Often done manually in spreadsheets.	X	X	X
Disaster recovery and business continuity: The cost of planning and testing for these items.	X	X	X
IT staff management. The fully loaded indirect costs of managing IT staff.	X	X	X

TCO Description	Cloud	COTS	Custom

Retirement costs

These are costs incurred when retiring software, for example:

- If you have grown out of one cloud product and moved to another. Old data must be available for several years for compliance reasons.

- If you are migrating from one help desk system to another, is it worth moving things like the knowledgebase?

Rather than migrating historical data to the new system, it may be preferable to keep the old system in an archived state for several years. There would be costs associated with that option.

	Cloud	COTS	Custom
Data export: You want to be able to export existing data in a usable format. Some vendors make it easy to get data into their systems, but with little incentive to make it easy to get data out again, exports can be expensive.	X	-	-
Archived systems: Data in the old system must remain available for reference, for example for compliance reasons. For cloud software, you want the system to be available for reference at a nominal cost. Unless this was part of the original contract, you could be forced to pay a lot more. For custom or purchased software running on servers, the associated data center costs are small. Note this cost continues as long as the system remains in an archived state.	X	-	-
Inactive licenses: You may need to keep all user licenses on the system to preserve audit trails, but you certainly do not want to pay full user costs for an archived system. Discounts for archived systems should be in the software contract.	X	-	-

Software ROI

The primary aim of a major software purchase is to meet expectations. One of those expectations is that the software ROI will be achieved, and that purchases with insufficient ROI are never made in the first place. It makes sense that software fully meeting expectations is going to return the best ROI.

Previous sections in this chapter provided two ways to estimate the value of a software project, and a method for estimating the TCO. Putting all of this together, we can estimate the ROI for the project:

Project ROI = (risk-adjusted value / TCO − 1) x estimated fit score x 100%

Note

- No product has a fit score of 100 percent and every purchase involves some compromises. Since the software has yet to be purchased, the estimated fit score above is the average of what you expect the fit scores of the top three or four products to be.

- At this point, you only have a rough estimate for ROI because the software has not yet been selected. You may even have three ROI estimates, one each for cloud, COTS and custom software.

- For the estimated fit score you could use:

  o Ninety percent is a generous value. If you select software that has a fit score of 90 percent or higher, you have found a product that fits your specific needs very well.

  o Eighty-five percent is middle of the road.

  o Eighty percent is on the low side. If the fit score of the best product was substantially less than eighty percent, the project scope should be examined because there is not a good fit with what the market can supply (See: Scope check on page 231).

At this point, you should examine the ROI and decide if it is indeed worth proceeding with the project. Bearing in mind that there are multiple assumptions in the ROI estimate, it is unlikely to be worth proceeding if the annualized ROI is less than about ten percent, and you may even set the bar significantly higher than this.

Estimating software ROIs

The fit score is a measure of how well a software product meets requirements (See: Actual and fit scores on page 214). It is expressed as a percentage where a fit score of 100 percent means that the software fully meets every requirement. However, no software product ever has a 100 percent fit score, so the individual software ROIs should be adjusted downwards based on their fit scores:

Software ROI = (risk adjusted value/software TCO – 1) x product fit score x 100%

Note

- The price of a software product is factored into its TCO, which is the *software TCO* in the above equation.

- Each software product will have a different ROI; usually the software product with the highest ROI is the one that is selected.

ROI example

To illustrate estimating the ROI, consider the example of Acme contemplating a new CRM system as part of a business development program. All values are per year, except where stated. Dollar amounts are rounded to the nearest million.

Hard benefits

Hard benefits are those benefits where a dollar value can be estimated.

Increased sales

Acme expects the new CRM will improve the efficiency of salespeople by reducing their administrative work. Acme expects this improvement to result in an effective increase of three salespeople. Salespeople average $12 million revenue each per year, with other Acme revenue coming from existing contracts. Thus, the outcome of the new CRM is an effective increase of three salespeople:

Three effective extra salespeople = $12 million x 3 = $36 million

Speed

Acme estimates the new CRM software will provide better visibility and management of the sales pipeline. The improved reporting will help resolve sales problems faster, and accelerate sales opportunities through the pipeline. Sales management anticipates this will improve the odds of winning business in competitive situations and estimates the annual value of this benefit to be $4 million.

Total hard benefits of new CRM = $36 + $4 = $40 million

Multiplier effect

The new CRM will integrate with the existing customer support system. Acme estimates this to be worth $4 million per year by reducing customer churn.

Adding the multiplier effect (+$4 million) = $44 million

Operational life

Acme is assuming an operational life of five years for the new CRM:

5-year operational life x $44 million = $220 million

Gross value of hard benefits from the CRM software project = $220 million

Eliminate egocentricity error

A large part of the value of this project will come from sales training and customer support training in addition to the value from the CRM itself. Acme estimates the new CRM itself will deliver 40 percent of the sales development program value.

$220 million x 40% = $88 million

Risk adjustment

Acme estimates the project has a 75 percent probability of delivering the planned ROI, and calculates the risk adjusted value of the project:

$88 million x 75% = $66 million

The risk adjusted value of the proposed Acme CRM system is $66 million.

Estimate project ROI

At this stage, Acme has not yet selected the software so they must use an estimate of the TCO for the five-year operational life, and then use this to estimate the ROI:

Risk adjusted value of project = $66 million

Assume the following:

- TCO over five-year operational life = $15 million

- Software fit score of 90 percent

Project ROI = (risk adjusted value/TCO – 1) x fit score x 100%

Expressed in numbers:

Project ROI = (66/15 - 1) x 90% x 100% = 306%

That is a project ROI of 306 percent over five years. To make for easy comparisons, express this as an annualized ROI using the formula below, where the operational life is specified in years:

$$Annualized\ ROI = \left[(Project\ ROI)^{1/Operational\ life} - 1 \right] x\ 100\%$$

Project Annualized ROI = 25%

Estimate software product ROI

The project ROI is a coarse estimate. Once the evaluation of potential software products is complete, estimates can be refined by factoring in the fit score and the TCO for each individual product being considered:

Product ROI = (risk adjusted value/product TCO – 1) x fit score x 100%

Using the risk adjusted value of $66 million for the Acme CRM project above and factoring in the fit score of each product, the individual annualized ROI for each product is shown in the table below:

Table 3: Annualized ROIs for individual software products

Software Product	Fit Score	5-year TCO	Gross Product ROI over 5 years	Annualized ROI
SellFit CRM	94%	$13 million	383%	31%
Prophecy CRM	90%	$18 million	240%	19%
Forceful CRM	84%	$14 million	312%	26%

This example illustrates estimating the ROI of individual software products. Breaking down the numbers in this manner helps achieve more accurate and defensible ROI estimates. To uncover potential problems, it is always a good idea to test your assumptions by inviting others to play devil's advocate and disagree with you. If this is going to be a major software purchase, critics are not hard to find!

Knowing when a selection project is worthwhile

With fewer than 10 percent of projects meeting expectations, the odds are not in your favor when making a major software purchase. Evaluation and selection projects are an enormous amount of work for any organization because there are so many factors to consider. It takes months from the start of the project to making the selection and purchasing the software. Is it worth doing all this work up front, either internally or by hiring outside consultants? Key to answering this question is determining the value the new software will provide to the organization.

The value of software comes from the benefits that result from using that software, and those benefits are maximized when the software meets expectations. The value of a selection project comes from purchasing software that meets those expectations, and then from reducing implementation project risks. Below is a list of situations to help decide if a selection project is worth the effort:

When a selection project is worthwhile

- **Bottom line:** If the new software will make a significant difference to the organization's revenue or profitability either directly or indirectly, you cannot afford to take the risk of the software not meeting expectations.

- **Excel and Access:** When there is a proliferation of spreadsheets and Access databases working around problems with the current system, that system does not properly meet requirements and needs replacing.

- **User resistance**: When substantial resistance to the new software is expected, the selection is an opportunity to create and nurture user buy-in. This is especially important if the new software will be used by many employees in the organization and failure is not an option.

- **Time constrained implementation**: Sometimes business reasons constrain implementation dates, for instance the software may go live before the financial year-end or a seasonal period. A selection process that collects critical information needed by the implementation reduces the risks of the schedule slipping.

- **Replacing existing software**: You may want to compare the value of existing software, an updated version of that software and potential replacement software products before deciding. If existing software is updated it can be a better fit than a new system, much cheaper, and less disruptive.

- **Reputation and status**: If a successful software project will enhance your organizational standing, but anything less would damage your career, a thorough selection project will minimize your personal risks.

When a selection project is not worthwhile

- **Low ROI:** If you estimate the annualized ROI of the project and it is too low, say less than 10 percent, you should not proceed with the selection project or buying any software.

Key lessons

This chapter begins with an explanation of why software should be purchased on value rather than price. That value is expressed as the ROI. Then we examined how to estimate ROI and decide whether it was worth proceeding with the project or not.

- Estimate the value of the software. The quick way to do this is to base the estimate on the purchase price. The more accurate way is to estimate the value of the benefits that flow from using the software.

- Estimate the TCO of the software for the implementation, operational life and retirement. Ensure all significant costs are factored into the estimate.

- Combine the value and TCO to estimate the project ROI. Only proceed with the project if there is sufficient ROI. If it is worth proceeding, complete the evaluation project, and then refine estimates with the ROI for each of the top three individual potential software products.

- A list of reasons is provided to help decide if it is worth proceeding with an evaluation project or not.

Chapter 6.   Software Strategy

No enterprise software purchase is done in isolation, and every major project should be considered from the perspective of how it aligns with and supports the business vision and strategy. This chapter will examine how the proposed software fits into the corporate vision. It also considers things that trigger software purchases, and concludes by examining the costs of delaying software upgrades.

The power of vision

For many organizations or departments, a vision or mission statement[1] is de rigueur. The problem, however, is it's not used to drive decision-making. Properly understood and used, a vision or mission can bring a laser-like focus to an organization, company, department, or even an individual and help achieve new heights and relevance.

In this book, vision and mission are treated as synonyms. The fundamental concept of a vision is that it can never be achieved except in a trivial sense. A vision or mission statement exists to translate core values into objectives, goals, projects, tasks etc., all of which can be achieved.

When a goal is achieved, the vision guides the selection of the next goal. It is this goal setting guidance that keeps the focus and alignment. When a company does not understand the difference between a vision and a goal, they can lose their way in the market.

Consider Microsoft in the late '80s and early '90s when their "vision" was "a computer on every desk and in every home." When a goal is far enough away, it can masquerade as a vision or mission and guide the company, and this is what happened to Microsoft. When a PC on every desk was achieved in the late '90s, they stumbled because they did not have the vision to guide them beyond that

---

[1]The Society for HR Management defines the mission statement as explaining the reason for existence while the vision statement describes a future successful state. The problem is that when the future state is achieved, what is next? These two definitions do not help guide the setting of future goals and objectives.

goal. That is why Microsoft went from being a market leader to a company fighting to stay relevant in the early 2000's. Lack of vision resulted in misaligned goals and lost focus.

Compare this with Apple, a company who used their vision superbly. To paraphrase Tim Cook's 2015 commencement address at George Washington University: "Most people have forgotten, but in 1997 and early 1998, Apple had been adrift for years. Rudderless. However, Steve Jobs thought Apple could be great again. His vision for Apple was a company that turned powerful technology into tools that were easy to use; that help people realize their dreams and change the world for the better."

Think of the products made by Apple with Steve Jobs at the helm: the iPod, iPhone, and iPad and how they made Apple one of the most valuable companies in the world. That shows the power of vision. In contrast, Steve Ballmer's reaction to the new iPhone was that it was way overpriced, and that he really liked Microsoft's phone strategy. He simply did not get Steve Jobs' vision. That lack of vision caused Microsoft to fail completely in the smartphone market, while Apple dominated it. That is the power of vision. (See: Ballmer laughs at iPhone: youtube.com/watch?v=eywi0h_Y5_U)

Defining the vision

The Microsoft and Apple examples above explain the vision concept at the corporate level, but the same principles apply at the departmental level and even at the personal level. A vision is built on the foundation of core values, and it determines how those values are expressed. You could think of the vision as the way core values are translated into executable tasks.

An essential point is that a vision must not be achievable, except in a trivial sense. If you can achieve a vision in a non-trivial sense, then it is a goal, objective etc. and not a vision. If a so-called "vision" is achieved, then it vanishes and must be replaced by a new one. Think back to what happened to Microsoft when their "vision" of a PC on every desk and in every home was achieved; they no longer had anything to guide them when setting new goals or objectives.

The essential point of a vision is that it can never be achieved, therefore, it continues to exist in order to guide the setting of new goals, objectives etc. which *are* achieved. The vision translates core values into objectives and goals that are aligned, achievable and measurable. The vision focuses effort and activities on things that matter while avoiding the waste and distraction caused by misalignment.

Ideally, the vision or mission statement is no longer than about 15 words, and should be written in a way that its meaning is immediately apparent to anybody in that field. Don't be deceived. While they look simple, there is usually a great deal of thought behind them and it can take months or even years of thought to get them right.

Many corporations don't understand the difference between a mission and an objective, for example, they will declare their mission is to become No. 1 in their market. The problem is that when they achieve that objective, they do not know what to do next and lose direction. However, by rephrasing this objective it can be turned into a mission. For example, "becoming No. 1 in the market" can be rewritten as "Leading the market in..." Notice how this statement guides and aligns the setting of new goals, and remains relevant even when the No. 1 position in the market is achieved.

Software selection strategy

The corporate vision guides the setting of objectives. The software strategy describes what needs to be done to achieve those objectives from the perspective of selection. When it comes to software strategy, it is never really about "technology X." There may be good reasons for "technology X" because it serves a function, it supports the business vision, improves efficiencies and reduces costs. But at the end of the day, it is never about technology per se. Rather it is about what technology can do for the business. After all, what software technologies from 10 years ago are still on the forefront today?

In the corporate world, new software is always purchased in the context of the business. Very few companies buy software for pride of ownership. Rather, software is bought to realize the benefits that flow from using it. For example, even if new software is purchased to ensure compliance with certain standards, ultimately its purpose is to avoid the cost of noncompliance. Selecting the software that best meets the functional and non-functional needs of an organization is a critical part of meeting objectives and executing on the corporate vision.

Software purchasing triggers

All companies need software to operate, but what events push them over the edge and trigger a major purchase? What are the real problems triggering the search for new software? Why is the project being undertaken now and not last year or next year?

Much of the time the trigger is some form of pain caused by existing software, but there are other reasons. Very often, there is more than one trigger behind the decision to move ahead with an evaluation and selection project.

The purchasing trigger can be sudden and urgent, for example a cloud vendor shutting down. More frequently, it is caused by software pains that gradually develop over time. Eventually, the organization decides to make a purchase, or at least investigate the possibility of a purchase. There are two types of purchasing triggers, internal and external. Many of the common triggers are listed below:

Internal triggers

- **Business growth:** For example, existing systems may not be able to handle the increasing volume of transactions. Growth may also expose other limitations of existing software, for example, where certain tasks were handled by spreadsheets outside the current software. When the company was smaller this worked, but spreadsheets do not scale up with growth.

- **Mergers and acquisitions:** For example, when two companies of comparable size merge, there is usually a desire to eliminate software redundancies, information siloes etc. For all the software products that are used by both companies, do they keep system A or system B, or do they use this as an opportunity to get an entirely new system C?

- **Business changes:** For example, moving into new markets, out of old markets, divesting a spinoff, or a company downsizes.

- **Cost savings:** Existing software has missing or inadequate functionality and the organization wants to streamline internal operations and reduce costs. For example, every month employees spend far too much time massaging data in spreadsheets to produce reports that could be automatically delivered by better software.

- **Software rationalization:** Various parts of the organization use similar software products that have a high degree of functional overlap. The same (or similar) data is collected by different systems in silos, and it is difficult to keep this data synchronized (See: Software rationalization on page 144).

    After a merger or acquisition, a company can have two (or more) different products that do the same things, e.g. multiple ERP systems, multiple CRM systems and so on. One large company in the life science field we are familiar with has been through multiple mergers and acquisitions over the years and at last count had a combined total of 46 CRM systems!

- **Replacing homegrown software:** The cost or effort of maintaining a homegrown application has become too high for the value that the application brings to the organization. Alternatively, a company may decide it no longer wants to be in the business of developing their own application.

- **Messaging:** Occasionally management uses a major software purchase to communicate to analysts or Wall Street that the company is "doing something" about lackluster results, and thereby hopes to maintain or push up its stock price.

    In February 2015, the CEO of Cubic Corporation based in Southern California announced they were purchasing a new ERP system that was supposed to save $16 million per year. In most quarterly reports since then the costs of this system have been broken out on its own line item. The way Cubic has trumpeted this new ERP has all the hallmarks of using this purchase to communicate a message to the market (See the introduction to Chapter 7: Project Management on page 117 for more on this slow-moving software disaster).

- **Continuous improvement.** Organizations that actively practice continuous improvement may identify software that is past its prime and needs replacing.

- **Vendor audits.** The threat of a software audit by a vendor can prompt an organization to take stock of their software and find a product that has outlived its usefulness and needs to be replaced.

External triggers

- **Regulatory changes**. For example, if the U.S. government decided to introduce federal VAT (value added tax), many companies might use this as an opportunity to replace existing software.

- **Software is obsolete**. Typically, this happens with on-premises software that has not been updated for years. Training costs have increased, there are no longer any security patches, and it has become difficult to maintain the underlying hardware and so on.

> *We were talking to a manufacturing client about new ERP software. In 2016, they were still using character-based IBM green screens to manage their manufacturing. They were complaining that it took at least four weeks to train new employees because nobody had experience with these old systems anymore. This and other pains eventually accumulated to the point where they decided to evaluate manufacturing ERP software.*

- **Vendor product vision changes**. A company wants one set of features out of their software, but vendor development takes the product in another direction. This also happens when a vendor loses their vision for a product. Lotus Notes was very popular in the corporate market, but a few years after IBM bought it in the mid '90s it just faded away.

- **Vendor slows development**. This is very common. A large vendor buys a smaller and successful vendor and then "milks" the product for revenue. Apart from security patches, most development stops, but customers continue to pay maintenance fees.

- **Vendor discontinues development**. The software is no longer updated, and security vulnerabilities are no longer patched. For example, think Windows XP.

- **Vendor goes out of business**. The software is no longer updated and security vulnerabilities are not patched. Source code can be lost.

- **Vendor costs**. Sometimes vendors raise their maintenance and support charges to the point where the organization will need to seek lower-cost software.

No discussion of purchase triggers would be complete without considering evaluation project timing. For selection project duration and common sources of project delays, refer to, Selection project duration on page 137.

The costs of not upgrading enterprise software

Some things in life are inevitable: death, taxes and obsolete software. Relentless and rapid innovation means constantly improving software. Newer products must do more, be easier to use and cost less than established products otherwise there is no reason to buy them. However, organizations know their software, and may hang onto it long past its prime. Though there are many reasons not to change enterprise software, the biggest is inertia. If it isn't broken, why fix it?

The cost of not replacing old software must be estimated to answer this question, especially for systems that have been in place for more than 5 to 10 years. Most companies underestimate the costs of inaction. This cost can be much higher than expected, and is incurred every year that the old software is being used. Start by estimating the common costs of obsolete software listed below. For an expanded treatment of estimating the value of software refer to Chapter 5: Select Software for Value, Not Price on page 81.

Increases in:

- **Revenue**. Would new software enable revenue capture that cannot be provided by the current system? That missed revenue is an opportunity cost.

- **Profit**. Would new software provide opportunities for increased profit, for example, by allowing premium services with the potential to earn greater profits?

- **Growth**. Is organizational growth being constrained by obsolete software? For example, is the company unable to tackle new markets because of software limits? This is another opportunity cost.

Target is a U.S. corporation that wanted to expand into Canada. Target's software had to be modified for the new location, for example to handle the metric system and the Canadian currency. Those modifications were far more difficult than anticipated.

When Target went live in Canada, the inability of their software to handle imperial and metric units correctly caused problems like accurately computing shelving locations. In turn, this caused items to back up in the distribution centers and leave store shelves empty. There is more to the story (see link below), but these software limitations caused the entire Canadian operation to fail, costing Target over $2 billion.

(See: Billion-dollar mistake: How inferior IT killed Target Canada: zdnet.com/article/billion-dollar-failures-how-bad-decisions-and-poor-it-killed-target-canada)

- **Retention**. Will the new system be better at retaining customers, e.g. by facilitating faster service? If you sell online, would the new software reduce abandoned shopping carts?

- **Stock price**. Sometimes companies want to use a major software purchase to send a message to Wall Street that they are "doing something" about a problem. They hope this message will boost their stock price (See the story of Cubic Corporation at the start of Chapter 7 on page 117 for an example of this kind of market messaging).

Reductions in:

- **Production costs**. Would new software allow production costs to be cut by reducing process steps?

- **Support costs**. Obsolete systems cost more to maintain than newer systems, because of the increased need for admins, developers, and help desk resources. Newer systems tend to cost significantly less to run because many of those complexities have been eliminated. What would the annual support cost difference be?

- **Training costs**. The cost of training new users on obsolete systems can be high. How much would a better user interface and less complexity reduce ongoing annual training costs?

- **Business risk**. Obsolete software may be running on obsolete hardware. If that hardware fails, everything stops. You may struggle to find replacement hardware and technical skills for repairs. Estimate the business cost of losing that system, and multiply it by the probability of the system failing.

- **Integration costs**. It can be costly when integrating obsolete software into more modern systems. This cost is incurred by having to pay more to write integration code or have data moved manually via spreadsheets. Estimate the annual costs of integrating the old system with new systems that are being deployed in the organization.

- **Software maintenance**. After about five years, most companies will have spent more on software maintenance than they originally paid for the software licenses. In addition, many organizations pay for maintenance that will never be used.

- **Time and effort**. Could new software enable existing work to be done faster and with less effort?

Improvements to:

- **Productivity and efficiency**. New software will usually enhance productivity and efficiency because of things like better user interfaces or improved workflows. Examine the anticipated productivity and efficiency gains from the new software, and estimate the annual cost of not having them.

- **Processes**. If the new software supports new or improved processes, what would these be worth?

- **Quality**. Would new software allow earlier detection and correction of defects in your system or production? How would that affect revenue and profitability? What effect would that improvement in quality have on reducing customer churn?

- **Reporting**. Modern software usually has far better reporting capabilities than older software:

  o Provides summary reports on dashboards, and supports drilling down to underlying data.

  o Reducing the work needed to generate reports.

- o   Making reports available sooner, for example in real time and not needing to wait for batch processes to complete, or eliminating manual data massaging in Excel.

- o   Providing information that is not available in the old system.

- **Information quality and currency**. Today, businesses run on information that must be comprehensive and current. Obsolete systems do not capture information in the detail required and are slow in providing it to other systems. For example, a batch job may only run at night, yet the business needs the information in real time.

- **Elimination of data silos**. Larger organizations often have silos of information that have built up over time. For example, if both sales and technical support have separate customer databases, will the new software allow these databases to be combined to provide a single source of information, removing duplication, and improving accuracy?

Creation of:

- **New products.** Would the new software allow the creation of new products? For example, if you are a service provider, would the new software allow the creation of a new service that could be added to your product line?

To estimate the cost of not replacing obsolete software, estimate the annual amounts for each item above that applies, along with those from any other situations specific to your organization. The total of all those items is an estimate of the annual cost of not replacing the software. The bigger this number, the more urgent replacing the obsolete software is. And remember, this is an annual hidden cost that does not show on the income statement.

Although some people might think that cloud software is constantly updated and will never be obsolete, there are still reasons for replacing it. A company can outgrow an existing system in the cloud and upgrading to new and more capable software could result in significant gains.

At a minimum, software older than 5 to 10 years should go through this exercise, which should then be repeated every three years. By failing to examine the cost of not replacing obsolete software, you may be leaving a lot of money on the table.

Key lessons

- Proposed new enterprise software must align with and support the business vision and strategy. If that alignment is missing, then the organization should not proceed with the purchase.

- Triggers for major software purchases can be from inside or outside the organization, and there are often multiple triggers behind a decision to select new software. Triggers can be the anticipation of gain, but more often they are avoiding pain.

- "If it ain't broke, don't fix it" thinking can cost an organization dearly. We described a method to estimate the cost of using enterprise software beyond its prime, and suggested that any software that has been used for more than five years should be examined every three years to see if it is still delivering a reasonable value.

- We considered the role timing plays in a successful software selection. We concluded that the better course of action was to undertake software selection projects sooner rather than later. It is crucial not to delay software selection projects until it becomes critical because time pressure is a major contributor to project failures.

Chapter 7.   Project Management

Based in Southern California, Cubic Corporation is a public company that operates in the defense and transport industries. In February 2015, the CEO announced steps to streamline operations to improve profitability, which was expected to yield about $16 million pre-tax savings annually starting in fiscal year 2016. This would be about $160 million savings over 10 years.

Bob provides an informal update on the status of the ERP project

The ERP project started in late 2014. Based on published financials, as of March 2017, Cubic had spent $61 million on the project. With completion estimated to be in 2018 (assume Q2) and extrapolating implementation costs, they will have spent a total of about $86 million. (This scenario was projected from publicly available information at the time of writing. The actual outcome of the Cubic ERP acquisition may be different.)

The same problems that caused the two-year extension to the implementation are likely to cause business disruption when the software goes into production; estimate $8 million for this cost. In addition, those same problems will reduce the value returned from the new software; estimate this to be $12 million per year instead of the anticipated $16 million.

If a 10-year lifetime is used for this software, what return can Cubic expect from their ERP investment? The purchase was made around Q4, 2014 and assuming they go live in Q2, 2018, they will have a working life of 6.5 years x $12 million value returned per year = $78 million, less the $8 million business disruption cost incurred when going into production. Over 10 years that is a loss of $16 million instead of a savings of $160 million. It is interesting to note that during the Q2 Fiscal Year 2017 results conference call the CEO said he was expecting "significant savings and efficiency."

Why will the expected savings of $160 million turn into a loss of $16 million? There would have been an inadequate requirements analysis, which meant that "new" requirements were discovered during implementation. Dealing with these "new" requirements takes time, which causes implementation schedules to slip. In an effort to rein in slipping schedules, items are left for "phase 2" and this is what causes business disruption when going live. The only winners in this affair are the software and implementation vendors.

The key to avoiding problems like the one above is in the software selection phase. This chapter focuses on the project management aspects of that process. Projects are executed by people, and we begin by examining their roles and how they affect the selection process.

People and role considerations

People play a significant part in bringing a software acquisition project to a successful conclusion. In this section, we examine the various project roles played by people both inside and outside the organization.

The role of the software selection expert

Using a software selection expert as project manager of the selection process is essential. This person must understand every step of the process because they will guide the selection to a successful conclusion. This person is usually a consultant because very few companies make a large enough number of major software purchases for an employee to develop the needed software selection skills.

With small to midsized projects, the software selection consultant manager can have enough experience to take on the role of subject matter expert. In these circumstances, they use the process of reverse engineering software features into requirements to help them understand organizational needs. In larger projects, this person may be assisted by one or more subject matter experts. In still larger projects, there may be several people under the project manager who host requirements weighting meetings with users. Running multiple requirements weighting meetings in parallel reduces the overall time taken by the project.

The role of software selection consultants

In many organizations, especially midsized or smaller companies, the people who will evaluate new software also have their daily responsibilities. When the work involved in a selection project runs into hundreds or even thousands of hours and resources are limited, is it any wonder that the new software so seldom meets expectations? If you have a major purchase on the horizon, it can be well worth using external consultants for the project work. The advantages are as follows:

- You avoid overloading employees who still have their regular workload to deal with. In addition, these employees are unlikely to have developed a mature software selection process because companies don't make major software purchases frequently enough.

- Consultants who specialize in software selection understand the process and have the experience to ensure that the value of the software acquisition is maximized.

- For the same work, consultants are faster because they know the process. In addition, they will have libraries that cover some or most of the requirements, which means spending less time developing requirements.

- Being outsiders, consultants avoid getting entangled in internal organizational politics.

For more on what questions to ask when interviewing software selection consultants check out Appendix A: Selecting Software Selection Consultants on page 283.

The role of subject matter experts

Subject-matter experts (SMEs) are familiar with both the type of software being considered and the business domain in which that software operates. Their expertise is used in the following places:

- SMEs assist in developing requirements using the reverse engineering process.

- SMEs verify requirements are complete and written to be implementable.

- SMEs provide out-of-the-box thinking. During requirements weighting meetings, SMEs provide perspectives from outside the organization and prompt users to consider each requirement in their current and future context, and arrive at the correct weight for that requirement.

Larger companies evaluating software like ERP may need the services of several SMEs, e.g. for finance, production, supply chain, etc. While SME's may be employees in larger organizations, in smaller ones they are usually consultants.

One error many organizations make is assuming SMEs are experts at software selection, which is seldom the case. Rather, SMEs specialize in a specific industry or business process like supply chain, finance etc. While they may have experience with multiple software products that pertain to their expertise, they are rarely skilled in the software evaluation process.

The role of users

Many people think that users are the best source of requirements, but they are not. Users know their pain points, but seldom know much more. While users who are new to the organization may have a broader experience from previous employers, those who have been employed for many years lack that perspective. For these reasons, users can only supply a very limited list of requirements. The primary roles of users in an evaluation are to:

- Weight requirements for importance to the organization.

- Provide feedback from software demos.

While users may not be able to supply more than a subset of requirements, it is critical to get their buy-in because they are the people who will be using the software. To get their buy-in, users must be part of the software selection process (See: Creating and nurturing user buy-in on page 122).

The role of the decision-maker

When following a data-driven process, the software selection decision is made by the gap analysis and confirmed by the software demo. The role of the decision-maker is to consider the gap analysis, factor in demo feedback and make the provisional software selection decision. Occasionally a committee may be part of that selection process, especially if there are two or three software products with comparable fit scores and similar feedback from users. Ultimately, the decision-maker executes the decision, which means approving or withholding payment for the new software.

The role of committees

When organizations use committees to select business-critical software, they are substituting a committee for a process. Experience shows this does not work as expected (See: Relying on committees to select software on page 27). Except as described in the role of the decision-maker above, committees should not be used to select enterprise software.

The role of software vendors

Software vendors are the companies that create the software. Smaller software vendors will handle the full sales and implementation process. Larger software vendors sell through their partners who also handle the implementation. However, you will be signing license agreements with the vendors, not the partner or reseller (See: Software contract risks on page 255).

The role of implementation vendors

As mentioned above, larger software companies sell their products through resellers who are the implementation vendors. These resellers respond to the RFI, close the sale, and implement the software.

Suppose you used an implementation vendor that did not respond to your RFI and the project failed, if you end up in court you are in a weak position. For example, if, based on the RFI, you expected the software to meet a specific requirement and it did not, the vendor can justifiably say they never claimed the software would meet that requirement. As this example shows, the vendor who responds to the RFI should be the one who does the implementation. This means you must perform due diligence on a vendor before inviting them to respond to your RFI.

One mistake made by many organizations is that of asking implementation vendors what software they should consider or buy. It's like asking a barber if you need a haircut! Don't do it. A vendor can only offer an opinion on software they are familiar with, and that won't necessarily be the best software for your specific needs.

Implementation resources

When building a luxury home, the key to quality construction is adequate planning. Likewise, the key to a successful software purchase is an adequate selection. Having a few IT people work on the project part-time in addition to their regular duties almost guarantees a failure, as does hiring consultants on the cheap. This is one reason so many major software purchases fail to meet expectations.

The question then becomes this, 'Given the desired return on your software investment, what resources and funds will you commit to the selection project?' Only you can answer that question, but the wrong answer can mean a lot of pain for you and your organization.

Creating and nurturing user buy-in

The lack of stakeholder involvement can doom new enterprise software. Who are the stakeholders, why must they be involved and how do you involve them? This is not a technical issue, but a people issue that directly affects the outcome of a software acquisition project.

A big mistake made with software purchases is leaving user buy-in until the implementation phase. When this happens, users feel the software is being foisted on them without their input. Some of them may be indifferent to the new software; others may actively push against it and refuse to use it.

A salesperson who had taken a severance package related the story of a major international pharmaceutical company that had implemented a new CRM sys-

tem. As the tale progressed, it was apparent the company had made many of the classic software selection mistakes.

Sales teams rejected the new CRM software that had been forced on them and continued to use their existing spreadsheets. To meet directives that they use the new software, they logged in once per week and updated data from those spreadsheets. Of course, this consumed a number of hours, time they should have been out selling.

The new CRM software did nothing to resolve the underlying problems. Sales continued to lag, which was reflected by a 25 percent decrease in stock price over a two-year period. That CRM was a very expensive software failure in terms of both stock price and market position.

Contrast this to the situation where users cannot wait to be trained and start using the new software. Much better, isn't it? So how do you achieve this buy-in? The answer is to involve users in the software selection process right from the start.

Who are the stakeholders?

Internal users: (also called end-users) Employees who make regular use of the system. In most projects, the internal users are the most relevant stakeholders. If they have truly bought into the new system, the probability of success is far greater.

Executive sponsors: They will invest their budgets in the new software. They want a sizable ROI; otherwise why bother with the project?

Indirect access users: Users of any systems that interface with the new software. For example, think of an employee using an expense claim system that connects to the corporate accounting system. Think of a salesperson using a CRM to update a master customer record in an ERP system. In this capacity, the employees are indirect access users of the underlying system.

External users: Non-employees who use the system. For example, they could be vendors, job applicants and customers tracking orders.

Why is user buy-in so important?

New enterprise software requires considerable effort from users, such as learning the new system, or using new and old software in parallel for a few months. When users are afraid the new software will cause them to lose their jobs, resent the extra work, have no interest in the new software or are actively working against it, the rollout to production is in serious trouble.

An important aspect of curating user buy-in is to avoid the situation where users want to recreate their old business processes in the new system, rather than exploring how the new system can improve those processes.

> *A West Coast manufacturing and general distribution company wanted ERP and was looking at JD Edwards, Oracle and SAP. They didn't put any requirements together. They started with demos, and then selected SAP "because they liked it." The consultant telling the story said, "What we saw was they wanted to reinvent their legacy system." They were not looking at how the new software could improve business processes.*
>
> *During the implementation, there was one change order after another. There was no user buy-in because they were reinventing the legacy system. This company paid for their lack of preparation with an ERP implementation that took a year longer than planned.*

How to create and nurture user buy-in

The key to creating and nurturing user buy-in is to involve users in the evaluation and selection process. When they take ownership of the new software it becomes theirs, and they will do what is necessary to ensure success. If this is left for the implementation stage it is far too late.

Users must know the software selection is driven by their needs and priorities. They must feel involved in the process; know they are being heard and that their lives will be easier after the transition. This must be done with a transparent and data-driven selection process that does not favor political or other interests over real needs.

Users must also understand that every major software purchase is a compromise, and that the aim of the selection is to minimize that compromise. Ensure soft-

ware that will be used by many departments is not selected by only one department. To maximize buy-in, everybody should be involved, which can be challenging in larger organizations. There are four places where user buy-in is created and nurtured:

1. Project kick-off meeting

This meeting formally announces the project, and is the first opportunity to
communicate with users. If the new software will result in jobs being eliminated,
ensure those employees will be retrained and redeployed. Let them know that
the software will do the tedious work, which frees them to be retrained for more
interesting jobs. It is an opportunity for them to improve their skills and grow
their income. Do not use the new software as an opportunity to reduce head-
count or the organization's credibility will be destroyed.

2. Initial requirements interviews

These interviews are an opportunity to build rapport with users. Unfortunately,
most users only know their pain points and few other requirements, so don't expect too much from them (See: Sources of requirements on page 174 for other
methods of gathering requirements).

3. Weighting requirements

Here different user teams like finance, IT, production, and so on are interviewed.
For each requirement capture the weight (how important it is), why it is important and to whom it is important. When users see their details written on
each requirement, they feel the organization is listening to them. This is the
most powerful step of all for creating and nurturing user buy-in.

4. Software demos

Software demonstrations typically have up to three products selected. Users are
reminded that the products are selected based on the gap analysis and that the
demo serves only to confirm that decision, not to make it. The demos are where
the excitement for the new system really builds in the user community (See:
Software demos on page 243). When user feedback is captured and summarized,
users really feel the organization is listening to them.

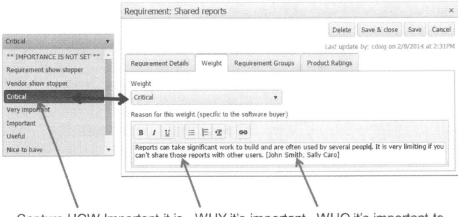

Capture HOW Important it is, WHY it's important, WHO it's important to.
(i.e. the weight)

Figure 2: Screenshot of requirement weighting

In one of our early projects, we were helping a company select an ERP system. The client team was weighting their inventory requirements. Buddy, a blue-collar worker whose "office" was the warehouse, was responsible for that inventory.

When Buddy saw his comments and his name written on the inventory requirements his eyes absolutely lit up. At that point, he understood the company valued his input and was factoring his needs into the selection. He became a passionate advocate for the new software because his input was invested in the decision. After seeing this scenario played out several times, we realized that involving users in the selection decision is a critical part of the ultimate success of the new software.

Other communication

It is understood that there needs to be constant communication with stakeholders all the way through the project. Best practice is to send that communication to users via a project status page and notify users of all updates by text or email.

Managing expectations

Closely related to maximizing user buy-in is managing user expectations. User expectations are managed by aligning them with the features that the short-listed products can deliver (See: Expectations management on page 245).

User adoption matters!

Process is the key to success

Imagine entering a courtroom where the trial consists of a prosecutor presenting PowerPoint slides. In 20 compelling charts, he demonstrates why the defendant is guilty. The judge challenges some facts from the presentation, but the prosecutor has a satisfactory answer to every objection. So, the judge decides, and the accused is sentenced. That wouldn't be due process, would it? (Analogy by Olivier Sibony of McKinsey from How CFOs can keep strategic decisions on track, from an interview by Bill Huyett and Tim Koller.)

If this process is shocking in a courtroom, why is it acceptable when selecting enterprise software? Substitute the prosecutor for the salesperson, the judge for the buyer and you have the same situation. Problems with selecting enterprise software are caused by a lack of process.

Erecting a large building is a complex process with thousands of tasks that need completing. Each task is a step towards meeting a requirement in the building design specification. Unless there is a process to manage these tasks, some will be missed and those requirements will not be satisfied. Unsatisfied requirements will cause problems when the building is handed over to the buyer.

Enterprise software is the same, with thousands of requirements that need to be satisfied. However, few organizations have a formal process to ensure those requirements are, in fact, properly satisfied. Unsatisfied requirements cause disruption to normal business operations when users start working with the new software.

The key to a successful enterprise software acquisition is to use a good process, one which has the characteristics listed below.

Designed for implementation

A major cause of implementation project delays is decision latency, which is the time needed for decisions to be made. Sometimes implementation teams end up waiting weeks for a decision to be made by the business. When these decisions aren't made quickly enough, delays start to pile up and schedules slip.

While decisions will always be made during the implementation, decision latency is reduced by designing the selection process to collect the critical information needed for the implementation.

- The requirements analysis must be broad enough. All significant requirements need to be identified, including unknown requirements. No significant "new" requirements should be found during the implementation.

- The requirements analysis must be deep enough. Requirements need to be written in enough detail to be implemented.

- Requirements should be weighted: include a measure of how important they are, why they are important and who they are important to. The weight and the reason a requirement is important will usually answer most implementation questions. When more detail is needed by the implementation consultant, the requirement contains the names of people who can answer their questions.

In addition to selecting the software that best meets the organization's specific requirements, the selection process should be designed to gather the critical information needed for the implementation process. A benefit of doing this decision-making in the analysis phase is the organization has more time to think about the ramifications of their answers. If decisions are changed before the software is selected, those changes will not cause any delays.

When things must be done

The process should describe what triggers a selection project (See: Software purchasing triggers on page 109), and when the work should be done, i.e. the order of tasks. When gathering requirements for new software there is always a strong temptation to improve business workflows. However, this would be working in a vacuum because the new software is yet to be selected. Rather, process re-engineering should be left for the implementation phase (See: Process analysis and optimization on page 31).

Who should do the work

The process should describe who is responsible for tasks, and the skills needed to complete those tasks (See: People and role considerations on page 118).

What must be done and how

The process should describe the steps needed in enough detail so they can be executed by a competent professional. It must not list vague, high-level generalities, such as "gather requirements" without describing how to do this.

Why things must be done

The process should describe why things must be done so it can be fine-tuned if necessary. Every step should be clearly explained, and there should be no steps that do not add value. In addition, the process should be documented so any competent professional can understand how and why it works.

The output of each process step should logically flow into the input of the next step, and everything should contribute to the outcome. The process should be designed to collect the information needed for the software implementation, which is used to minimize the risk of slipping schedules, increasing costs and business disruption when going live.

Deterministic

The selection process should be deterministic, which means the decision is driven by the data collected rather than by the professional opinions of those involved. If a different team in the same situation used the same process, they would arrive at the same conclusion. In addition, the selection should be transparent and auditable, and it should be possible to see how the fit scores were calculated.

The place of the demo

Starting a software selection with demos is absolutely the wrong way to go about the project, and is such a 20th century approach to buying software. While most of today's buyers are typically well-informed about a number of products and their competitors, when it comes to selecting software far too many organizations still operate in the last century.

Of course, vendors want to start with a demo of all their glitzy features and are very happy to oblige. They want the opportunity to influence you with their "reality distortion field," they want to build the relationship and grow your trust in them. And once they have your trust, the sale is primed to close.

Vendors focus on emphasizing their unique features and persuading you that those features are critical to your success. When other vendors do not have those features you might think they are out of the running, but don't be fooled. The path to success is a robust selection process that includes a gap analysis which *measures* how well the software products meet *your particular needs*. The decision is made based on the gap analysis and the demo confirms that decision. Don't short circuit the process or you will end up with software that doesn't meet expectations.

A mature software selection process

Many organizations never give a thought to the maturity of their software selection process, which is one of the reasons why so few major software purchases meet expectations. Based on CMMI publications we have developed the Software Selection Maturity Scale (SSMS) to measure the maturity of the software selection process. While CMMI for Acquisition covers processes for acquiring products and services, SSMS described here covers just enterprise software selection. Note that there is not a one-to-one correspondence between CMMI and SSMS.

SSMS has six levels, numbered 0 to 5 as shown below. As you move up the list, processes are more mature and project risks reduced. Each level adds to the one below.

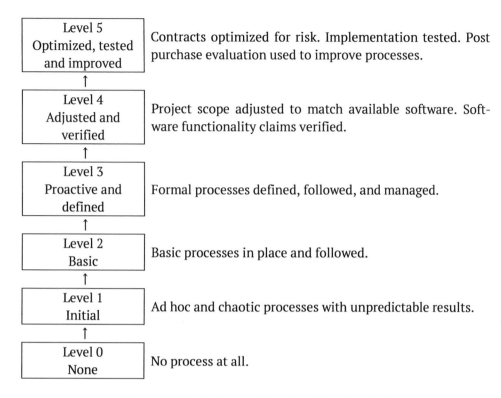

Figure 3: The Software Selection Maturity Scale

Level 0 - None

There is no process in place for evaluating and selecting software. Selection is based on experience or the advice of others; referrals from colleagues, product reviews or salespeople. Software may be selected for unethical reasons like favors or bribes. If there are demos, the most persuasive pitch wins.

Risks

- Implementation schedules always slip, and budgets are exceeded.

- There is invariably business disruption when going live.

- There is a major risk of the new software failing to meet organizational needs adequately.

- There is little leverage over vendors who over promise and under deliver.

Level 1 - Initial

Evaluating and selecting software is ad hoc and chaotic, with success depending on individual efforts. Even if a software purchase meets expectations, there is no ability to repeat that success with the next project.

Characteristics

- IT usually manages the selection project with little planning for needed resources. Minimal project management.

- Inability to articulate organizational needs. Poorly defined requirements written at too high a level, usually in Word documents or spreadsheets.

- Software is informally evaluated against high-level requirements. If used, scoring is rudimentary.

- Software selection is subjective and unrepeatable, and may be chosen by a committee. May also be selected based on previous experience, e.g. "I know what I am doing" (See: Dunning-Kruger effect under Cognitive bias on page 23), but with little attempt to examine organizational differences.

Risks

- Implementation schedules slip and budgets are exceeded.

- Serious risk of business disruption when going live.

- Serious risk of the software not properly meeting organizational needs.

- Little leverage with vendors who over promise and under deliver.

Level 2 - Basic

A basic software evaluation process is established and followed. Organizations can achieve partial success, but usually fail to meet the ROI used to justify the software purchase.

Characteristics

- Informal ROI estimate. Some project management. Limited IT resources with no specific software selection training.

- Mainly functional requirements are gathered mostly from users and stakeholders. No process in place to discover unknown requirements.

- Requirements managed in spreadsheets in moderate detail, and may be weighted for importance.

- Moderate product research into alternatives. Basic gap analysis done: products may be scored with a simple system (often just yes or no).

- Non-functional requirements like security, support, licensing, etc. tend to be examined only superficially.

- Somewhat subjective software selection process that is not readily repeatable. The selection decision is often made by a committee.

Risks

- Implementation schedules often slip, and budgets are exceeded.

- Moderate risk of software failing to properly meet organizational needs.

- Significant contractual risks.

Level 3 – Defined

A software evaluation and selection process is established, followed and managed.

Characteristics

- Formal ROI estimate before a project starts.

- Reasonable project management in place. Adequate resources are available that may include external consultants. Resources are trained on the principles of evaluating software. Some resources are familiar with the type of software being evaluated.

- The organization understands the value of a thorough requirements analysis. Requirements are well written and captured in enough detail to be implemented. External sources of requirements may be used, and requirements are reverse engineered from potential products. Requirements are weighted for importance to create the requirements profile and traceability matrix.

- There is adequate research into potential software products.

- Products are rated by how well they meet requirements. Formal gap analysis is done and products ranked by fit score.

- The organization knows how well the software will work for their specific needs before making the purchase. The selection decision is data-driven, objective and repeatable.

- All significant requirements were captured in the analysis phase. No significant "new" requirements are found during the implementation, which is within budget and on time.

Risks

- There is a risk of some vendors not responding to RFPs or RFIs, which can lead to the best-fit software being overlooked.

- There is the risk of vendors misrepresenting their software because RFPs or RFIs are not audited to expose "overoptimistic" responses.

- There is the risk of a mismatch between the requirements and available software because a formal scope analysis is not done (See: Scope check on page 231).

- There is a risk of inexperienced implementation consultants being used.

- Typically uses the vendor's purchasing contract, which is very one-sided in favor of the vendor.

- Inadequate user acceptance tests increase the risk of business disruption when going live.

Level 4 – Verified and adjusted

Vendor claims are verified. Project scope is adjusted if there is a mismatch with what the market can supply.

Characteristics

- There are adequate project resources and adequate project management.

- Requirements analysis process is designed to collect critical information needed by the implementation team.

- Adequate requirements analysis especially using reverse engineering.

- Due diligence performed on implementation vendors before inviting them to respond to an RFI.

- Formal requirements scope analysis and adjustment ensures that requirements are matched to software features the market can deliver (See: Scope check on page 231).

- Expectations are formally managed: the evaluation of the selected software defines expectations (See: Expectations management on page 245).

- Objective, data-driven and repeatable decision-making selection process (See: The gap analysis on page 218).

- The winning vendor RFI or RFP is audited to verify that vendor claims are realistic and the software has not been misrepresented (See: How to audit an RFI on page 248).

- Non-vendor supplied reference customers are identified and interviewed (See: How to find independent references on page 253 and Appendix C: Questions for Software References on page 294).

- The winning evaluation is used to prime the implementation for success. No significant new requirements are discovered during implementation (See: Implementation handover on page 272).

- User acceptance tests are not created as part of the requirements.

Risks

- The buyer accepts more risk than necessary because they do not negotiate the contract to transfer some risks to the seller.

- Implementation contracts are written in terms of milestones rather than outcomes. It is too easy for vendors to meet milestones while missing outcomes.

Bridgestone Tires had contracted with IBM to implement SAP, but after working on the implementation for three years, the project was deemed a failure. After spending more than a year negotiating with IBM and being unable to reach a settlement, Bridgestone filed a civil lawsuit against IBM.

IBM, Bridgestone stated, claimed it was just there to work by the hour, meet milestones, and collect over $78 million. Furthermore, Bridgestone said that IBM claimed to bear no responsibility for the damages they caused.

In filing a motion to dismiss five of the six Bridgestone claims, IBM said it had no obligation or duty to disclose potential problems! However, the judge dismissed only one of the six Bridgestone claims.

(upperedge.com/ibm/bridgestone-vs-ibm-bridgestone-wins-round-one-and-increases-the-pressure-on-ibm)

Level 5 – Optimized, tested, and improved

Software acquisition risks are managed and minimized. The purchase contract is optimized to share risk with the implementation vendor. Testing verifies the software's business performance. Post purchase selection process improvement is undertaken.

Characteristics

- Purchase contracts are written to share project risks with the implementation vendor. The purchaser pays more in exchange for reduced risk of project failure. Contracts are written based on business outcomes, as opposed to meeting milestones.

- The implementation is verified against requirements with formal user acceptance tests. The purchase contract includes terms that require the software and / or implementation vendor to achieve a particular score on those tests, and a failure to meet agreed scores triggers penalties.

- Post implementation analysis is actively used to improve the software acquisition process.

- After the software purchase, requirements common to enterprise apps like security, usability, licensing, etc. are collected in libraries for future projects.

- Post implementation analysis identifies gaps in requirements and acceptance tests. These are added to libraries for future software selections. The library is moderated for quality.

Use the SSMS to measure the maturity of your software selection process. Note that different projects within one organization can operate at different places on the scale. For example, an organization operating at Level 3 may hire a new VP who buys a particular software product that he likes, without considering alternatives. That project will have performed on a Level 0 or 1.

Use the SSMS as a road map for improvements to the software selection process. As an organization moves up the SSMS scale, the ROI tends to improve and implementations tend to be completed on time and within budget. A mature software selection process helps an organization meet or exceed the ROI that was used to justify the software purchase in the first place.

Selection project phases

Every selection project should start with an ROI analysis before proceeding with a software selection. Projects with insufficient ROI should be eliminated (See: Chapter 5: Select Software for Value, Not Price on page 81). Once the decision has been made to proceed, there are four phases in a software selection:

Phase 1: Requirements: Requirements are to software selection as plans are to a construction project. Details matter (See: Chapter 9: Requirements on page 165).

Phase 2: Evaluation: Measure how well potential software products, software and implementation vendors meet requirements (See: Chapter 10: Evaluation on page 208).

Phase 3: Selection: Purchase the software product that best meets your needs. Your evaluation of that product defines your expectations (See: Chapter 11: Selection and Purchase on page 242).

Phase 4: Post purchase: The evaluation and selection are designed to collect critical information, which is used to prime the implementation for success (See: Implementation handover on page 272).

Selection project duration

Providing you are following a mature selection process (See: page 130), when it comes to major software purchases there is an inverse relation between time and risk. The more thorough the selection process, the lower the risk. Most software selections are significantly more work than expected and run out of time, which means they are not as thorough as they should be. For this reason it is better to start sooner rather than later. Starting early avoids being forced into taking shortcuts with the inevitable painful consequences. It also allows employees more time to consider requirements and the scope of the project.

Bear in mind that undertaking an evaluation and selection project does not commit you to buying software. At the end of the evaluation, you may conclude that no new software provides enough of an advantage to justify a purchase. You may decide to remedy the weak areas of the current software with one or more add-on products, e.g. by employing a third-party reporting tool. You could decide to develop your own software. You may even decide that the advantages of the new software are so great that you need to move ahead as soon as possible. However, the only way to find this out is to do the evaluation!

Software selection projects can take considerable time. Some of that time is spent working, but other time is spent on things like waiting for vendors to respond. As a *very rough* guide, you can assume the project duration will be about a month for every 250 to 500 requirements. For example, when selecting ERP software you can expect:

- Small company: 1,000 - 2,000 requirements, 3 - 6 months

- Medium company: 2,000 - 4,000 requirements, 4 - 8 months

- Large company: 4,000+ requirements, 6+ months

Single function enterprise software products like CRM, HRIS and all the other acronyms typically have less than half the number of requirements compared to ERP products, and take correspondingly shorter times.

Common sources of selection project delays

Some project delays are inevitable. This is a list of the most common causes of delays to software selection projects.

Scheduling employees to weight requirements

You can estimate weighting about 30 requirements per hour, and each employee team involved in the project will have several hours of work. When team members are often unavailable, it takes longer to schedule those meetings.

Scheduling conference rooms

When there is a shortage of conference rooms they tend to be reserved well in advance, which means project meetings are scheduled later rather than sooner.

Selecting implementation vendors

Where the implementation will be handled by a company other than the software vendor, a suitable implementation vendor must be found for each software product being considered. That vendor will be the one responding to the RFI. Identifying such vendors and performing due diligence on them can take considerable time, and this must be completed before RFIs are sent to them.

Vendor RFI responses

Even when RFIs are designed to reduce the work vendors need to do when responding, they typically take two to four weeks to respond to those RFIs.

Scheduling software demos

Demo schedules must fit in with vendor, employee, and conference room availability. In practice, it can take two to four weeks to get them on the calendar.

Where the project time goes

Adequate requirements are the foundation for successful software acquisitions and at least half of the work in most projects is in developing those requirements. Where does this time go, and how is it estimated?

Developing requirements

Reverse engineering requirements averages 10 to 15 minutes per new requirement created. At the start of each product considered it is very quick to capture requirements, but the pace slows as you get deeper into that software.

One way to save time is by using libraries of requirements. Web research may yield RFPs that are a useful source of requirements, or requirements lists can be purchased. You can also create your own libraries, for example, of security, usability, contractual etc. requirements that are common to most software purchases. These libraries can be reused over multiple projects.

Weighting requirements

Expect to complete about 30 requirements per hour when weighting requirements for importance to the organization. That means about 30 hours of work per 1,000 requirements. Having users weight requirements is the most important part of nurturing their buy-in to the new software, so don't rush through these meetings (See: Creating and nurturing user buy-in on page 122 and Weight requirements for importance on page 201).

Auditing vendor RFIs

Vendors have been known to misrepresent what their software does and tell customers what they want to hear. The only way to verify the software performs as claimed in an RFI is to audit that RFI (See: How to audit an RFI on page 248).

When auditing an RFI, you want to verify all showstopper requirements and possibly include critical requirements as well. That could be as much as 10 percent to 20 percent of the total number of requirements, and could take as long as 10 to 15 minutes per requirement. On an ERP evaluation of 2,500 requirements, that could amount to 500 requirements or about 100 hours of work. However, considering the TCO over the lifetime of an ERP purchase, spending that time is a small price to pay for minimizing project risks. One way to reduce overall time is to have several consultants auditing the requirements in parallel.

Selection project costs

Software selection costs are more than offset by avoiding the four costs of poor software purchasing. For example, ERP projects usually take at least 25 percent or more time to implement than planned. If the implementation budget was $2 million, typical delays would mean an unanticipated expense of at least $500,000 or more. If a thorough selection project reduced this overage by half that would save $250,000, which is more than what would be spent on the software selection itself. In addition, completing the project earlier would mean achieving the benefits of the new software a few months sooner than otherwise would have been the case. There would also have been a corresponding reduction in business disruption when going live. These are very conservative numbers, and the savings that are the result of the software selection project are usually much greater (See: The four costs of poor software purchasing on page 83).

If requirements are not found in the analysis phase they will be found during implementation where satisfying them costs much more, so it is well worth spending the effort on requirements development. From a financial perspective, for every $1 *not spent* on requirements analysis:

- $10 is spent on extra implementation cost and delayed ROI.

- $100 is spent in business disruption costs on going live.

- $1,000 is spent in hidden costs of not meeting expectations over the life of the software.

Types of software selection projects

Keep or replace?

Many new software purchases are triggered by outgrowing existing systems. Another problem is that software is customized and consequently not updated. Eventually it becomes too difficult to interface that software with others systems that are being purchased. At some point the question gets asked: Should the existing software be kept or replaced? The first way to answer the question is to estimate the value of the benefits that the new software would bring (See: Benefits value estimate on page 86). If that estimate is too low, stop right there and save your organization a lot of unnecessary work and costs.

If there is enough value in the new software estimate, proceed with a software evaluation. Ensure the current software is one of the products evaluated, along with potential replacements. Once the gap analysis is complete, compare the fit score of the current software with that of the highest scoring replacement.

- If the fit score for the current software is just a few percent less than that of the top scoring replacement product (e.g. 5 percent), it is unlikely to be worth proceeding.

- If there is a substantial difference in fits scores (e.g. 30 percent) then it is likely to be well worth proceeding.

As a final check, you can use the following formula to estimate the number of years it will take for the new software to reach breakeven:

$$\frac{TNSC}{(FSR/FSC - 1) \times CV} + DIMP = Breakeven\ years$$

TNSC is the total new software cost, including implementation. If the software is purchased, add the maintenance fees over five years, or if the software is in the cloud, add subscription fees for five years.

FSR is the gap analysis fit score of the proposed replacement software.

FSC is the gap analysis fit score of the current software.

CV is the annual value returned by the current software. One way to estimate the upper limit of the CV is to consider what the cost of that software failing would be. Be aware that the software is just one link in the value chain; i.e. not all that value comes from the software.

DIMP is the duration of the new software implementation, expressed in years.

The breakeven is the number of years it will take for the gain from the new software to return the total cost of that software.

Example: Suppose the current software had a fit score of 60 percent and the proposed replacement software had a fit score of 90 percent. Assume the annual value from the current software was $1 million, the cost of the new software including implementation was $800,000, and the implementation project would take six months.

$$\frac{\$800,000 \; cost \; incl. \; implementation}{(90\%/60\% - 1) \; \times \$1 \; million \; per \; year} + 0.5 \; yrs \; implement = 2.1 \; years$$

As the above example shows, the new software would have paid back its cost after two years. Bear in mind that this is an estimate and doesn't factor in things like system administration, e.g. the old system may require a full-time admin, but the new system only needs half that amount of time.

Build or buy?

While many companies regret building enterprise software because it turns out to be much more expensive than originally expected, there are times when custom software is best, for example where the new software will provide a competitive advantage in the market.

> *I worked at Netflix in the early days. They wrote their movie selection software to give them an edge in the market. To their customers, that software "is" Netflix. The competitive advantage it provided helped them defeat Blockbuster, the video rental market leader at that time. However, for things like accounting and HR, Netflix bought software because there was no advantage to be gained from developing those products themselves.*

If a company has an in-house development team, there is always the push to build because they can supposedly satisfy all needs. However, from my experience and observation, it is usually far cheaper and faster to buy than to build. After all, if a problem has been adequately solved in a commercial product, why solve it again? Why not get the development team to work on new and more interesting problems that do provide real advantages in the market?

The build or buy question is seldom clear cut and it is too easy to make the wrong choice. There are two responses to the question:

- Make an emotional decision that "feels right."

- Make a rational decision driven by data.

Most decisions are a blend of the two extremes, but many companies, especially those with in-house software developers, lean too far in the emotional direction. When hard data is available, making an emotional decision is not good business practice. Building the software "because it is cheaper than buying." very rarely turns out to be the case.

Many organizations have an immature software selection process. Evaluations start with spreadsheets, but as the work proceeds, limitations become apparent (See: Spreadsheet limitations on page 158). People realize how much work is involved in the evaluation, and lack a clear idea of how to proceed. In the end, they may do a very high-level analysis, but underneath it is an emotional decision based on what "feels the best." In contrast, a rational build vs. buy decision starts with a thorough evaluation as described in Chapter 9 and Chapter 10. If you have existing homegrown software, include that in the evaluation. Once the evaluation is complete, the fit scores are used to make a rational build or buy decision.

For example, if several commercial software products have fit scores of 90 percent or above, then buying is the best decision. Under these circumstances, internally developed software is unlikely to offer any advantage in the market. If all commercial products score lower than about 60 percent, there are three possibilities:

- Reduce the scope of the project by eliminating certain functionality.

- Combining a commercial software product with a small custom code module.

- Combining two or more commercial products.

Each of the above increases the fit score. If none of these approaches works well enough, then building the app is the best decision. And if a build decision is made, the development team is starting with a very comprehensive list of requirements.

As a rule of thumb, a company should only develop code if it will provide a competitive advantage in the marketplace. *You should never, ever build software because it is cheaper than buying.* Writing code always costs much more than you expect. If you do decide to build rather than to buy, consider writing the new software on a platform product, as opposed to creating it from scratch. The coding effort will be focused on where value can be added, rather than being wasted on recreating the basics. For example, FinancialForce ERP was written on the Salesforce platform rather than being created from scratch.

Software rationalization

From a high-level perspective, IT budgets have two parts: maintenance and strategic initiatives. Maintenance tends to grow at the expense of strategic initiatives and, left unchecked, ultimately stifles all innovation. In mid to large IT organizations, this has resulted in the emergence of Application Portfolio Management (APM). APM is a disciplined approach to aligning enterprise applications to maximize business value while minimizing operational costs like software maintenance and support.

A lack of APM results in uncontrolled application growth (also called application sprawl), which gives rise to multiple problems listed below. Note that APM is a continuous process and not an objective.

> *In fiscal year 2015 the federal government spent about 75 percent of their total IT budget on operations and maintenance. Such spending has increased over the past seven fiscal years, which resulted in a $7.3 billion decline from fiscal years 2010 to 2017 in development, modernization and enhancement activities.*
>
> *(See: Federal Agencies Need to Address Aging Legacy Systems, May 2016 www.gao.gov/assets/680/677435.pdf)*

Common causes of application sprawl

1. Mergers and acquisitions.

2. Business strategy changes.

3. Business growth and the need for immediate solutions leads to software purchased just to solve a problem. In turn, this leads to application overlap and data siloes.

4. In-house software developed as point solutions. Technology siloes develop where project teams fail to communicate.

5. New software that has better features and is easier to use is bought to replace existing applications, but the old applications are not retired.

6. Compliance requirements cause obsolete applications to stay around. Access is not disabled, and some people continue using them.

7. Organizational siloes where different departments bring cloud applications online to solve similar problems.

8. Political purchases. New executives introduce software because it worked well at their previous company. This new software turns out to be a poor fit for the organization so the original software that was supposed to be replaced can't be retired.

Typical problems caused by application sprawl

1. Unnecessary software costs for underused applications. This takes the form of annual software maintenance paid to vendors, or subscription fees for cloud applications.

2. Increased administration costs. All applications require some level of system administration, and these costs are often overlooked because they tend to come out of general IT budgets.

3. Increased support costs. Each system requires help desk staff to support it. Employee turnover means training new help desk staff in these applications.

4. Increased training is required for new users – they must be trained in a greater number of applications. In addition, when there are too many applications, people tend to use each application less frequently and forget how to do things.

5. User confusion caused by duplicated software functionality. Different departments use different applications for the same business processes.

6. Denormalized data. The same information is stored in different systems in different formats. For example, after a merger two different sets of customers exist in two different CRMs. Some customers can be in both systems. Even if each customer is in one or the other system, automated reports covering the whole customer base cannot easily be obtained.

7. Reduced efficiency. Older applications often don't have the functionality or ease of use delivered by current applications. Older applications usually take more work to achieve the desired results.

8. Increased interface costs. As the number of applications increases, the costs of those applications exchanging data increases exponentially. Data tends to be in different application siloes, which prevents users from getting the big picture.

9. Increased development costs. Custom applications developed in-house may have to work with denormalized data in multiple repositories with different APIs and data schemas. This significantly increases the cost of internal software development.

10. Reduced security caused by an increased attack surface. More applications running mean more potential security holes that hackers can exploit.

11. Unnecessary data center resources consumed. Organizations find the number of virtual machines (VMs) explodes, but also find the usage of those VMs (and the applications that run on them) is lower than expected. More applications mean more systems to back up, and more effort to manage those backups.

Rationalizing software

Several situations call for software rationalization:

- Some applications have a low business value to operational cost ratio, and they can be eliminated. These usually tend to be older applications bought or created to solve a specific business problem.

- There is significant functional overlap between two or more applications. For example, we were speaking to a client who said they had three treasury applications they felt could be combined into one.

- New, integrated applications have duplicated the functionality of existing applications, e.g., new HR software may have a time keeping module that duplicates the functionality of existing time keeping software.

The core of a software rationalization project is to optimize the business value to operational cost ratio of applications used. The steps in a software rationalization project are as follows:

1. Software inventory

Create an inventory of all enterprise applications. This can be as simple as a spreadsheet, or it can be portfolio management software. For example, Innotas is recognized by Gartner as a leader with their APM product. Note that APM is often a subset of features in a larger application.

2. Review applications

A straightforward way to identify applications in need of rationalization is to plot them on the quadrant chart below in terms of operational costs and business value. Operational costs include all regular, ongoing direct and indirect costs associated with an application. They do not include one-time costs like implementation or initial training (See: Estimating the TCO for enterprise software on page 91). Business value is the total value of the benefits that flow from using the software.

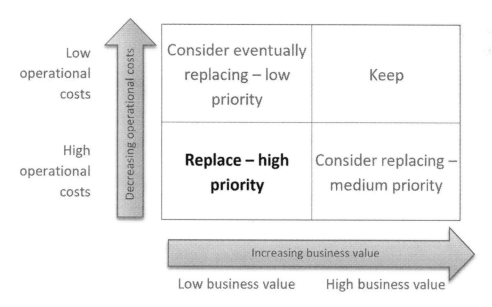

Figure 4: Application Review Quadrant Chart

3. Manage the application portfolio

Applications in the bottom left quadrant are prime candidates for rationalization. They could be replaced with other existing software. Alternatively, two or more of them could be replaced by an entirely new software product. In each case, estimate the ROI of the project, which is the basis of the business case for undertaking software rationalization (See: Software ROI on page 98). Start with the highest ROI projects because they will bring the greatest return for the effort.

4. Retire obsolete applications

Before retiring an obsolete application, consider the risks. Verify that it no longer has any business use. Sometimes people do tasks they have always done, but there is no longer any business value in those tasks and they can be eliminated. Obsolete reports that are no longer read by anybody are a good example. Other times the few tasks that remain in the obsolete application can be migrated to another application.

5. Replace low value applications

Some applications may have a low business value to operational cost ratio, for example caused by a poor functional fit or the software may be difficult to use. It may be possible to move those business processes to an existing application or a new application may need to be purchased. Either way, this will trigger an evaluation and selection project to identify replacements (See: Chapter 10: Evaluation on page 208).

6. Consolidate overlapping applications

Where there are significant functional overlaps between software applications, it may be possible to consolidate them. Again, this will trigger an evaluation and selection project. Part of the work will include using the process of reverse engineering features of the existing software to help create a comprehensive list of requirements for the replacement software (See: Reverse engineering on page 177).

Suite or best of breed

No software product is an island; all software products must interface to other systems. The question is this: where do the boundaries between systems lie?

Chapter 7: Project Management

On one hand, there is a "suite" of products from one vendor that does everything needed, but there are significant limitations in several areas. The downside of suites is that you end up with the vendor's weaker products along with its stronger products. Also, larger vendors that buy smaller vendors have been known to claim their new products are integrated with their existing products when they are not. It is all too easy to end up with software that does everything, but is not particularly good at anything.

On the other hand, you could purchase multiple "best of breed" products from different vendors, and resolve those limitations at the expense of making the systems work together. Smaller products are faster to bring online and have less risk, but then there are issues with things like integration and reporting that straddles system boundaries.

Key to answering this question is using the gap analysis to measure how well the suite and best of breed products meet your requirements. Remember that best of breed software does not necessarily mean that software is the best at meeting your specific needs. With a gap analysis, you can make a rational, data-driven decision as to where the boundaries between the systems should lie. This allows you to avoid the problems at the two extremes:

- An inflexible monolithic strategy.
- A chaotic situation with every department selecting their own software.

These days even if a suite is selected, a company will still end up with some best of breed products. The aim is to maximize the value of the benefits that flow from using the software, and minimize the cost of managing those systems.

> *Charlotte-based Coca-Cola Bottling Co. Consolidated, the largest independent Coca-Cola bottler in the U.S., used SAP. They found the SAP expense claims module did not meet their needs well enough. Adoption of the legacy procurement system was low because it lacked the mobility needed by their field users who relied on iPads and iPhones. Although they considered extending SAP, in the end they chose Coupa, a cloud-based expense management system. Patrick Hopkins, the bottler's procurement director said, "I've been involved in a variety of computer related system installations since the late 1970s, and this was the smoothest go-live that I have experienced." (See: Coke bottler picks SaaS over SAP: computerworld.com/article/2495293)*

Try before you buy

Many cloud vendors offer free trials of their software, often without even asking for a credit card. What is wrong with trying a pilot project? The answer to this question comes down to the value of the benefits that are expected to flow from using that software.

For any vendor you might be considering, there are likely to be several other vendors in that same space, and there could be dozens. How do you pick one of them? If you run a pilot there is a good chance you will stay with the first product you try. But if you do stay, you will never know if it is the best product for your specific needs.

For an example of using value to decide if a selection project is worth the effort, consider a company with 50 users. Suppose they were looking for help desk software, they read the reviews and ran a pilot, they could be satisfied. Spending the time evaluating help desk products and picking the best one for their needs may not be worth the effort for 50 users; they just need to solve the problem and move on. But if a company had 5000 users, that is a completely different scenario and it would be well worth spending the time evaluating help desk alternatives.

If a company was looking at ERP systems, trying one is a recipe for disaster for several reasons:

- ERP is critical to the business. The wrong choice could cause the company to fail, and the risk is proportionally greater for smaller companies because they have more limited resources.

- Unknown requirements are likely to cause significant problems.

- Learning to use the new software and then adapting work processes to fit with that software takes considerable effort for end-users. It is simply too much to expect users to go through this for more than one product.

- Implementation costs, training costs, business disruption costs etc. are sunk costs and spent again every time you try a new system.

From this we can conclude that deciding if a software selection project is worthwhile depends on the value of the benefits that will flow from using the software.

If the value of the benefits is relatively small and implementation costs are low to none, you can be guided by reviews etc.

However, an effective approach we have found when dealing with low value projects is to focus only on functional requirements. Examining the features of multiple products and rewriting those features as requirements (i.e. reverse engineering, see page 177) can help you decide very quickly which products are suitable or not. We *always* find there are some features we don't know we need until we see them. It is much better to know about these unknown requirements before you try the software than after you start using it.

Key lessons

Software selections are projects, and must be managed as such. Since people are an essential part of projects, we examine their roles in selecting software.

We also considered diverse types of software selection projects, for example the decision to keep or replace software, answering the "build or buy?" question and when to rationalize a software portfolio.

The chapter concludes by comparing software suites to best of breed products and considering the role of "trying before you buy." Here are some of the key lessons from this chapter.

- Creating and nurturing user buy-in is an essential part of rolling out new enterprise software. This must be part of the selection project, and not left to the implementation.

- Do not start a software selection project with product demos. That invariably allows the vendors to take control of the purchase.

- The key to successful software acquisitions is to use a robust evaluation and selection process.

- Software selection projects involve a substantial amount of work, and always take longer than expected. Many of the delays are outside your control.

- The money invested in software selection projects is typically returned many times over in the form of reduced implementation times, reduced business disruption on going live and avoiding the costs of unmet expectations.

- When software has been used for 5 to 10 years or more it is well worth the effort of estimating the ROI of new software.

- Application sprawl needs to be continuously managed and software rationalized to keep operational and maintenance costs under control.

- We considered a process to rationalize an organization's application portfolio. Applications with high operational costs and low business value can be eliminated freeing up funds for more innovative projects.

Chapter 8.   Software Selection Toolbox

Enterprise software selections involve extensive work and many people. Fortunately there are tools to help with the task. Some tools are complicated, and that complexity can get in the way of completing the project, for example comparing products from almost any conceivable angle. If an organization is considering a major software purchase, only one software product will be bought. Most tool users are not really interested in the arcane details of how products compare. Generally, they just want to guide the project to a successful conclusion.

There are two approaches when it comes to tools for evaluating software:

1. Provide ways to examine the products being evaluated from multiple angles, e.g. compare how products fit the needs of different departments.

2. Reduce the evaluation down to a single number, the fit score, which measures how the software meets needs across the entire organization. Then rank software products by fit score, and select the best-fit product.

While being able to "slice and dice" an evaluation from many angles is enticing, it does not really help with the final decision. Only one software product will be selected, which should be the one that best meets the needs and minimizes all compromises across the organization. To do that you need to take the second approach above, which is reducing everything down to one number, the fit score.

Software selection tool core features

This list of core features needed in a software selection tool focuses on what is essential for an evaluation, and not the "bells and whistles" that these tools might have.

Capture requirements

The tool must be able to capture requirements in enough detail (See: How to write good requirements on page 187). One very common limitation is that there is not enough screen real estate where the requirements can be captured, along with examples, use cases, notes, general reasons why a requirement may be wanted etc. For project management purposes, the tool should track the total number of requirements captured.

Weight requirements

The tool must allow requirement weights to be set. For project management purposes, the tool should track the number and percentage of requirements weighted. A common limitation of these tools is there is not enough screen real estate to capture specific reasons why the requirement is important to the organization, along with who it is important to and why it is important. This is all information used by the implementation team.

Requirement groups

Enterprise software selections contain many hundreds or thousands of requirements. The only way to manage these requirements is to collect them in groups and subgroups, nested as deeply as needed. To prevent unnecessary duplication, it is essential that one requirement can appear in multiple groups. It is important that groups have names *and* descriptions of what they are for, because the meaning of a group name can get lost with time (See: Requirement groups on page 198).

Requirement lists

Because one requirement can appear in multiple groups, the tool should be able to display a list of requirements in both grouped and flat formats. It should be possible to change the list sort order, e.g. by clicking on column headings. For example, in flat format if you sort by last edit, you can see the most recent changes.

Weight requirements groups

Typically, all requirements groups start off with a weight of one, and this is adjusted up or down as necessary. The ability to set a group weight to zero is particularly useful, because this effectively removes the requirements in that group from the evaluation without deleting them when reducing project scope (See: Scope check on page 231).

Capture products

The tool must be able to capture the software products being evaluated. For each product, there should be a place to summarize conclusions about that software.

Capture product appraisal ratings

The tool should be able to capture the product appraisal rating (or product rating for short) for a particular requirement, e.g. "fully meets," "partly meets" etc. Along with the requirement weight, this rating is used when calculating a product's fit score.

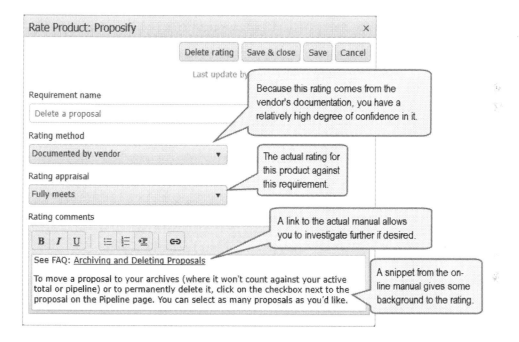

Figure 5 Screenshot illustrating a product appraisal rating

A product rating without any source or reference is not particularly useful because there's no way to know if it's anything more than an opinion. The tool should be able to capture the source of the information used to make the rating, e.g. a few lines of text copied from an online manual, a link to a product documentation page etc.

The rating method records *how* the rating was made. The tool should have the ability to select the product rating method from a list, because that allows you to search on rating methods. For example, if half of the showstopper ratings came from email correspondence with the vendor, you would want to verify those ratings before selecting that product. In particular, the product rating method is used to audit vendor RFI responses (See: How to audit an RFI on page 248).

For evaluation purposes, the tool should track the percentage of requirements that the product has been weighted against.

Filters

For any lists, e.g. requirements, groups, products or product appraisal ratings, the tool should allow the list to be filtered. Examples of filter uses are:

- **Keywords:** The list of requirements can be filtered by keywords to see if specific requirements have already been entered. Filters can also be used to find requirements.

- **Requirement weights:** List of requirements can be filtered by weight, e.g. "showstopper" or "important." You can focus on unweighted requirements by filtering out those already weighted.

- **Product appraisal ratings:** A list of product appraisal ratings can be filtered by weight, e.g. you can see how well a product scores for "showstopper" requirements only. You can focus on un-appraised requirements by filtering out those that have already been rated for that product. In particular, you want to ensure 100 percent of the showstopper and critical requirements have been rated for each product that is being seriously considered for purchase.

- **Product rating method.** The tool should allow a list of product appraisal ratings to be filtered by the rating method, e.g. find ratings where a salesperson claimed their product fully met the requirement in an email or phone call. These ratings can then be checked when auditing the RFI, e.g. against user documentation.

Note that when a filter is applied to, for example, product appraisal ratings, the tool should display the appropriate scores for the items in the filtered list. That allows you to examine ratings from different perspectives, e.g. how does this product meet showstopper requirements only.

Multi-user

Evaluating enterprise software is a huge task. Whatever tools you use, they should allow multiple people to work on various parts of the project simultaneously. While this is seldom a problem for tools in the cloud, beware of desktop tools like Excel spreadsheets that only allow one person at a time to work on the evaluation.

Spreadsheets in the cloud solve the multi-user problem, but are always far too slow when the number of requirements in the evaluation climbs into the thousands.

Software selection tools

While the vendors below have a somewhat different philosophy to the one described in this book, they do have good tools. No one software tool does everything, which is one reason we developed our own app (wayferry.com/app). You can combine several tools to cover most of your needs for selecting software.

Requirements management tools

When considering requirements management systems, you may consider tools that are designed for software development. Blueprint (blueprintsys.com) has an excellent requirements management tool that even deals with business and IT alignment. While these kinds of tools excel at requirements management, they tend to be optimized for software development and lack gap analysis features.

Gap analysis

- **SelectHub** (selecthub.com) is a software selection management platform aimed at larger organizations, especially those with a centralized IT group with multiple stakeholders spread across multiple departments and geographies. Their workflow spans requirements gathering, vendor short-listing, RFIs, RFPs, proof-of-concepts, and final vendor scorecarding. SelectHub also sells libraries of requirements.

- **Technology Evaluation Centers** or **TEC** (technologyevaluation.com) is based in Montreal. They have a gap analysis tool with a free version available. A more comprehensive version is available to purchase by project, e.g. ERP, CRM etc. TEC also sells libraries of requirements.

RFP tools

There are several cloud-based RFP or procurement systems. While providing some functionality, they tend to be optimized for the RFP process.

Spreadsheet limitations

Evaluating enterprise software is a lot of work. Managing this work in a spreadsheet seems the obvious choice, but that is deceptive. While spreadsheets are excellent tools on a small scale, they do not scale up to handle the many hundreds or thousands of requirements found in a typical enterprise software evaluation. In fact, the work required to develop a large software evaluation spreadsheet is not that much less than the work required to develop a software evaluation app. In this section, we examine the limitations of using spreadsheets to evaluate enterprise software.

Manual work

Both the strength and weakness of spreadsheets is that they are so manual. When you start building an evaluation in a spreadsheet the ability to reorganize things manually as you go is very useful. However, when there are many hundreds or thousands of requirements, things get out of sync and errors creep in. The amount of manual work that is required in large evaluations is what causes the problems, and it is *always* far more work than expected.

Version nightmares

If the information collected for a large evaluation is managed with an Excel spreadsheet, it doesn't take long before there are multiple versions of the spreadsheet and nobody knows which the "real" one is. A huge amount of time can be wasted on resolving version discrepancies.

Multi-user problems

Cloud spreadsheets allow multiple people to edit the same spreadsheet simultaneously, a huge advantage because it prevents multiple versions of the spreadsheet from proliferating. However, enterprise evaluations are large and cloud spreadsheets can be excruciatingly slow. (Microsoft has finally rolled out real-time collaboration in Excel 2016 desktop, but you need an Office 365 and OneDrive subscription to use it. See: computerworld.com/article/3212262)

Audit trails

With spreadsheets, it is difficult to see who made changes. While Google spreadsheets have a limited audit trail, in Excel, there is no audit trail of individual changes to show who did what and when.

Updating requirements lists

After creating the list of requirements in a spreadsheet, the list is typically copied and pasted once for each product being considered. However, as products are evaluated, new requirements will be discovered. If those new requirements are added to the master list, they must also be added to each product being evaluated. It is all too easy to get out of sync and not evaluate some products against some new requirements.

Limited cell formatting

Software selection needs well-written requirements. Text size limits in each cell and very limited text formatting can be real problems (See: How to write good requirements on page 187).

Limited links

In spreadsheets, you can only have one link per cell; you cannot add inline links to words or terms in the cell text. However, you might need more than one link:

- When writing requirements, rather than explaining acronyms and terms used, you may want links to external references like Wikipedia.

- When rating a product against a requirement, you might want to include links to online manual pages and links to videos explaining that feature.

As a workaround, you can add extra columns to the spreadsheet to hold extra links but this can rapidly become unmanageable.

Limited data structure

Relational databases have the concept of normalized data, where each data item exists only once in the data set, e.g. one requirement exists in multiple groups. Denormalized data is where multiple copies of data items are used, for example, where one requirement is *copied* into multiple groups.

The limited data structure of spreadsheets means that data is denormalized and multiple copies of requirements are inevitable. When a requirement is changed, it must be found and manually updated in multiple places to keep everything consistent, which is difficult if not impossible. This flat and non-relational data structure is a core problem with spreadsheets.

Spreadsheets often start with all products being evaluated on one tab, but limitations quickly lead to a separate tab for each product. When you consider that every requirement on an evaluation should appear on a master list, and again on a tab for each product being evaluated, the problem of manually updating multiple requirements starts to become apparent.

Requirements in multiple groups

To help manage large numbers of requirements, they are always organized in groups and subgroups. In our experience, around 15 percent of requirements belong in two or more groups. With denormalized data, that requirement must be found and updated in multiple places. However, with normalized data, edit the requirement anywhere and it updates everywhere that requirement is used.

Denormalized data makes it difficult to find and remove duplicated requirements, especially where the same requirement is expressed multiple times with different wording.

Group weights

Group weights tend to be hard coded into spreadsheets. When a group weight must be changed, it must be changed in multiple places. Again, manually keeping denormalized data consistent is difficult.

Product scoring

A core concept of a software selection project is the gap analysis, but when doing this on a spreadsheet, a scoring system must be designed. Unfortunately, spreadsheet formulas lack variables. The workaround is to add an extra column to hold the value, and then hide that column. Manually keeping scoring formulas consistent across a large evaluation is difficult. Even if you manage to make formulas consistent, there is no straightforward way to *know* those formulas are, in fact, consistent.

Search

Enterprise evaluations are large, and you always need to search requirements. A simple search is easy in a spreadsheet, but advanced searches need to be built. While this is not particularly difficult, the spreadsheet is starting to turn into a programming project.

Error checking

It is very easy for errors to creep into spreadsheets because they are so manual. Most error checking must be manually coded, which is where the spreadsheet morphs into a full-blown programming project. Usually the person in charge of the software evaluation is responsible for this work, which requires a great deal of time. As a result, error checking is typically not done at all.

Progress tracking

Enterprise selections are a lot of work that sometimes never seems to end. Spreadsheets have no tools built in to track progress, making these projects more difficult to manage.

Spreadsheet summary

While spreadsheets are tremendously useful for some kinds of problems, selecting enterprise software does not play to their strengths. They are too manual and simply do not scale up to large selection projects. Using spreadsheets for enterprise selections takes an already large project and adds another layer of work and risk.

The place of product reviews and analyst reports

When the favored enterprise software receives complimentary reviews from analysts it's tempting to skip an evaluation project, but doing so invites failure.

In the context of purchasing enterprise software, a review is an examination of one or more software products written to help organizations make a buying decision. Reviews may include comparisons with other products, benchmarks, strong and weak points of each product, and may include charts that graphically compare products.

Who writes reviews and analyst reports?

Reviews are written for online publications by journalists working for those organizations or by consultants wishing to share their expertise. Reviews are sometimes commissioned by software vendors, and those tend to be biased in favor of that vendor. Occasionally, reviews are written by knowledgeable users of a product who want to share their experience for the benefit of the community.

Products are researched and reviewed by analysts at companies like Gartner, Forrester, IDC, etc. Sometimes companies researching software for purchase will buy these reports. However, usually vendors must "pay to play" to be included in analyst reviews. If a vendor does not pay, their software is not reviewed. So, if a software product is not featured in an analyst review, it may simply be that the vendor did not pay.

Vendors who do well in these analyst reviews often buy them so they can put them on their websites. When you find such reviews, they can be a goldmine of information that will not cost you anything. If you do find relevant reviews, download and save them. Evernote and Microsoft OneNote are good tools for this, especially if the information is not in pdf format. Usually these reviews are available for a limited time only, and if you do not save them after finding them, the information may not be available when you need it.

Limitation of reviews and analyst reports

Reviews and analyst reports have significant limitations:

- The most important thing about reviews is to realize they must be written for the "average" users of the products being reviewed. And you are never the "average" user. You will always have some requirements that are specific to your situation.

- Different analysts can reach conflicting conclusions because they write for different audiences.

- Reviews are always high-level overviews of products. They simply do not have the space for the necessary detail, and, we all know, the devil is in those details.

- Great reviews can instill a false sense of security when selecting a product. Just because a product has great reviews does not mean it is a good fit for your specific requirements.

- People sometimes use reviews to justify their software selection. All this shows is that they have not done their homework. If somebody tries to justify purchasing software based on reviews that is a red flag. You can be sure that project is already in trouble!

- Reviews can be biased, especially when commissioned by vendors.

All software has weak points, and one way to spot fake or biased reviews is to look at how evenly weak points are treated across the various products. If the review omits or glosses over the weak points of one product, but goes into a greater detail of the weak points of other products, it is likely to be a mediocre or even a fake review. However, knowing the weak points of those other products is still very useful information.

Where reviews and analyst reports are helpful

While it is never a good idea to purchase enterprise software based solely on reviews, they are an excellent place to start product research. For example, reviews can alert you to new features or problems that might affect the use of the software, and new products that are worth evaluating.

A technique for finding relevant reviews on the web is to search for the names of two or three software products in one search phrase. Reviews that include these products appear near the top of the search results.

When searching, pay attention to the review date; for example, a 6-year-old review is much less useful than one that is six months old. In addition, some reviews have comments at the bottom, which often mention other products that were not reviewed. Read the information in the comment area carefully, for example somebody in Australia might mention a local product that would not be suitable in the U.S.A.

Use reviews in the initial stages of gathering information, but do not make the mistake of thinking that because a product is recommended by several reviews you cannot go wrong. The TCO of enterprise software purchases often runs into tens of millions of dollars, and maximizing the ROI demands a thorough software selection process.

How to find software products

Product searches usually start on the web, but how do you find out about other products you aren't aware exist? Use the search method mentioned above, but use different combinations of two or three product names in one query. By doing this you will often find reviews that include other products with which you are not familiar.

Another way of finding products is using software comparison and research sites. These often have tools to help refine your search, but those tools are limited because they operate at such a high level. In addition, using these sites for selecting software does not gather critical information for the implementation. Still, they are an excellent starting point for your research, particularly if you are looking for more niche enterprise products. The software comparison and research sites below are listed alphabetically:

- Capterra (capterra.com)
- Compare Business Products (comparebusinessproducts.com)
- GetApp (getapp.com)
- G2Crowd (g2crowd.com)
- ITCentralStation (itcentralstation.com) Focused on technology rather than business.
- pFind (pfind.com) Focused on marketing and small business.
- Siftery (siftery.com)
- Software Advice (softwareadvice.com)
- TopTenReviews (toptenreviews.com) Focused on personal and small business, but does have useful information for certain types of software.
- TrustRadius (trustradius.com)

Depending on the type of software needed, analyst companies like Gartner and Forrester are another useful source of information. These companies sell their analyst reports, and they are not cheap. However, the research tends to be in far more depth than anything on the software research sites and the source of the information is known.

Key lessons

- Selecting enterprise software requires considerable effort. We listed the core features needed by software selection tools to help make the work easier, and several commercially available tools that can help facilitate the process.

- While spreadsheets can be used to collect requirements at the start of a project, they are too manual to scale up for large software selections.

- While reviews or analyst reports are an excellent place to start product research, you never want to use them to make a software selection decision.

- We listed several sources of information for software product research.

Chapter 9.   Requirements

Requirements are to acquiring software as plans are to constructing buildings. If a builder has inadequate plans for your dream home, do you think it will meet your expectations? If your organization has inadequate requirements when selecting software, do you think the new software will meet expectations?

Most people think requirements are used for selecting software, but that is only half the story. The requirements development process should also be designed to gather critical information needed for the implementation. Well-written requirements will significantly reduce the amount of work the implementation team must do, and the risk of the implementation schedule slipping.

Enterprise software purchases usually take much longer to implement than planned. Most of the delay is caused by finding "new" requirements during implementation when they should have been discovered during the analysis phase. The time taken to deal with those new requirements is what causes the delays.

Either those new requirements were missed, or they were written at too high a level to be implemented. Satisfying too many new requirements causes schedules to slip and costs to rise. In an effort to meet schedules some items get left for later and this causes unnecessary business disruption when going live. Requirements will always be found: during the analysis, implementation, or in early production. However, the later they are found, the more they cost to satisfy (See: Selection project costs on page 140).

> *The later requirements are found in the software acquisition process the more they cost to satisfy.*

When coding software, requirements development usually starts by asking users and working towards the finished product. Many people assume this applies to buying software. That may have been the case in the last century, but today it is far better to start with potential products and work back towards users. This is how you find requirements you don't know you need.

Developing adequate requirements for a major software purchase takes months, and is usually around 50 percent of the total work in a selection project, but may be more. With projects like ERP, the cost of the software selection is usually more than recovered by reducing or eliminating delays to the implementation schedule.

However, if an organization is unwilling to spend the time and money needed to develop the requirements, the project is in trouble from the start. Those decision-makers who take shortcuts with this foundational step take unnecessary risks for their organization and their careers.

If you search the web for help with developing requirements you will find statements like "write well-defined requirements" or "write detailed requirements." This advice is not actionable because it does not tell you what well-defined requirements are, or how much detail they should contain. Most advice on the web is not actionable because it is too high-level. It might tell you what you want, but it does not tell you why you need it or how to get it.

Then there is advice like, "don't waste time on basic functionality." You *will* get into that basic functionality when doing the implementation, so why not make it part of developing requirements up-front, and avoid the problems caused by selecting software that does not implement that functionality in a way that works for you? Details matter. Following this type of bad advice always leads to implementations that take much longer than planned.

This chapter describes an actionable approach to creating a comprehensive list of requirements, and even how to find requirements you don't know you need. In addition, it describes why the process works.

Requirement definitions

Requirement: A specific capability or characteristic of the software or vendor that may be needed by the software purchaser to solve a problem or achieve an objective.

Significant requirement: A requirement, that if not adequately met, will cause some measure of business disruption when the software goes live.

Need: A more general, high-level requirement, for example "easy to use software" is a need, but "a calendar pop-up for date fields" is a specific usability requirement.

Requirements specification: A documented collection of requirements.

Requirement weight: A measure of how important a requirement is to the organization purchasing the software.

Requirements profile: A comprehensive list of requirements that have been weighted by the software purchaser. A requirements profile is broad enough to include all significant requirements related to a specific type of software purchase. It is also written so that all requirements can be implemented.

Requirements are questions

All requirements are questions, although they are seldom written that way. The implied question is, "How well does the software meet this requirement?" Questions can be open or closed. Open-ended questions allow the person answering to give their opinion. An open-ended question can be phrased as a statement that requires a response. Examples of open-ended questions are:

- How well does the software...?

- Describe your software testing philosophy.

Closed questions are answered with a *yes* or *no*, by picking a point along a scale or with a specific item of information. Examples of closed questions are:

- Does the software comply with...?

- Does the software include a module that handles...?

- Does the software...? Which is answered by selecting from a sliding scale, e.g.: "fully meets," "partly meets" or "does not meet."

When you are writing requirements for evaluating software, phrase them as closed questions that can be answered on a sliding scale.

Phrase requirements as closed questions that can be answered on a sliding scale. Answers can then be used to calculate a product's fit score.

When evaluating a software product, how well the product rates for each requirement is multiplied by the requirement weight to generate a score. Scores from hundreds or thousands of requirements are rolled up to calculate the fit score, which *measures* how well that software product meets those particular requirements (See: Actual and fit scores on page 214).

If requirements are phrased as open questions, there is no way to combine the responses mathematically into a fit score that measures how well the software meets those requirements.

Answers to requirements phrased as open questions can't be factored into the fit score calculation.

Why requirements are important

Few organizations realize just how critical the step of developing requirements is to the ultimate success of a major software purchase, where success is defined as fully meeting expectations (See: Software success defined on page 5). Inadequate requirements can cause the wrong software to be selected and an organization might find they have bought a square peg for a round hole. That immediately reduces the value of the benefits that will flow from using the new software, i.e. the return on a substantial investment has been diminished (See: The four costs of poor software purchasing on page 83).

Whether best-fit software was selected or not, requirements not discovered during analysis will be found during implementation or when going live. The software will not meet those requirements out-of-the-box because, if it did, there would be nothing to do.

As noted, discovering significant new requirements triggers meetings to decide how important those requirements are, and what must be done about them. If these new requirements are weighted as important or higher, the implementation team will attempt to satisfy them with system configuration, developing code, business process re-engineering, workarounds, or purchasing add-on modules or third-party products. If a requirement is not discovered until you're already in early production, it will cause business disruption.

New and unplanned requirements take longer to implement than if they had been planned for up front. For example, if an implementation was planned to take six months, inadequate requirements could cause it to take nine months. Had those requirements been discovered in the analysis phase and been part of the original project plan, implementation could have been about seven months.

As noted, discovering too many new requirements will cause implementations to take longer and cost more than originally planned, but it gets worse. As delays mount, in an attempt to meet schedules, some implementation tasks are left for later, which increases the business disruption experienced when the software goes live. Invariably functional fit is compromised which means users are dissatisfied and their buy-in dissipates. And this is only the start of the pains that will be experienced when new software does not meet expectations (See: Software purchase pains on page 7).

> *A company expected to spend around $1 million purchasing ERP software and $2 million on implementation. Consultants had quoted about $200,000 for the evaluation and selection project, but the company decided this was too expensive and selection was done using internal resources.*
>
> *Because of an inadequate requirements analysis, the best software for their needs was not selected. Implementation took 50 percent longer than planned and cost an extra $1 million. Business disruption on going live took a chunk out of annual revenue. Users were unhappy with the new software, but by then it was too late to do anything about it. In hindsight, that consulting would have been a very prudent investment. Not only did they end up spending more, but they wasted an opportunity for the business to "kick it up a notch."*

Where requirements are used

Knowing where requirements are used in the software acquisition process explains why it is worth spending significant effort developing them.

Where requirements are used in the selection

1. Weighting requirements

We have found that separating requirements capturing from requirements weighting is better and faster than trying to do both at once (See: Weight requirements for importance on page 201). When a requirement is weighted, the organization captures who wants it, why they want it, and how important it is to them. This information is used in the following places:

- The requirement weight is used in the product fit score calculation, which is used to select the software (See: A scoring system for rating products on page 208).

- When employees see their names written on the requirements, they feel the organization is listening to them. That builds buy-in, essential to the success of a major software purchase (See: Creating and nurturing user buy-in on page 122).

- Scope creep is reduced by keeping users focused on what potential software can do, rather than asking them to think up requirements (See: How to minimize requirements scope creep on page 186).

2. Vendor responses

Requirements are used when a vendor responds to an RFI or RFP. When vendors encounter incomplete, ambiguous, or badly worded requirements, they are quite entitled to interpret those requirements in a way that favors them rather than the buyer. Inaccurate RFI or RFP responses caused by inadequate requirements can result in:

- Expectations not being met. No vendor can be held accountable for not meeting unstated requirements.

- The wrong software being selected.

3. Gap analysis and software selection

In the gap analysis, potential software products are evaluated against the requirements and a fit score is calculated. The fit score is an *objective measure* of how well potential software products meet the requirements profile. The software with the highest fit score is the product that best meets the need, and is usually the one that is selected.

4. RFI or RFP Audit

In the RFI or RFP audit a sample of requirements is selected for verification (See: How to audit an RFI on page 248). The vendor is asked to provide evidence that their software does indeed meet the requirements as they claimed in their RFI or

RFP response. If a vendor misrepresented their product, the audit will discover this.

5. Setting expectations

Managing expectations is critical to the ultimate success of a software purchase. Selecting enterprise software always involves some degree of compromise, and the purpose of the gap analysis is to minimize that compromise. The gap analysis used to purchase software defines and documents the expectations of the organization down to how that software meets individual requirements. Knowing the compromises before the purchase keeps expectations aligned with reality and prevents buyer's remorse (See: Expectations management on page 245).

Where requirements are used in implementation

One way to reduce the risk of implementation schedule slipping is to design the selection project to collect the information needed by the implementation team.

6. Project planning

Once the software has been purchased, the winning evaluation is handed over to the implementation project manager, who uses that information to plan and estimate the implementation project (See: Planning the implementation schedule on page 273).

7. Software implementation

Questions always arise during software implementation. When a consultant has a question, knowing the weight of a requirement and why it has that weight may help answer the question. If still more information is needed, knowing who wants that requirement allows the consultant to easily contact that person for clarification (See: Answering implementation consultant questions on page 274).

8. Acceptance testing

One of the last steps in taking a major software purchase live is that of customer or user acceptance testing. Each requirement should be written so that an acceptance test can be developed to verify that the software unambiguously meets that requirement.

The ability to measure how well software meets requirements can help avoid problems like lawsuits with software vendors and implementation consultants. The only winners in such lawsuits are the lawyers.

> *Marin County hired Deloitte Consulting to implement SAP ERP, but after several years the project was declared a failure. Marin County's top administrator, Matthew Hymel, told the County's board that the SAP solution did not fit the needs and should be replaced with something better and more cost effective. Marin County then sued Deloitte Consulting for $30 million, but in a settlement agreed to accept $3.9 million, which was less than their legal fees of $5 million.*
>
> *Had Marin County properly defined their requirements at the start of the project, they would not have gotten into this mess in the first place. But even if they did end up in court an adequate requirements analysis would have won them a larger judgment.*

Where requirements are used in production

9. Maximize software value

By the time an organization gets to the end of a major software implementation project, everybody involved is relieved it is over and only too keen to move onto something new. This can lead to valuable software features being overlooked and never implemented.

Having a comprehensive list of weighted requirements along with a measure of how well the software meets them can prevent that functionality from being lost. When those features are later implemented the value of the software is maximized.

When to start requirements gathering

When it comes to selecting software, the sooner requirements are discovered the lower the cost of satisfying them. The best time to start gathering requirements is when you first realize you are outgrowing the current software, which is usually long before a decision is made to find a replacement. The reason is that from time to time problems will occur, and requirements can be written around those problems while they are fresh in your mind.

Reading articles in industry publications or thinking about the topic can result in new requirements being identified. Provided there is a system in place to capture those requirements, the longer this process runs, the better the requirements that are collected.

However, in practice, requirements gathering usually starts only after a decision has been made to acquire new software. It is important to realize that if requirements are not found in the analysis phase, they *will be found* during implementation, or when going live (See: Selection project costs on page 140). The problems with finding requirements later rather than sooner are:

- The wrong software may be purchased.

- New requirements found during implementation means the schedule slips, costs increase and there is excessive business disruption when going live (See: Why requirements are important on page 168).

- Expectations will not be met.

An adequate requirements analysis takes time, but that preparatory work means the new software gets into production sooner rather than later. It also helps ensure expectations are met.

Requirements are used both to select software,
and then to implement that software.

When to weight requirements

Speaking with users creates an opportunity to begin capturing requirements, but should the requirements be weighted for importance at the same time? In our experience, we have found it better to split requirements capture from requirements weighting for the following reasons:

- Requirements captured from users are in first draft form. Subsequently they may be revised, split into several detailed requirements, or combined with similar requirements from other users. They may even be completely rewritten. These actions would invalidate the weighting.

- Gathering requirements from users is slow and tedious. Asking them to weight the requirements makes the process take even longer. Overall it is faster to first gather requirements and later present users with a list of requirements to weight them.

- Apart from requirements based on their pain points, most users have trouble articulating what they want. Giving them a well-written list of requirements will allow users to easily express how important each one is to them.

- Teams are likely to weight requirements differently from individuals. This kind of discussion is good because it moderates those people who claim all their requirements are showstoppers.

- Many requirements will come from sources other than users, and will need meetings to weight them anyway.

For the above reasons, we have found it faster and more efficient to first capture requirements and then to meet with teams of users who weight them for importance to the organization.

Sources of requirements

The key to capturing a comprehensive list of requirements is to understand that, for any given type of software, every organization has the same requirements.

The difference between organizations is expressed in the requirement weights. For example, all organizations have security requirements, but a small retail chain will have very different security requirement weights to that of a national bank.

The source of the requirements does not matter; what does matter is that they are captured. Knowing this allows you to use requirements from any source.

For any type of software, everybody has the same requirements. It is the requirement weights that are unique to each organization

When purchasing software, there are five sources of requirements, each with its strengths and limitations.

Chapter 9: Requirements

1. Asking users

When it comes to gathering software requirements, the first step is to ask users. Some consultants believe that users are the only true source of requirements, but there are limits to what users can offer. Most users only know requirements based on their pain points. If there are any employees who used similar software in previous jobs, they can provide valuable input, particularly if that experience is recent.

While asking users is a slow process that will yield too few requirements, it is a vital step in building user buy-in (See: Creating and nurturing user buy-in on page 122). If consultants are used for requirements development, this is an opportunity for them to build rapport with users.

Broadly speaking there are two types of enterprise software users, each with different perspectives on requirements. Both perspectives are necessary, and some users are a blend of each.

- **Hands-on users:** These are employees who use the software daily as a critical part of their job. They will often have strong and detailed opinions, but a narrow focus. Best-fit software can make them much more efficient in their jobs.

- **Management users:** These employees have a broad and strategic view of requirements, and can have a valuable perspective on future needs.

While necessary for building rapport, asking users for requirements can be extremely time consuming. An efficient approach is to keep initial requirements gathering interviews short, for example 15 to 30 minutes with either individuals or small teams from one department or group. Focus on requirements related to their pain points. Then use the other techniques below to gather the remainder of the requirements.

2. Business process analysis

Business process analysis is a critical source of requirements when designing software, and usually it is followed by business process optimization. When developing software, only optimized business processes should be coded (See: Work done in the wrong order on page 29).

However, when *buying* software, business process analysis and optimization are unnecessary in the requirements analysis phase. Gathering requirements is already slow enough without this added burden. Process analysis and optimization are best left for the implementation phase for the following reasons:

- Unnecessary work may be done. The purchased software may have best practices that reduce or eliminate much of the business process analysis and optimization work.

- Best practices can be software specific, and it may not be possible to optimize them until the software is selected. If you try to optimize processes before selecting the software you are operating in a vacuum.

For the purposes of selecting software, all that is needed is to know how well the potential software can perform those business processes (i.e. "fully meets," "mostly meets," "partly meets," etc.).

Requirements need to be written so they are implementable (See: Implementable requirements on page 197). If you find yourself needing to know how the processes should be performed, the requirements have not been written in enough detail to be implementable.

3. Integration requirements

Existing software that might need to interface with the new software should be reviewed for requirements. For things like ERP this involves an inventory of all existing software, and reviewing each of these software products in turn.

For smaller software purchases, ensure all existing software that could integrate with the new software is reviewed. The last thing you want to discover when implementing the new software is that there are several legacy systems that now must be interfaced to it.

> *Some years ago, Thompson Reuters bought SAP to operate as ERP/MIS for their headquarters in Minnesota. Before the purchase very little discovery had taken place to determine how SAP would interface with legacy data collection systems in the book production plant. Initial implementation estimates were for about one year, but SAP did not have interfaces with any of the legacy bookmaking software. Developing these interfaces was a major source of delays which caused the implementation project to take 2 ½ years instead of one.*

4. External sources

External sources of requirements range from those extracted from RFPs found on the web, getting requirements from colleagues who have done similar projects or buying requirements libraries from vendors. Other external sources are hiring consultants who already have libraries of requirements from similar projects.

External sources of requirements can be useful even if they are poorly written because they can help find unknown requirements. Poorly written requirements can always be improved (See: How to write good requirements on page 187). If you can find or buy requirements, get them, you'll find it's the fastest and most economical way to develop what you need.

5. Reverse engineering

Reverse engineering is the process of formally examining the features and functions of multiple potential software products and writing them as requirements. It is like running software development backwards.

Imagine you moved to a new city and wanted to buy a home. You would not call up an architect to design your perfect house, and then try to find the house that best matched that design. But that is how most organizations buy software; they start by developing their requirements and then working towards the products. The reason this happens is that when developing software, you must start with the users, and most organizations extend this thinking to buying software.

However, since the software is being bought rather than built, a better way is to start with the products on the market and work back towards the requirements.

Returning to the house analogy, you would first outline your requirements and then start looking at properties. As you looked, you would refine your requirements. That is exactly how the process of reverse engineering works.

Discovering unknown requirements during implementation is the primary cause of schedule delays, cost overruns, and business disruption when going live. Reverse engineering is a very valuable technique because it discovers requirements an organization does not know they need before the implementation phase. It also ensures the latest innovations on the market are captured as requirements. However, the process of reverse engineering requirements takes time; for example, it can take 150 to 200 hours per thousand requirements captured.

> *A few years ago, we were working with a client in the civil engineering space who was considering project management software. At that time, some of the newer cloud vendors had software that worked on smartphones, and when the client saw this, their eyes lit up.*
>
> *Field access was something they had never considered. Previously, they needed to run internet connections to their site offices in the field, and that was not always practical. And then, when on site, project managers had to go to the site office to get the information they wanted. However, with the project management software available on smartphones, they had immediate access to the information needed on the building site, and that had immense value for that client.*

Limits to reverse engineering requirements

Reverse engineering will only find functional requirements if at least one of the products reverse engineered expressed that requirement as a feature. In the Thompson Reuters story on page 176, it is very unlikely that any ERP system would have had interfaces to legacy bookmaking software and therefore reverse engineering would not have found those requirements.

For other types of requirements that would not be found by reverse engineering, such as requirements for new business processes, use the same requirements discovery techniques that would be used when developing software.

Where to find requirements

Software features and functions can be found in user documentation, which some vendors make available online. Another source of requirements is from training or demo videos. A YouTube video on a software product longer than about 10 minutes can be a tremendous source of requirements. Shorter videos tend to be marketing focused rather than feature focused, and are seldom useful.

Requirements can also be discovered from watching live software demos, although recordings where you can stop and take notes are much more useful.

Requirements from current software

When contemplating replacing existing software that has been outgrown, reverse engineering features from the existing software can establish a requirements baseline. This helps prevent selecting software that remedies the pain points of the old software, but does not have all of its functionality.

In addition, existing process and data flow documentation should be reviewed for potential requirements. However, there are some limitations:

- The documentation is usually out of date and incomplete.

- The documentation describes the existing system, and improvements are a primary reason for replacement. There is little point in re-implementing the existing system on new software without taking advantage of what the new software offers.

Nevertheless, if the documentation exists it is well worth reviewing for requirements. When gathering requirements from existing documentation avoid writing system specific requirements, for example if the existing system requires X, don't write that as a requirement. Find out why X is required and what it is used for. Then you can decide if X is a true requirement or if it was only a requirement caused by limitations of the existing system.

Types of software requirements

Some types of software requirements apply to all purchases while other types are specific to the cloud or the data center. Here is a partial list of different requirements types:

- **Functional requirements:** Specify what the software must do. When considering requirements, most people think of functional requirements. These are the most important types of requirements because if the software does not do what is needed it will not be selected and then the other requirements do not matter.

- **Usability requirements:** User interface, navigation, searching, user help and searching user help, languages.

- **Vendor requirements:** Due diligence, implementation, support, payment arrangements, and application ecosystem; things like user groups, add-on products from other vendors.

- **Hardware requirements:** If an organization is going to manage the hardware on which the software will be run, that hardware must be capable of adequately supporting the software now and in the future.

- **System requirements**: Performance, monitoring, integration, configuration, compatibility, architecture (front and back-end), user management, backups.

- **Compliance requirements:** Vendor compliance, quality, standards (ISO, SOX, HIPAA, 21 CFR Part 11, etc.), vendor standard operating procedures (SOPs), audit trails, tracking end-user training.

- **Contractual requirements:** Legal, license, performance, contract terms and termination (all contracts eventually end, make sure there is a graceful way to exit).

- **Security requirements:** Especially in the case of cloud or hosted applications: physical and logical security, configuration, security testing and audits, logging and reporting, authentication and passwords, encryption.

- **Training requirements:** Content, delivery, training management.

Who should write requirements?

Writing requirements is a skill that can be developed, and is best done by those who enjoy writing.

Requirements are often written by IT or Line of Business employees. However, given the hundreds of hours of work needed to develop requirements for selecting software, it is unrealistic to expect these employees to do a decent job without offloading some or most of their normal responsibilities. But that seldom happens, which results in an inadequate list of requirements. This leads to implementations that take longer and cost more than expected, and business disruption when going live.

A better solution may be to use outside consultants who specialize in software selection. They have the time, skills and experience, and will complete the work faster. They usually have libraries which can save time. In addition, requirements written by outside consultants will be free of institutional jargon that can be a source of misunderstandings.

How many requirements are needed?

When it comes to enterprise software, details matter, and one of those details is the number of requirements. So, when developing requirements for a major software purchase, how many requirements should there be?

Software with inadequate high-level features and functionality is eliminated early in the evaluation process. However, without adequate requirements, software that does not function as expected can get selected.

> *The work of capturing requirements is always done.*
> *It just costs a lot more when they are discovered*
> *during implementation or when going live.*

While one purpose for requirements is to select the software, the other purpose is to implement that software. If there are too few requirements, missing requirements will be discovered during implementation, which causes a number of issues.

It is never a good idea to skimp on the number of requirements. Larger numbers of more detailed requirements mean:

1. Requirements can be created faster when each requirement does not contain as much information. Larger requirements can be split into several smaller requirements.

2. Weighting requirements is faster. Requirements written at too high a level tend to be debated extensively when being weighted.

3. Rating potential software products against requirements is faster. Vendors take less time when responding to RFIs (See: Maximizing vendor responses on page 226).

4. The evaluation is a more accurate measure of how well that software product will meet those needs.

5. Software RFI audits that verify the vendor did not misrepresent the product are faster and more accurate when requirements are greater in number, but each requirement includes less (See: How to audit an RFI on page 248).

6. Implementation project schedules and cost estimates are more accurate (See: Planning the implementation schedule on page 273).

7. If the implementation is by fixed contract, the number of change orders is minimized, which reduces cost increases.

8. Implementation is faster because there is more requirement detail that describes how the software should be implemented.

9. Working around unexpected software limitations is minimized.

10. Acceptance testing is faster, again because there is more detail that describes how the software must operate in production.

For example, suppose there was a requirement to capture transaction dates in a field. Instead of manually typing in the date, a pop-up calendar is faster and less error prone. Suppose that many of the transactions clustered at the start or end of the month. A three-month pop-up calendar that showed last, this and next month would save even more mouse clicks. Where there are many operators entering dozens of transactions per hour, minimizing the number of mouse clicks or keystrokes can add up to significant savings. If these usability factors are important to your organization, you need to go down to that level of detail when specifying requirements. If they are not important, such detail is not needed.

If requirements are written at too high a level, a vendor can truthfully claim to meet them, but they still will not satisfy your needs. No vendor can be held accountable for not meeting unstated requirements.

As a buyer, it is your responsibility to specify requirements in enough detail to ensure the software purchased can be implemented in a manner that works for your organization.

The above point cannot be emphasized enough. Inadequate requirements are the largest source of problems by far with new software implementations.

There are many cases where a software implementation fails and the purchaser takes the implementation vendor to court. This has happened with large companies like Bridgestone Tires taking IBM to court for a failed SAP implementation. It has happened to smaller companies like Kentwool's failure when implementing NetSuite. If the requirements had been spelled out in enough detail to implement the software the way the buyer wanted they would not have ended up in court. The only winners in these kinds of court cases are the lawyers (See the Marin County court case on page 172).

When to split requirements

When developing requirements, a decision must be made about whether a requirement should be split into multiple detailed requirements. The answer to this depends on how the requirement will be implemented. For example, consider the case of a requirement for a mobile app. This requirement could be split into several levels of detail, depending on the actual needs.

Level 1 - One requirement

It could be written as a single requirement, for example, "mobile app for iOS and Android." If a software product had a mobile app for only one or the other, it could be rated as "Partly meets." If it has mobile apps for both, it could be rated as "fully meets."

Level 2 - Two requirements

If 90 percent of potential users had iPhones, you might want to split it into two requirements, and weight the iPhone requirement as "critical," while the Android requirement was only "important."

Level 3 - Four requirements

If there is a need to use the app on tablets, and putting a phone app on a tablet is not good enough, this could be split into four requirements: iPhone app, iPad app, Android phone app, Android tablet app. Each could have their own weights.

Level 4 - More than four requirements

If you need to perform specific tasks on phones and tablets, you want to specify those tasks in detail for each of the four device options. For example, the tablet apps may need the ability for people to fill out forms and to capture signatures.

As you can appreciate, if your requirements are written at Level 1, but you really need the detail of Level 4, there will be problems during implementation.

For another example, consider the requirement that "the software must be easy to use." What vendor would give themselves anything but a "fully meets" on that requirement?! We have developed a library of over 180 usability requirements that provide an objective way to measure ease of use. That one "easy to use" requirement was split into 180 detailed requirements.

How a requirement is split into detail depends on how it will be implemented, what it will be used for and the weight of that requirement. But remember, it's far better to capture too many requirements up front than to discover new requirements during implementation where they cause problems and pains.

Obvious requirements

When collecting requirements, should you include obvious ones? The answer is yes, for the following reasons:

- In a hierarchical requirements structure, obvious requirements are used as *containers* for more detailed requirements. For example, if you are evaluating accounting software, you will have accounts payable. The accounts payable requirement is a container for detailed requirements related to paying accounts.

- One of the reasons for capturing requirements is to collect the information needed for the implementation. An obvious requirement must be stated so that the information about it can be gathered:

    o How the software meets the requirement, which is used for implementation planning, such as if a feature must be configured to meet the requirement.
    o Who wants that requirement, why they want it and how important it is, is used by consultants during implementation.

- It is too easy to exclude something that seemed obvious, and then to discover the selected product does not meet that requirement. Vendors responding to an RFI or RFP cannot be held accountable for not meeting requirements that the buyer didn't think it necessary to document.

How to know when you have all requirements

When writing software all requirements cannot be known, but when buying software, in principle, they can. An organization will be considering a list of potential software products with a finite number of features. The requirements that could be satisfied by the individual features of those products define the complete list of requirements for that software acquisition.

If users want a feature not present in the range of products being considered, the absence of that feature will not affect which product is selected (because no product has it), although it could change the project scope or the range of software products being considered.

Reverse engineering (see page 177) features into requirements is effectively running the software development process in reverse. When multiple potential products have been identified and all their features have been reverse engineered into requirements, all requirements have been captured for that project.

This can be tested: if further product research reveals one or more potential product candidates, and the reverse engineering technique yields no significant new requirements, this confirms that all requirements have indeed been captured.

Although it is possible to capture all requirements, in practice time constraints usually mean taking a risk-based approach, and that means a trickle of new requirements are usually found during the project. The goal is to capture all *significant* requirements as early as possible, and reverse engineering is well suited to that task.

> *When reverse engineering new products finds no significant new requirements, you know you have found all significant functional requirements.*

How to minimize requirements scope creep

The success of a major software acquisition depends on managing risks like scope creep. Scope creep is defined as adding significant new requirements after the requirements analysis phase. If the requirements scope grows too large, it can cause a project to fail. While this is always a danger when developing software, it can also happen when purchasing cloud or off-the-shelf software.

When users think the new software is their one and only chance to solve all of their problems, they may continually add new requirements from selection through to implementation. After all, from a user perspective, what is unreasonable?

The first part of controlling scope is to develop a comprehensive list of all significant requirements using the reverse engineering process. The second part of controlling scope is to keep users focused on weighting requirements that can be satisfied as opposed to their wish lists. This works because reverse engineering exposes requirements users did not think of themselves. If users working through requirements are finding ones they did not think of themselves, they are not tempted to dream up new requirements.

Scope creep is reduced by keeping users focused on requirements that can be satisfied.

What to do with requirements found after the analysis

Although the aim is to discover all significant requirements during the requirements analysis, new requirements will likely be found along the way. These are prompted by real-live situations users encounter. After RFIs have been sent to vendors, most of the time new requirements will not affect the software selection, but they should still be captured and weighted, as should requirements that are found after the software has been purchased. These will all be used during the software implementation (See: Implementation handover on page 272).

When requirements are added after the analysis phase it's usually more about refining or expanding existing requirements, rather than adding significant new requirements. However, if there is a valid business reason for a significant new requirement, it should be added and weighted because it can affect which software product is selected (See: Scope check on page 231).

How to write good requirements

It must be stressed that this book covers requirements for selecting software, not for coding software. Although both types of requirements share some characteristics, such as they must not be ambiguous, there are several differences. In general, requirements for selecting software are not as finely detailed as requirements for writing software.

When developing requirements for a major software purchase, how much detail should there be in each requirement? To answer this question, we must examine why description detail is important and where it is used. Then we can look at how to write good requirement descriptions.

Why description detail is important

By analogy, compare a list of requirements to directions for a journey. Have you ever followed directions and yet not arrived at the desired destination? The problem can happen because directions are at too high a level, there are unexpected detours along the way, you get lost and so on. Sometimes when you arrive, the place is not what was expected and you abandon the trip.

The problem is similar when purchasing software. You want to realize the benefits that will flow from using the new software. You want the implementation project to be within budget, on time and with a minimum of business disruption when going live. Well-written requirement descriptions play a crucial part in achieving these goals.

When writing a requirement, focus on what must be satisfied, and, in general, why it should be satisfied. Include an example to provide context to help readers fully understand that requirement.

It is best practice to include examples that show how the requirement might be satisfied because that helps set the context. However, the "how" should always be in examples and not in the requirement itself.

If you find yourself writing how in the requirement description, ask yourself why the requirement must be satisfied in this way. You may find you need to break the requirement into several more detailed requirements. Alternatively, you may be revealing a bias based on your experience. Whatever the cause, the how should only appear in examples.

Requirement description detail

When deciding how much detail a requirement description should contain, it is not necessary to go to the level needed for coding software. However, if you later decide to build rather than to buy, you will have an excellent foundation for software development requirements although they may need further work to make them suitable for coding. When writing descriptions keep in mind what they are used for, and include enough detail so that:

1. The organization acquiring the software can decide how important the requirement is to them, and give it a weight.

2. An evaluator can objectively and accurately rate how well a potential software product meets that requirement. This person usually is a vendor responding to an RFI.

3. When auditing an RFI or RFP, an auditor can verify that a product rating is an accurate measure of how well the software meets that requirement.

4. An implementation project manager can estimate how long it will take to implement that requirement.

5. A software implementation consultant has enough information to implement the requirement with the selected software, for example by configuring the software or by writing scripts.

6. A user acceptance tester can verify the implemented software meets the requirement as described.

Do not make requirements too high a level, but split them into multiple more specific requirements (See: When to split requirements on page 183).

> *To illustrate the level of detail needed in requirements consider this story: We were evaluating software for creating consulting proposals, and one of the requirements was the ability to embed an image into a proposal. With one product, we found an image could be added to a proposal, but you could only resize the image larger, which made it pixelated. You could not resize it smaller than the native size. This was an entirely unexpected limitation, and caused us to modify the detail of the requirement to specify that embedded images should be able to be resized larger or smaller. This is an example of the level of detail needed to ensure a requirement can be implemented as expected.*

It's the unexpected limitations that cause the problems when implementing software.

Parts of a well written requirement

Buying a car is much simpler than building one. Likewise, requirements for buying software are much simpler than requirements for building software. But don't let that fool you. Poorly written requirements can mean the purchased software does not meet expectations. Painful consequences include selecting the wrong software, extended implementations, unrealized ROI, and occasionally outright failure (See: Software purchase pains on page 7). Writing good requirements accelerates software selection and implementation projects and reduces overall risks.

Chapter 9: Requirements

> *We were working with a client team to weight requirements for their organization when we came across one incomprehensible requirement. The name of the author was on the requirement and he was in the meeting. When asked to explain he answered: "I have no idea what I meant!" We ended up deleting it from the list because it had no meaning for that project. He simply could not remember what he was thinking of when he wrote it.*

This type of situation is all too common. Why does it happen, and how can you avoid it? The answer is that requirements have meaning in a context. When writing the requirement, the context was assumed. Over time, the context changes or is forgotten, and the meaning of the requirement dissipates.

It takes some practice, but one of the secrets of good requirements is to write them so they include the context, and can stand alone without the support of external context. The ability to stand alone is particularly important if requirements will be collected in a library and reused on subsequent software evaluations.

The parts of a well-written requirement are listed below. Note that while a well written requirement does not have to have all these items, it should have the first three, and several of the others.

1. **ID:** Every requirement should have a unique ID that does not change. Requirement titles can and do change as evaluations progress, and the requirement ID allows you to unambiguously identify a requirement for example, in an exported spreadsheet.

2. **Title:** A short descriptive name for the requirement, preferably less than about five or six words. The title is the shorthand way to refer to a requirement in conversation, emails, etc.

3. **Description:** Amplifies the title and removes ambiguities. The description should be written with enough detail so that how well software products meet or do not meet that requirement can be assessed (See: Requirement description on page 188). If a description contains acronyms, buzzwords or concepts, there should be links to resources like Wikipedia to explain them. There can also be links to articles from technical publications that provide background to the requirement.

4. **Reasons:** Requirements should include *general* reasons why the requirement might be wanted. Reasons *specific* to why an organization may want a requirement should be part of the requirement weight.

5. **Use case example:** Wherever possible, when writing a requirement include an example of where a feature satisfying that requirement would be used. This provides the context in which to understand the requirement, amplifies the description and helps remove ambiguities.

6. **Design example:** Include examples of how the system might be designed to satisfy this requirement. This helps understand the requirement, and to be consistent when rating how well software products meet that requirement.

7. **Notes**: Any notes about the requirement that clarify it, limit, or extend its application, remove potential ambiguities, etc. Typically, notes take the form of bullet points.

8. **Evaluation note:** Specific instructions on how to rate a product against the requirement. For example:

   - Does not apply to cloud software, rate as "not applicable."

   - If the product only does X, rate it as a "mostly meets." If it only does Y then rate it as "partly meets."

9. **Audit trail:** An edit history that shows changes to a requirement, who made them and when they were made. It should allow earlier versions of a requirement to be viewed. It should also allow a requirement to be rolled back to an earlier version.

Characteristics of well written requirements

Unambiguous requirements

Adequate and well-written requirements are the foundation for selecting enterprise software that meets expectations. A frequent problem with requirements is that some are ambiguous. While ambiguities are easy to see in requirements written by others, they are difficult to spot in your own writing.

Ambiguous requirements are defined as requirements where:

   - A single reader can interpret the requirement in more than one way, and is unsure which interpretation is intended.

- Several readers interpret the requirement differently from each other.

Ambiguities are difficult for a writer to see because, when writing a requirement, they have a specific context in mind. The ambiguity is visible to anybody who does not have this context. That is why writers may be able to see ambiguities if they reread their requirements after a few weeks, when they will have forgotten the assumed context.

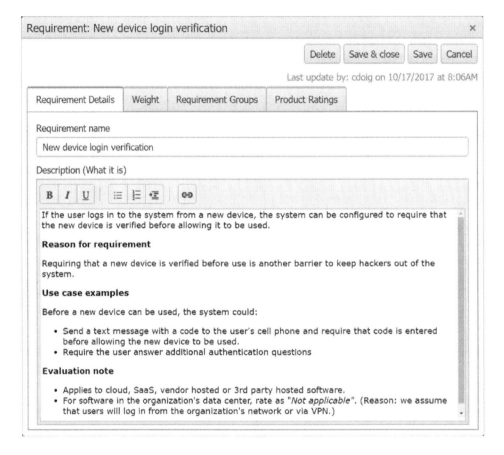

Figure 6: Screenshot of a well written requirement

A well written requirement has a single reasonable interpretation in a specific context, and that context is part of the requirement, as in an example. Some factors that cause requirement ambiguities are:

- A context is assumed, but not all readers will know that context.

- The requirement is written at too high a level, for example "the software shall be easy to use" or "the software must be flexible."

- An incompletely written requirement or one that is not explicit enough.

- Poorly structured requirements, for example having unclear antecedents, being written in the negative, using often confused terms or abbreviations.

How to write unambiguous requirements

Below is a summary of dealing with ambiguous requirements. For a more comprehensive treatment of this topic see: Ambiguous software requirements lead to confusion, extra work by Karl E. Wiegers, Ph.D. on techtarget

Use examples

Examples are one of the most powerful ways of removing ambiguities because they provide the context in which to understand a requirement. Include one or more examples of how features that satisfy a requirement might be used by the organization. Also, you can include examples of how features satisfying the requirement could be implemented by a software vendor.

Be explicit

Minimize the use of assumptions because they invite misinterpretation. Instead, explicitly state what is being assumed, and do not worry if you are being repetitive. You're not writing a novel. Your writing does not have to be "interesting."

Bridgestone Tires took IBM to court for a failed ERP implementation. Imagine you were in a comparable situation and the outcome of your case depended on whether you could show the software vendor had misrepresented what their product could do. The more explicit the requirements, the better the odds you would have of a favorable judgment. Keep this in mind when writing or editing requirements.

Avoid adverbs

Adverbs are subjective and result in ambiguity when people interpret them differently. For example, "the system must refresh the data reasonably quickly" is vague because the word "reasonably" is ambiguous. If it used to take eight hours of computing to refresh the data, and now the vendor does it in 10 minutes, is that reasonable when the organization wants a real-time response? If an organization wants real-time responses, it must specify that explicitly by saying, "The system must refresh the data within 0.5 seconds." It is also helpful to explain why such a fast response is desired. The reason could be "because customers are on the phone." Avoid adverbs like generally, usually, normally, frequently, occasionally and so on when writing requirements.

Be very careful with pronouns

A pronoun refers to a previously used noun, and that noun is called the antecedent. Pronouns can be ambiguous when their antecedents are unclear. Here's an example from a requirement with a pronoun whose antecedent is unclear:

> European users differ from American users in that they expect...

Here the "they" could refer to either American or European users. Readers outside the organization and unfamiliar with the behavior of the two groups will not know the intended meaning. Tools like Grammarly can be very good at catching unclear antecedent errors.

Use consistent terms

Do not be creative and vary your writing to keep reader interest. Avoid ambiguity by using terms and phrases consistently throughout the requirements. If the requirements use several similar, but not identical terms, create a glossary to define exactly what those terms mean.

Avoid negative requirements

Negative requirements say what the system should not do, rather than saying what it should do. For example, if the requirement stated, "The system should not allow external users to access..." does that mean that consultants working on-site get access or not? The requirement is better phrased as, "The system will only allow employees to access..." Note that the word only is what creates the limitation. Avoid double negatives, which are even more ambiguous.

Avoid confusing abbreviations

The abbreviations e.g. and i.e. are often confused. While e.g. means "for example" and will be followed by one or more illustrations that clarify a concept, i.e. means "that is" and should be followed by a complete list of items. To avoid confusion refrain from using these abbreviations.

How to find ambiguous requirements

Several useful techniques for finding ambiguous requirements are:

- Reread your requirements after two or three weeks. By then you will have forgotten some of the contexts and will be able to see the ambiguities.

- Have co-workers read the requirements.

- When teams meet to weight requirements for importance to the organization, team members will often see ambiguities, which can then be corrected before vendor responses are solicited.

Ambiguous requirements can cause unexpected and unnecessary problems when acquiring enterprise software. As a software purchaser, it is your responsibility to write well-written requirements that avoid ambiguities. By following the above guidelines, you can reduce the ambiguities in your requirement writing, which helps ensure the new software will meet organizational expectations.

Complete requirements

Incomplete requirements are those where significant details are not included. There are two types of incomplete requirements:

- Requirements that do not include all the details in the requirement.

- A set of requirements where some members of that set are missing.

The cause of incomplete requirements can be unstated assumptions, or requirement details that have been overlooked. Some examples are:

- Suppose the requirement was for "the ability for people to sign and approve the document online." However, the buyer needed a document with at least three signatures to be approved, but this was not stated in the requirement. That requirement was incomplete in its detail.

- Suppose there were requirements for the system to use Chrome or Firefox browsers. However, there were some users on Macs that used Safari browsers. That set of requirements was incomplete.

If incomplete requirements are discovered during implementation they will cause pain. One of the best ways to ensure you have complete requirements is to use the reverse engineering technique (See: Reverse engineering on page 177).

Verifiable requirements

In addition to being unambiguous and complete, requirements must be written in such a way that an evaluator or auditor can verify if a potential software product or vendor meets them. They must be explicit and detailed, and not high-level. For example, the requirement "the screen shall refresh quickly" is not verifiable, but "the screen shall refresh in 0.5 seconds" is.

Consider the case of a budgeting module where there is a need to assign budget development to specific people by role or by name. Most budget developments are assigned by role, but there are always a few department heads who want to delegate budget development to specific people in their departments. This could be written as two explicit requirements:

- The system should be able to automatically assign budget development to the heads of departments.

- The system should allow the head of a department to delegate the budget development to a specific person in their department.

Both requirements can be easily verified from the user documentation or by testing the software with a sandbox account.

If the requirement was written as "the system should allow budget development to be assigned" it is possible to meet this phrasing without meeting the intent because if budget development could be assigned only to department heads and not be reassigned, then the real need of the organization would not be met.

When writing requirements, continually ask yourself, "How can I know if a software product could meet this requirement or not?"

Independent requirements

Requirements should be written in such a way that they are not dependent on a specific system to be implemented. This is very important because the whole purpose of writing requirements is to select software. If some of the requirements are written in such a way that only one software product can meet them that is tantamount to bias. If requirements are found to be written so that only one system will satisfy them, you need to ask why that is the case. If no valid reasons can be supplied, the requirements need to be rewritten to remove that dependency.

Implementable requirements

Functional requirements must be written in such a way that they can be implemented in the new software. If you cannot devise a way to verify that a software product can implement a specific requirement, that requirement should be revised or removed altogether.

---

*Requirements must be written
so they can be implemented.*

It is best practice to include an example of how the requirement might be implemented. If you find you are unable to write such an example, you have probably written the requirement at too high a level and need to break it down into requirements that are more detailed.

If requirements are not implementable, when the selected software is being implemented, the organization will find that what is needed cannot be done and workarounds must be developed. That is when the implementation schedule starts to slip. If the schedule slips too far, certain things are left undone and that is what creates excessive disruption when the software goes live.

Other characteristics

Acronyms and jargon

Acronyms save space when writing, but can be difficult for outsiders to follow. Reduce the use of acronyms, or at least make them into links that point to explanations of what they mean. Wikipedia is a useful source of explanations for industry specific acronyms.

Since requirements will be going to vendors in the form of RFIs, ensure they do not contain organizational acronyms or jargon. People outside the organization will not know what those things mean.

Should or must?

When writing requirements, they can be phrased with the words "should" or "must." Which is the better way?

Using the word "must" implies a requirement is a showstopper, but when requirements are written authors are not concerned with their weight; they are focused on capturing the requirements. Also, in requirements specifications the weight of the requirement is captured by another field and is not determined by the text of the requirement itself. For those reasons, it is preferable to use the word "should" and avoid the word "must."

Proofreading requirements

Use a grammar checker like Grammarly to clean up text when writing requirements and it will catch the worst problems as you write. However, grammar checkers don't always catch errors like typing "you" instead of "your," so text-to-speech is and extremely useful proofreading tool. You hear what you actually wrote, and mistakes, poor phrasings and the wrong order of ideas are suddenly apparent.

There are an optimum number of words to use when writing requirements. Too few words and people don't understand the message, too many words and the message is diluted. When the computer reads your requirements aloud, you easily find those places where you have used the wrong number of words.

There are several tools that will read your text aloud. One example is if you are using Microsoft Word, customize the Quick Access toolbar to include "Speak." If you are working in a Chrome browser, you can try iSpeech.

Managing requirements

While you can start collecting requirements in spreadsheets, those spreadsheets are simply too manual to handle even moderately sized enterprise evaluations (See: Spreadsheet limitations on page 158). Consider using tools specifically designed for managing requirements (See: Software selection tools on page 157).

Requirement groups

Enterprise software evaluations have hundreds if not thousands of requirements. The most practical way to manage these large numbers is to organize related requirements into groups and subgroups. For example, you could put all requirements related to security in a group, and requirements related to passwords in a subgroup of security.

Depending on the software being evaluated, we find about 10 percent to 20 percent of all requirements belong to more than one group, and some requirements belong to several groups. The inability to have one requirement in multiple groups is one of the limitations of using spreadsheets for software evaluations (See: Spreadsheet limitations on page 158).

Naming and organizing groups

Best practice is to give each group a name, a default weight of 1.0 and a description of what type of requirements should be in that group. Descriptions also provide a place for recording the names of users responsible for the specific areas of the business that correspond to that group. These names are used by the implementation team when they have questions.

Depending on the software tool used to manage requirements, groups can be nested where they can contain subgroups and sub-subgroups and so on. You can think of this structure as branches of a tree, and requirements as leaves on the branches. You could also think of them as a Windows folder and file structure, where each requirement is a small file.

Alternatively, groups can be "flat" as in the example below. Flat groups are easier to manage because there is no need to expand them to see subgroups.

Example: A table of requirement groups for: Usability \Data entry

Group Name	Weight	Group Description
Usability \Data Entry	1.0	Requirements related to making data entry and editing faster and more accurate.
Usability \Data Entry \Address	1.0	Requirements related to entering addresses into the system, and using address information from the system.
Usability \Data Entry \Currency	1.0	Requirements related to using multiple currencies with the system.
Usability \Data Entry \Date and Time	1.0	Requirements related to viewing and entering dates and time values.
Usability \Data Entry \Forms	1.0	Requirements related to using forms to enter data.

Group Name	Weight	Group Description
Usability \Data Entry \Lists	1.0	Requirements related to selecting items from lists, e.g. like drop-down lists, combo boxes, pick lists, etc. Also related to editing items in list, table, grid, or view formats.
Usability \Data Entry \Numeric	1.0	Requirements related to entering numeric values.
Usability \Data Entry \Phone numbers	1.0	Requirements related to capturing phone numbers in the system.
Usability \Data Entry \Text	1.0	Requirements related to entering textual data.
Usability \Data Entry \Undelete and delete	1.0	Requirements related to deleting data, and then recovering from that deletion.

One requirement in multiple groups

Best practice is for the requirements management system to have the ability for one requirement to exist in multiple groups, for example "user inactivity timeout" could belong to both "compliance" and "user Management" groups. Collecting related requirements in groups allows duplicates to be weeded out.

Why duplicate requirements are a problem

- Duplicate requirements mean unnecessary work. For example, if the requirement is for a pop-up calendar on date fields, if every place there is a date field requirement there is also a pop-up calendar requirement, there could be many more requirements to manage.

- Duplicated requirements can be rated inconsistently. When rating a product against the same requirement in various places, that product may get different ratings. Which then, is the correct rating?

- Duplicated requirements can be implemented inconsistently. For example, requirements covering date formats could be implemented differently by two consultants working in two different areas of the software.

There are two types of duplicated requirements:

- Requirements that are copied between groups, i.e. they have the same wording. This is very common where requirement lists began in spread-sheets.

- Requirements that are the same concept but are expressed in different words. Usually these are created by different people.

How to de-duplicate requirements

De-duplicating requirements is a manual process. When related requirements are collected in groups, duplicates can be observed and these can be merged to-gether. Usually this happens all the way through the evaluation.

False duplicates

There are some requirements that might appear to belong in multiple groups, but do not. Putting such requirements in multiple groups causes errors. This is best explained with an example.

Consider the case of enterprise software that needs a mobile app to collect sig-natures. You might think this is one requirement for the iOS and Android groups, but it is actually two requirements because each OS can be rated differ-ently.

A potential software product could be rated as "fully meets" for the iPhone, but for Android could be rated as "does not meet." If that was *one requirement in two groups*, rating it as "does not meet" on Android would also rate it as "does not meet" on the iPhone, which is wrong. Such requirements must be split into indi-vidual requirements for each group.

Weight requirements for importance

Too often, RFIs (or RFPs, or RFQs) are just lists of requirements with little thought of how important those requirements are to the purchasing organiza-tion. In the absence of weights, all requirements must be treated equally. This is never accurate because some requirements are always more important than oth-ers.

To select software that will meet expectations, requirements must be weighted for importance to the organization, and that critical information comes from the users. When faced with a list of well written requirements, users can usually say how important each requirement is to them.

Weighting requirements means capturing who wants them, why they want them, and how important they are. In doing this, the organization is exploring, discovering and documenting their needs. Weighting requirements should be done by the business process owners assisted by subject matter experts if necessary. Usually this is done in team meetings.

The use of requirement weights

1. Eliminate unimportant requirements

Weighting requirements allows unimportant requirements to be eliminated, which reduces the work of evaluating products. It also creates an audit trail. Anybody can come back later and see that the requirement was considered and deemed unimportant, why this decision was taken, and who made it.

2. Auditing vendor responses

Occasionally vendors misrepresent their products in their RFI or RFP responses. Requirements with the greatest weights are audited to verify accuracy (See: How to audit an RFI on page 248).

3. Manage scope creep

Making users articulate why a requirement has a particular weight helps keep unreasonable requirements under control, and this reduces scope creep.

4. Create and nurture user buy-in

When users are the ones doing the weighting and they see their names written on the requirements and their reasons why the requirements are important, they feel the organization is listening to them. This creates and nurtures the user buy-in that is critical for a successful software launch (See: How to create and nurture user buy-in on page 124).

5. Data-driven software selection

The requirement weight factors into the fit score calculated in the gap analysis. By *measuring* how well potential products meet this comprehensive list of weighted requirements, an organization can identify the software that will work best for their specific needs.

For governmental organizations, this analytical approach can demonstrate the software was selected based on documented requirements, and not with any improper influence.

6. Software implementation

After the software is purchased, that evaluation is exported and given to the implementation team. For each requirement, the reason it is wanted and how important it is guides them. If a requirement is weighted as a showstopper far more care must be taken with implementation than if it is only weighted as important.

With the evaluation export, consultants can see why the requirement is weighted so highly. If still more information is needed to implement, the consultants have the names of the requirement owners to contact. Having this information readily available to consultants reduces implementation time and cost overruns.

7. Requirements traceability matrix

Regulated industries need the ability to trace requirements back to owners, which is captured when requirements are weighted. If a requirement does not have an owner, it should be weighted as "no interest." If any requirements later need refining, the owners of those requirements are known and can be approached for further information.

How to weight requirements for importance

The requirement weight is a measure of how important a requirement is to an organization. Best practice for weighting requirements is to gather input from business process owners, other stakeholders, and subject matter experts. With discussion, teams may weight requirements differently from individuals, and this moderates those people who feel all their requirements are showstoppers.

Typically, this means setting up a meeting in a conference room or it can be done online. Keep team sizes to less than a dozen people, and focused on their subject areas/skills. For example, the finance team weights financial requirements, the IT team weights security and usability requirements, and so on. If teams get too large, they slow down.

In requirements weighting meetings, focus on one requirement at a time, and ask attendees to weight that requirement, and give their reasons for that weight.

On the requirement itself, capture the names of the people who want it, why they want it and the weight. When multiple people have different weights, the convention is to select the greatest weight.

Requirements on wish lists can be "nice to have," but sometimes there are valid business reasons behind them. Making users articulate why they want a specific requirement helps get a more accurate weight. Requirements weighted less than "important" can be ignored when selecting software.

Whenever somebody says they do something in a particular way "because they have always done it that way," they really have no idea of why it is done that way. There may be a valid reason, but that reason must be determined. Other employees may need to be asked, experts consulted or process analysis may need to be done.

When weighting requirements, consider how important each requirement is now, and how important it will be in the next 3 to 5 years. Subject matter experts provide invaluable input here. If there are no employees with deep enough experience in specific areas, use outside help in the form of consultants.

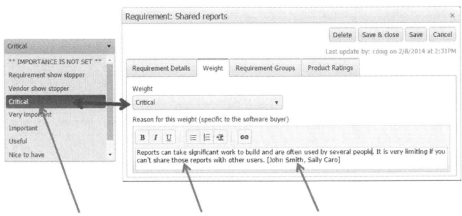

Capture HOW Important it is, WHY it's important, WHO it's important to.
(i.e. the weight)

Figure 7: Screenshot of requirement weighting

Ensure all people use the same scale when weighting requirements. Create a requirements weight chart with explanations of what each rating means (see the example below). The weight of each requirement is used to calculate a score when rating software products against that requirement.

Requirement weighting meetings go faster if there is one person managing the meeting, and a second person capturing user responses to the requirements. We budget weighting 30 requirements an hour, but that can vary tremendously.

Example: Table of requirement weights, names and descriptions

Weight	Weight Name	Description
7	Showstopper	If this requirement is inadequately satisfied, the software is automatically excluded
6	Critical	There would be significant limitations to using the software if this requirement were not adequately met. Substantial effort would be needed to work around the limitation.
5	Very important	If this requirement were not adequately met, there would be significant effort expended in working around the limitation.
4	Important	If this requirement were not adequately met, some effort would be needed to work around the limitation.
3	Future need	This requirement does not need to be satisfied as part of the implementation but is expected to be needed at some point in the next 2 - 5 years.
2	Useful	Somewhat important. If the requirement were not satisfied, there would only be a minor inconvenience in working around it.
1	Nice to have	Nice to have if this requirement is met, but nothing to worry about if it is not.
0	No interest	No need for features that satisfy this requirement, do not care if it is included or not. This weight verifies the requirement has been considered for a particular person or group, and they have no need of it.

In general, the more detailed the requirements are, the less time weightings take because the scope of each requirement is smaller. Broad requirements tend to be endlessly debated.

> *The act of deciding how important requirements are to the teams helps them fully understand their needs. In going through this exercise, several finance executives have told us that they found this process very valuable because it forced them to think through issues they otherwise would not have considered.*

A thorough requirements analysis is the critical step that helps an organization fully understand what they need. For this to be effective, the requirements must be comprehensive and cover all software usage areas in sufficient detail.

Weight requirement groups for importance

As mentioned on page 198, requirements are organized into groups. Best practice is to give each group a weight of one to start with. Once the gap analysis and the scope check are completed, group weights may be adjusted.

- Some groups, such as security requirements, are always going to be important. These groups can be given a higher weight at the start of the project.

- If it was decided there are other groups that need to be emphasized, the weights of those groups can be increased to two or three or more. If some groups need to be de-emphasized weights can be reduced to 0.5 or 0.2. This typically happens when there are several products with very similar fit scores. Adjusting group weights can separate product scores from each other.

- If it was decided to reduce the scope of the software and eliminate some requirements, rather than deleting those requirements the group weights can be set to zero. In that way, the audit trail of examining those requirements is retained. Also, if a requirement existed in multiple groups and it was deleted, it would be deleted from the other groups as well. Setting the group weight to zero avoids this problem.

If group weights are changed from the default value of one, e.g. a group weight is set to zero or two, best practice is to update the group description with the reason for that change of weight.

The requirements profile

The output of this requirements development process is a requirements profile that accurately describes the organization's specific needs in adequate detail.

This is the organization's unique reference standard and all potential software products are compared against this standard. In addition to being used for the selection, this information is also used when implementing the software (See: Implementation handover on page 272).

Key lessons

- Adequate requirements are the foundation for a successful software acquisition. They are used to select AND implement that software.

- The work of capturing requirements is always done. If requirements are missed in the analysis phase, they will be found in the implementation phase or when the software goes live. When discovered later, new requirements cause delays and increased costs. Increasing pressures on schedules cause shortcuts to be taken and work to be deferred, which causes business disruption when the software goes live.

- One goal of the analysis is to gather requirements in enough detail so that no significant new requirements are found during implementation. Use the reverse engineering technique (page 177) to discover unknown requirements.

- Another goal of writing adequate software requirements is to collect the information needed for implementation. This is why requirements must be described in enough detail to be implementable. It is always the unexpected limitations that cause problems when implementing software.

Checklist

At this point in the evaluation and selection project, the following should have been completed:

- There should be a comprehensive list of well-written requirements.

  o Requirements should have been written to be implementable.

  o Requirements should have been collected in enough detail so that no significant new requirements will be discovered during the implementation (See: Sources of requirements on page 174).

- The list of requirements should have been weighted for importance to the organization, which creates the requirements profile.

Chapter 10.   Evaluation

All major software purchases have some degree of compromise. The aim of an evaluation is to minimize that compromise by *measuring* how well potential software products meet requirements, and guide you to select the software with the smallest compromise. This is accomplished with a method of measurement called gap analysis. Gap analysis summarizes the entire evaluation into a single number, called a fit score, which measures the degree of compromise.

Although it may seem like a gross simplification, no matter how many ways you slice and dice the evaluation data, only one software product will be purchased, and usually that is the one with the highest fit score. More complex scoring systems only get in the way of that selection decision and slow the project down.

The core of this chapter is describing how a software selection decision can be made using a rigorous and objective data-driven analysis rather than with a more subjective approach. It means you can know exactly how well the software will work for your needs *before proceeding with the purchase.*

This chapter describes a method of scoring products, benefits of using vendors to gather information needed to evaluate software, and how to compare existing software with potential replacements.

The chapter concludes by describing a technique to verify the requirements scope is well matched to what the market can provide. You want to avoid buying software that does everything, but doesn't do any one thing particularly well.

A scoring system for rating products

The section Weight requirements for importance on page 201 describes how requirements should be weighted to reflect their importance to the organization. Requirements should be written as questions that can be answered by selecting a value from a drop-down list. The next step is to design the drop-down list so software products can be evaluated against the requirements.

> *To measure how well software meets requirements, those requirements must be written so a product can be rated against them by selecting a value from a drop-down list.*

Each potential software product is rated against each requirement in turn and assigned a value from the product ratings dropdown list. That value reflects how well the software meets the requirement, and rolls up into the fit score calculation. In addition, those ratings are used to plan the implementation (See: Planning the implementation schedule on page 273).

Any tool designed to evaluate software products will have this built in, however here we will examine the principles behind the scoring to explore how it works.

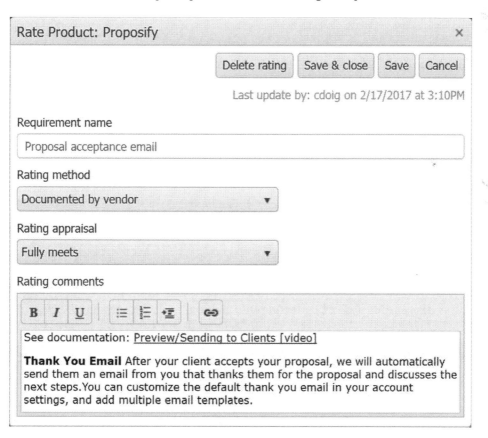

Figure 8: Example of a product rating form

Parts of a product rating

An example of a product rating form from the Wayferry software evaluation app is shown above. This information is collected every time a software product is evaluated against a requirement.

Every product rating has at least three parts to it:

1. Rating method

Describes how the rating was made, for example the salesperson mentioned the requirement was satisfied on a phone call or in an email, it was a response from an RFI or it was verified by the purchaser. This is an item selected from the rating method list (see below). This information is used when auditing a software product to verify it does perform as claimed.

2. Rating appraisal

A measure of how well a product meets a requirement. This is an item picked from the product rating list (See: The product rating appraisal list on page 212), and is used to calculate the fit score of that software product.

3. Rating comments

A rating is of little value if the source of that rating is unknown. This field captures the source of the rating information, for example a snippet of text from the user documentation. Often includes links to that documentation. This information is used if there ever are questions about the rating, for example, when auditing the RFI.

The rating method list

As your search begins, the list of potential software products is large, and in the initial stages the speed of collecting information on those products is more important than the accuracy. The aim of the process at this point is to eliminate clearly unsuitable products. However, once a software product has been provisionally selected, you want to verify the information is indeed accurate.

The key idea behind the rating method is to manage the accuracy of the information received. Having a salesperson claim "the software fully meets that requirement" in a conversation is very different from watching a training video that demonstrates how the software meets that requirement. You may even decide after watching that video that the requirement is not a "fully meets," but really is a "partly meets." For this reason, every rating appraisal has the rating method captured.

Example: Table of rating methods

Rating Method	Description
Audited	The software has been verified to meet this requirement as described by the rating appraisal. This feature has been adequately explained in user documentation, shown in a training or demo video, or it has been verified using a sandbox account.
Recent experience	The information for this rating appraisal was from a user who has recent firsthand experience with the software.
Informal test	The information for this rating appraisal was from an evaluator with a sandbox account.
Vendor detailed documentation	The information for this rating appraisal was found in product user guides, manuals, or demo videos. The information provides a detailed explanation of how the requirement is satisfied and is good enough for validation (although validation will only be done if the software is provisionally selected).
Vendor summary documentation	The information for this rating appraisal was found on product marketing web pages and claims the requirement is satisfied but provides no supporting details. This documentation is NOT good enough to validate how well the requirement is met.
Live demo	The information for this rating appraisal was adequately demonstrated, and there was ample opportunity to have questions answered.
RFI	The information for this rating appraisal was from the vendor's RFI response.
3rd party	The information for this rating appraisal was from 3rd party websites that document the features, e.g. vendor partner videos, reviews, blogs, etc.

Rating Method	Description
Verbal or email	The information for this rating appraisal was informally supplied by the vendor. It could have been in person, by phone, email, a chat session etc. and is usually from a sales or tech support person.
Presumed	The information for this rating appraisal is based on industry standards, and the product is expected to satisfy this requirement. There is no evidence that it does, but there is also no evidence the capability is missing.
Competitor	The information for this rating appraisal was from a competitor to the vendor, often as a competitive analysis.
Not mentioned	No mention of the feature(s) needed to satisfy this requirement can be found on the vendor's website or in any other vendor documentation.

The product rating appraisal list

For greater fidelity, the product ratings drop-down list should always display the rating name, and not just the weight. To ensure rating consistency and accuracy, rating descriptions must be available. When vendors respond to requirements on the RFI or RFP, they select a rating from the drop-down list. See the example below.

Example: Table of product ratings

Weight	Rating Name	Rating Description
7	Fully meets	The software adequately meets this requirement as it is supplied "out-of-the-box" without compromise. Setup or configuration may be necessary.
6	Fully meets (code)	The product can fully meet this requirement with a "reasonable" amount of code. Note: the product is designed to support these code fragments, for example a macro triggered on a certain event. It does not refer to customizing the source code of the product.
5	Fully meets (add-on)	When optional modules or 3rd party products are added to the configuration, the software adequately meets the requirement without compromise.

Weight	Rating Name	Rating Description
4	Fully meets (customize)	The software can fully meet this requirement with reasonable custom code developed by the purchaser, for example by modifying existing tables in the database or by editing product source code. Note: • Only applies where the purchaser has source code access, and never to cloud products. • You really want to avoid customizing source code because it makes future upgrades much more difficult and risky. For that reason, you may reduce the weight of this rating substantially or even make it zero.
3	Mostly meets	The software meets this requirement to a substantial extent. Deficiencies can be reasonably overcome with minimal effort.
2	Partly meets	The software has significant deficiencies in meeting this requirement, but they can be overcome with considerable effort.
1	Slightly meets	The software has the required feature, but serious deficiencies exist in the implementation that can't easily be worked around.
0.5	Future release	This feature is not currently in the product, but is planned in a future release.
0	Does not meet	Product does not meet the requirement at all, or the feature is completely missing.

Weight scales

Both requirement importance weights and product rating weights use numerical scales. These scales can be linear or logarithmic. For example:

- Linear values: 0,1,2,3,4,5,6...

- Logarithmic values: 1,2,4,8,16...

Nonlinear scales can be used to change the weight of the ratings relative to each other. They can be useful if several products have similar fit scores and you want to move the fit scores away from each other. However, we prefer linear scales because they are simpler, and are consistent between evaluations.

How product scores are calculated

The purpose of scoring is to measure how well software products meet requirements, and then rank the products so the best-fit software can be selected.

Scores are "rolled up" from the bottom and used to calculate the product's score. The requirement score is a measure of how well a potential software product meets an individual requirement, and is the lowest level of scoring. It is calculated as follows:

Requirement score = Requirement weight x product score

Requirements are collected in groups. Individual requirement scores are rolled up into group scores, and a group weight is applied. The group scores are calculated as follows:

Group score = (sum of requirement scores in group) x group weight

All group scores are rolled up into a product score, calculated as follows:

Product score = sum of all group scores

Normalized scores

The product score is an arbitrary number that can vary all over the place, depending on the number of requirements and how the requirements and groups are weighted. To make these numbers more meaningful they are normalized.

A normalized score is a score expressed on a standard scale, e.g. as a percentage. Normalized scores provide an absolute way to measure how well a product meets requirements, and a straightforward way to compare and rank software products. The normalized score is calculated by dividing a product's score by the maximum possible score and expressing the result as a percentage.

Normalized score = (Product score / Maximum possible score) x 100%

Actual and fit scores

For a better perspective, there are two ways to view product scores:

- The **actual score** is the product's normalized score measured against all requirements. Unrated requirements score zero in the calculation. The greater the number of unrated requirements, the lower the actual score.

- The **fit score** is like the actual score, but includes only rated requirements. Unrated requirements are ignored.

The fit score is a useful estimate of what the actual score might be before the product evaluation is completed. As the percentage of requirements rated increases, the fit score approaches the actual score. When a product is rated against all requirements, the fit score and the actual score are identical.

The fit score allows products to be compared before they are fully evaluated. For example, if one product has been evaluated against 65 percent of the requirements, and another product against 75 percent, they can be compared with each other even though they have been evaluated against different requirements.

If more than 90 percent of all requirements are rated, the fit score is usually accurate. However, verify that 100 percent of the showstopper and critical requirements have been rated.

For smaller software purchases where you are evaluating software yourself (as opposed to vendors responding to RFIs) the fit score is a useful measure of where the product's score is trending. For example, after rating a product against half the requirements, if the fit score is below 50 percent, you can be sure that software will not be selected. That evaluation can be halted, which reduces the total work needed on the project.

When evaluating software yourself, the fit score tends to be higher early in the evaluation, but drops significantly towards the end. The reason is that at the start of the evaluation you are focused on what the software can do. This information is easy to find because vendors like to describe their product features. At the end of the evaluation, you are discovering what the product does not do and vendors are not forthcoming with this information. This causes the "fully meets" ratings to cluster towards the start of the evaluation and the "does not meet" ratings to cluster towards the end.

Where product appraisal ratings are used

1. Fit score

Product ratings are used to calculate the fit score, which measures how well potential software products meet the requirements. This is the core of the software selection, and the most obvious use of product ratings.

2. RFI audit

Product ratings are used to audit an RFI to verify the vendor did not misrepresent their product (See: How to audit an RFI on page 248).

3. Implementation planning

Product ratings are used when planning the software implementation, which is often overlooked and is one of the major reasons why implementations usually take longer than planned (See: Planning the implementation schedule on page 273).

When rating a product, how the product meets each requirement is captured by selecting a value from a list (See: The product rating appraisal list on page 212). This information is used by the implementation project manager to estimate the time and resources needed to meet each requirement as follows:

Example: Table of product ratings and implementation tasks

Rating Name	Implementation Tasks
Fully meets	No implementation work is needed, or may require configuration. If necessary, estimate the time and resources needed to configure the software to meet this requirement.
Fully meets (code)	Estimate the time and resources needed to write the code to meet this requirement.
Fully meets (add-on)	Estimate the time and resources needed to configure the option or 3rd party product to meet this requirement. If necessary, verify the 3rd party product has been purchased.
Fully meets (customize)	Decide if customization can be avoided by re-engineering the business process. If it can, estimate the time and resources needed for re-engineering. If not, estimate the time and resources needed to customize the code.

Rating Name	Implementation Tasks
Mostly meets	
Partly meets	
Slightly meets	Estimate the time and resources needed to re-engineer the business process to work around the software's limitations.
Future release	
`Does not meet	

The implementation project manager uses the product ratings when planning the implementation project. These estimates are accurate because:

- There was an adequate requirements analysis and no significant new requirements will be found during the implementation to cause delays.

- Since requirements were written to be implementable, the project manager can accurately estimate the work needed to meet each requirement.

This level of detail captured during the product evaluation helps ensure implementations are completed on time and within the budget, and the software goes live with a minimum of business disruption.

Rating method

Software product scores are made up of numerous ratings against individual requirements. The source of this information is tracked in the rating method field, and is used to ensure the vendor is not misrepresenting their product.

For example, suppose a product was provisionally selected. If a sizeable number of showstopper requirements had been rated as "fully meets" and the source of many of those ratings was a salesperson, you would want to verify that those requirements really deserve that rating. This is auditing the evaluation, and is covered in detail in: How to audit an RFI on page 248.

The gap analysis

The gap analysis is where software products are evaluated by measuring the fit with the requirements profile, and products are ranked by fit score. While it is unnecessary to fully rate every product in the evaluation, potential winning candidates should be rated against all showstopper and critical requirements, and against about 90 percent of all requirements in total. Once the gap analysis is complete and applications are ranked by fit score, things start to get interesting.

The fit score objectively *measures* how well applications meet the requirements profile, and allows those applications to be compared and ranked. For example, take a post-merger scenario where an organization is deciding between two existing ERP applications, or if both ERP applications should be replaced.

- If both existing ERPs have a very high fit score, e.g. greater than 90 percent, then it does not matter which is selected. Both will do a decent job, and the decision is reduced to one of cost.

- If one ERP has a significantly lower fit score, e.g. less than 80 percent while the other has a high fit score of greater than 90 percent; pick the ERP with the highest score.

- If both existing ERPs have relatively low fit scores, e.g. less than 75 percent, and a replacement ERP has a high fit score greater than 90 percent, then it is probably worth selecting that replacement ERP.

- If all ERPs evaluated have relatively low fit scores, e.g. less than 75 percent, then the scope of the evaluation needs to be adjusted. Alternatively, other products that could better meet the requirements may need to be considered.

- If all applications have exceptionally low fit scores, e.g. less than 60 percent and adjusting the scope of the evaluation does not make a significant difference, then you have a prime candidate for software development.

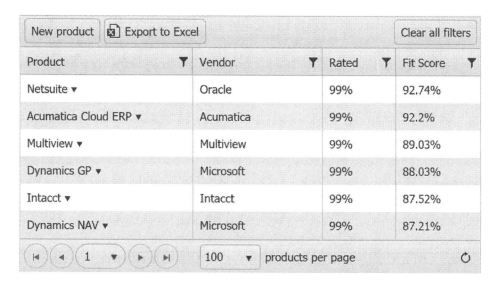

Figure 9: Gap analysis showing products ranked by fit score

Dealing with vendors

A successful implementation is a necessary part of a major software acquisition, and there are three parties involved:

1. The software vendor
2. The implementation vendor
3. The software purchaser

For smaller or more specialized software products, the implementation is often done by the software vendor themselves.

Implementation vendor conflict of interest

While there are several reasons why software implementations take longer than planned, one trap buyers fall into involves a conflict of interest, which occurs when the software implementation vendor's interest is diametrically opposed to yours. When you allow this to happen, you have set yourself up for an implementation that will take longer and cost more than expected.

The software selection trap

Software companies pay implementation vendors large sales commissions. Vendors have a strong incentive to sell you the product that maximizes their commission and implementation billing hours. While obviously they would like your project to go well because it makes them look good and can be useful marketing collateral, they have no other interest in you selecting the software that best meets your specific needs. They would rather you purchase software that was not a good fit with your needs because there is more money to be made from the implementation.

Conflict of interest

You want the software that best fits your specific needs but vendors want to sell software that maximizes sales commissions and implementation billing hours.

Solution

To help you select enterprise software, use consultants who specialize in software selection only. Avoid hiring vendors who sell, implement, or support software for the selection because you will have limited yourself to that vendor's products before the project has even started. For example, if an implementation vendor lists several ERP vendors as partners on their website, you can be sure they would recommend a product from one of those vendors because that is how they make money.

You also want to avoid consultants with vague processes and subjective opinions that are not backed up with a meaningful analysis. Instead, hire consultants who use an objective and data-driven selection process. Ask them to show you how their process works. Examine the process and verify that the output of each step is logically part of the input of the next step. There should be an obvious reason for each step; if there are steps without apparent reasons find out how they contribute to the output. Vague answers are red flags. Each step should have enough details to be actionable. A few examples of problem steps are:

- "Gather requirements" is too high-level to be actionable because it does not tell you how requirements should be gathered.

- "Gather requirements in the right level of detail." This is un-actionable because the "right level of detail" is unspecified. Requirements need to be gathered (written) in enough detail to be implementable.

- "Identify appropriate requirements in drafting the RFP." is un-actionable because there is no guidance as to what appropriate requirements are.

- "Interview users for requirements" is a necessary step, but they also need to say how they will discover requirements users don't know they need.

The hourly billing trap

When vendors are paid hourly for implementing software, the more hours they spend on the project, the more money they make. They have no incentive to work quickly. Instead, every "i" is dotted and every "t" is crossed, and they look good because they are perceived as being thorough. The implementation ultimately costs much more than planned, and any business plans that depend on the new software are delayed.

During the sales cycle, implementation vendors parade their best consultants. A common complaint is that once the project gets underway, those experts are nowhere to be seen. Instead, there are junior consultants who cost the vendor less. They work more slowly than skilled consultants do, and that increases hourly revenue. Also, these junior consultants are learning at your expense.

Conflict of interest

You want the implementation project to be on schedule and on budget. The implementation vendor is billing hourly and wants to stretch the project out as long as possible.

Solution

Pay the software implementation vendor by the project, not by the hour. Of course, the quote will be much higher than hourly billing estimates, but ask yourself how many implementations are completed as planned? The final amount paid for ERP implementations is often 50 percent or even 100 percent more than initial hourly estimates.

When implementation consultants are paid by the project their interests are aligned with yours. Both of you want the project completed as fast as possible.

The vendor will use the best consultants available. If the implementation is completed early or on time everybody wins. If the implementation takes longer than expected, at least the implementation budget is not impacted.

A note on change orders

When a vendor quotes a fixed price for a project, that vendor expects change orders to increase project revenue. Costs increase because most implementations start with an inadequate list of requirements. Instead of all significant requirements being discovered during the analysis, new requirements are found during the implementation. The vendor needs change orders to accommodate these new requirements, and implementation costs increase.

To avoid this problem, make sure you perform a thorough requirements analysis. For example, use the reverse engineering method (See: Reverse engineering on page 177) to discover unknown requirements. If you do your homework with the analysis, no new significant requirements will be found during implementation, and that minimizes change orders that increase costs.

Conclusion

To select the software that best fits your needs and to keep implementation costs within budget, avoid conflicts of interest and ensure implementation contracts are structured to align vendor interests with yours, and everybody wins.

Implementation vendor due diligence

A major software purchase usually involves an implementation vendor as well as a software vendor. Typically, the implementation vendor will respond to the RFI, do the demo, sell the software, and earn a commission from the software vendor, and then implement the software.

While software vendor due diligence is part of the software evaluation, implementation vendor due diligence is separate and is done before inviting a vendor to respond to an RFI. The only exception is when the software vendor also implements their software, which is typical of specialized or smaller software products.

You want the vendor who responds to the RFI to be the one that implements the software. You do not want to use a different vendor for implementation because there is no leverage if the first vendor misrepresented the software in the RFI or demo.

Vendor due diligence is a huge topic for procurement, and could be the subject of a complete book. However, when approaching it from the perspective of software implementation it is simpler. The purpose of due diligence is to assess the risks of dealing with vendors and factor those risks into the implementation vendor selection. From the software implementation perspective, these risks occur in several categories, for example:

- Financial
- Operational
- Legal
- Security
- References and reputation

Do not skip implementation vendor due diligence, because even large and well-respected companies can sometimes make atrocious implementation partners. For example, see the comment on IBM performance while implementing SAP for Bridgestone on page 135.

Due diligence considerations

For an implementation vendor (and for a software vendor that implements their own software) some of the things to consider are:

- Is the vendor too large? If things went wrong, would they lose interest in your project and just let things drag on?

- Is the vendor too small? If things went wrong, would they have the resources to solve the problems? Can they provide adequate support?

- Do they have sufficient experience implementing their software in your industry with companies of comparable size to yours?

- Do they have sufficient experience implementing their software? For example, if they had recently started representing NetSuite, you might not want to be their first NetSuite client.

- Will they present their "rock stars" during the demo and when closing the sale, but the actual people used on your project would be juniors without the necessary experience.

Soliciting vendor input

When enterprise software requirements are complete and defined in enough detail to be implementable, there will be hundreds or even thousands of requirements. Evaluating software against those requirements is significant work. Rather than doing that evaluation work yourself, the most effective way to proceed is to have the vendors evaluate their software against the requirements. The reasons are:

- Vendors know their products, and have ready access to the necessary information.

- Vendors will earn substantial revenue from selling and implementing the software. They are therefore prepared to do the evaluation work in the hope of landing the business.

- The evaluation work is outsourced to participating vendors rather than being done using limited internal resources.

- When RFIs or RFPs are sent out the evaluation is done by vendors working in parallel. If your organization evaluated the software, it would tend to evaluate one product after the other, which would make the evaluation take much longer.

- Provided the contract is structured correctly, it should be possible to hold vendors legally accountable to their responses to the requirements.

RFI or RFP?

Soliciting this information from vendors usually takes the form of an RFI or RFP. What is the difference between an RFI and an RFP, how do they fit into the software purchasing process, and which should be used?

An RFI collects information about a software product and vendor, and occurs in the software evaluation phase. RFIs usually include software requirements, although the level of requirement detail can vary considerably. Typically, the format of the RFI is designed so that potential products can be compared with each other. While pricing information may be requested, only guidelines are expected at this stage.

The RFP can include the purchasing organization's strategy and business objectives to help vendors frame their response. It includes everything in an RFI, and requests additional information like detailed pricing, terms and conditions, licensing terms and restrictions, contract termination conditions and so on. In addition, the RFP will usually request information to help assess the vendor, for example their strategy, history and so on. Typically, the RFP occurs when negotiating the software purchase.

When buying software, the terms RFI and RFP are often used interchangeably, but the RFP is substantially more work for the vendor and takes longer to prepare. Using an RFI is preferred because it results in faster turnaround and encourages more vendors to respond.

RFI design

If you use an online RFI product, the way the RFI is presented to the vendor is built into the product and there is nothing more to do. However, spreadsheets are still very common for RFIs. The RFI spreadsheet should have the following columns:

- ID: Allows the requirement to be identified even if the requirement name changes.

- Name: The name is used as a shorthand way to refer to requirements when people are discussing them.

- Description: This amplifies the name and removes ambiguity from the requirement. Includes general reasons why that requirement might be important.

- Importance: This describes how important the requirement is to the organization. Some people like to exclude the requirement importance, but including it provides the vendor with a better perspective for their response.

- Importance reason: This explains specific reasons why the requirement is important to the organization, which helps the vendor put the requirement in context and understand what it is getting at.

- Rating: This column is used to capture the vendor's appraisal rating for their software. It should be a drop-down list as shown in the screenshot below. This is the only input the vendor need provide for each requirement.

- Comments: Do not allow the vendor to add comments to their ratings (See: Do not allow product rating comments on page 227). Comments are used by the software purchaser for rating traceability, things like links to user documentation, reference to the vendors RFI etc.

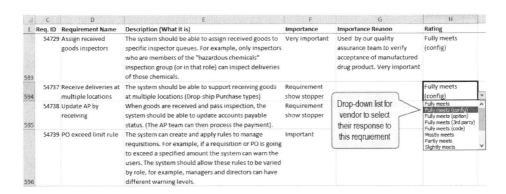

Req. ID	Requirement Name	Description (What it is)	Importance	Importance Reason	Rating
54729	Assign received goods inspectors	The system should be able to assign received goods to specific inspector queues. For example, only inspectors who are members of the "hazardous chemicals" inspection group (or in that role) can inspect deliveries of those chemicals.	Very important	Used by our quality assurance team to verify acceptance of manufactured drug product. Very important	Fully meets (config)
54737	Receive deliveries at multiple locations	The system should be able to support receiving goods at multiple locations (Drop-ship Purchase types)	Requirement show stopper		Fully meets (config)
54738	Update AP by receiving	When goods are received and pass inspection, the system should be able to update accounts payable status. (The AP team can then process the payment).	Requirement show stopper		
54739	PO exceed limit rule	The system can create and apply rules to manage requisitions. For example, if a requisition or PO is going to exceed a specified amount the system can warn the users. The system should allow these rules to be varied by role, for example, managers and directors can have different warning levels.	Important		

Drop-down list for vendor to select their response to this reqruiement

Fully meets
Fully meets (config)
Fully meets (option)
Fully meets (3rd party)
Fully meets (code)
Mostly meets
Partly meets
Slightly meets

Figure 10: Fragment of a spreadsheet RFI

Maximizing vendor responses

The primary goal of an RFI is to collect information from vendors, but because of the amount of work involved, they may decline to participate. To make matters worse, some RFIs start with this kind of discouraging preamble, quoted from a U.S. Government RFI:

> *The notice is issued solely for information and planning purposes and does not constitute a Request for Proposal or a promise to issue a Request for Proposal in the future. The RFI does not commit the Government to contract for any supply or service. The U.S. Government will not reimburse the vendor for any effort completed under this RFI.*

Responding to an RFI is significant work for vendors and it usually takes them a few weeks. Especially for smaller purchases, vendors may be reluctant to respond at all, and this can cause best-fit software to be overlooked. The key strategy is to make it as easy as possible for vendors to respond to the RFI, and to minimize the amount of work they need to do.

Make communication easy

When you make a major software purchase, you will be in a partnership with the vendor for a long time. Good partnerships start with effective communication.

Let the vendor know what is driving the project, what problem you are trying to solve, and your primary pain points. Provide enough information in terms of user counts, etc. so the vendor can supply realistic budgetary estimates. Most vendor questions can't be answered by procurement. When the vendor can speak to the person managing the software selection, they are more likely to respond to the RFI if they feel their product is a reasonable fit.

Do not allow product rating comments

When responding to an RFI, vendors should use a drop-down list to rate how well the software meets each requirement in turn. See the spreadsheet screenshot above. For an example of the drop-down list contents, see: The product rating appraisal list on page 212. The list allows the vendor to qualify their response beyond a "yes" or a "no" by selecting the appropriate value, for example "fully meets (code)" or "partly meets."

When a vendor responds to requirements, they may want to add qualifying comments. Do *not* allow this. Let the vendor know that any qualifying comments will be ignored. The reasons are as follows:

- Excluding product-rating comments significantly reduces the work a vendor must do when responding to an RFI. They are more likely to respond and their response will be faster.

- There is no way to factor qualifying comments into fit score calculations, so they cannot be used.

- Although you never want to reach that stage, if you ended up in court, you do not want the vendor using qualifying comments to escape culpability for misrepresenting their software.

- These comments are seldom thoughtful responses to the requirement. Typically, they are boilerplate text that has limited value.

The purpose of comments on product ratings is not to qualify the rating. Rather, it is to provide source information so the product rating can be verified if it is audited.

Two rounds of RFIs

Especially with smaller purchases, it can be a challenge to get vendors to respond to an RFI, and this can cause best-fit software to be overlooked. One way to resolve this is to use two rounds of RFIs:

- The first RFI includes only showstopper requirements (usually this is about 10 percent to 15 percent of all requirements).

- The second RFI includes the remaining unrated requirements.

Since there is much less work, more vendors will respond and they will take less time doing so. The second round of RFIs is sent to the top six or eight products from the first round.

Software vendor due diligence

It is too easy to be caught up in the excitement of a new purchase and not perform due diligence on vendors. This can be a big mistake, especially when buying business critical software from more specialized and smaller vendors.

> *We were helping a client select call center software. Several products looked great from a feature perspective. However, when we looked at the vendors, I was left feeling as if I was buying a second-hand car. How much do you trust a secondhand car salesperson when they glibly assure you that some noise in the vehicle is nothing to worry about? What kind of support do you get from the car dealer when you take a car back after three weeks with a major problem? It is much better to avoid getting into these situations in the first place.*

When considering a long-term relationship, what signs might suggest there are storm clouds on the horizon? Even if there is nothing underhanded or unethical about the vendor, you don't want to discover after the purchase that the vendor is not as substantial as thought. Due diligence can help avoid these problems, and best practice is to make it a standard part of the evaluation process.

Below is a partial list of due diligence requirements that can be used to get started. These can be weighted just like software requirements, and vendors can be rated against them just like software products. In other words, vendor due diligence is just another part of the evaluation.

At least five years in business with the same name. A vendor that has weathered a few years in the market has less risk. Disreputable vendors regularly change their name to escape a bad reputation. You would like the vendor to have been actively operating under the same legal name and "trading as" name for at least the past five years. To get an idea of their history, see when their website was registered. Note: this does not apply if the vendor is:

- A corporate spinoff or the result of a corporate breakup.

- A startup funded by recognizable sources like well-known venture capital groups.

Investor team. This only applies to private companies. Well-known investors add a great deal of credibility to a company. Investors who understand the business can help it, and you can judge this from perusing other companies in the investor's portfolio.

Broken links, spelling errors on the website. Use a "broken links checker" tool to test for broken links on the website, and none should be found. If there are broken links or spelling and grammatical errors, this suggests a level of sloppiness in the vendor that can extend to the product and tech support.

Poor corporate communication. Things like minimal or no postings on Twitter, no press releases page on the website, only occasional corporate blog postings, for example three or four per year. This is an indication that the vendor does not put much effort into customer communication, which can suggest a lower quality tech support experience.

Inadequate LinkedIn presence. You are looking for stability and growth. The company should have an established LinkedIn presence with a current corporate page. There should be an appropriate number of employees listed on LinkedIn, and some of them should have been with the company a reasonable length of time.

You can also search LinkedIn for people who worked at the company, but have left, and try reaching out to them. If they will talk with you they might provide invaluable insight into that vendor.

Presence on reference sites. Established companies are always listed on Hoovers.com, but companies that change their name because of a bad reputation may not be listed. Hoovers is also another way to get a company address if it is not listed on their website. The free version of Hoovers provides good basic information, and you can always purchase a detailed report.

Glassdoor reputation. Glassdoor is a place where employees anonymously rate a company. You are looking for an average rating of three out of five or higher and ratings from at least 15 to 20 employees.

If employees are not happy working for the company, you can be sure things like tech support and the product development roadmap will suffer.

Job postings on external sites. Does the vendor have any postings on public job sites like LinkedIn, indeed.com, monster.com, or the more specialist job sites? A lack of any job postings is not necessarily bad, but it does warrant further investigation.

Some active job postings suggest the vendor is growing. Note that job postings on the vendor website do not count for this requirement because they might not be real jobs. However, jobs posted on the job sites cost the vendor money, and are much more likely to represent real jobs.

Management team. Does the vendor website list their management team, along with biographies? If not, why not? What are they hiding? When researching VoIP phone services and SaaS call center software very few companies have anything about their management teams, which doesn't inspire confidence.

Management should also have their resumes on LinkedIn, and most of them should have 500+ connections. It's hard to fake this, so that lends credibility to the management team and the vendor.

Phone numbers listed. Does the vendor provide phone numbers? Have you called them, and did you get the expected response, or do you always get voicemail? You will be surprised how many smaller cloud vendors do not list a phone number. This could suggest they are more interested in your money than having you as a customer.

Street address listed. If it is, what evidence is there that the company is at that address? For example, are they listed on Google Maps, or can you see a confirmation of that address in Google street view (i.e. can you see the name of the company on a sign or building)?

Check on LinkedIn: How many employees are at that location? If very few or no employees list the corporate location as their own location on their personal LinkedIn page, you can be confident that something is not right.

Pre-sales access. Particularly for cloud software, the vendor should provide pre-sales access to the system. If they do not, how do you know it is a current product, and not still under development? Likewise, the vendor should provide pre-sales tech support so you can verify how well they respond to significant issues encountered evaluating the products, and the quality of that response.

While a low score on any one of these individual factors is not a big deal, you are looking at the overall score of the due diligence requirements group. For example, vendors that score less than 50 percent are best avoided while vendors that score more than 80 percent will have a reduced risk of problems after the purchase.

Rating enterprise software vendors against these requirements, particularly more specialized or smaller vendors, helps prevent you from buying from a vendor who is ultimately unsuitable in the long term.

Evaluating current software

Potential new software products are evaluated by vendors submitting RFIs. However, if there is a reasonable chance the existing software may be kept, that software should also be evaluated. Knowledgeable users who know the current software should rate it against the requirements.

Once the current software has been evaluated, it can be compared with other products to decide if there is sufficient justification for replacement. For example, if the current software fit score was 75 percent and the best replacement product fit score was 90 percent, it is probably worth buying new software. However, if the current software fit score was 80 percent and the best replacement software fit score was 85 percent it is probably better to stay with the current software. Note there may be other reasons for replacing the current software, e.g. it was internally developed and the company wants to get out of the software development business.

Scope check

No software product does everything and all purchases involve some degree of compromise. The aim of a software evaluation is to minimize that compromise.

Sometimes an organization has requirements that are too broad, and they want more than the market can provide. Even if the best-fit product was selected, the compromise would be too great and the organization could find they have purchased software that does many things, but is not particularly good at anything.

All software products have boundaries to their functionality. The aim of the scope check is to verify that the functional boundaries of the requirements match what the market can provide, and, if not, adjust those boundaries to minimize the amount of process re-engineering that must be done when implementing the new software.

> *We were helping a client select a clinical trials management system (CTMS). Documentation management is a critical part of the clinical trial of any drug or medical device. This client wanted the CTMS to manage documents in compliance with government rules so they could phase out their old document management system.*
>
> *All CTMS vendors said their software had basic document management features, but if the client wanted to comply with those government rules, they needed to interface the CTMS with an external document management system that was compliant. We advised the client to remove those requirements from the CTMS evaluation. After removal, the fit scores of all products rose. The client decided to continue using their old document management system, and said that it could be replaced later.*
>
> *A key part of controlling scope is expectations management. That client no longer expected their CTMS to include document management.*

The *Table of requirements scope adjustments* below describes when scope should be adjusted based on the highest scoring product on an evaluation. The first column lists the highest actual score from the evaluation. The second column lists the scope adjustment that should be done. For example, if the highest fit score on an evaluation was 76 percent, the scope of the requirements should be reduced to raise that fit score.

Table of requirements scope adjustments

Highest Actual Score	Scope adjustment	Comments
90% +	Not needed.	Success. The software meets the requirements very well.
85% - 90%	Worth checking.	Compromises will be noticed by users, but there is negligible risk of them causing project failure.
80% - 85%	Should be done. Some process re-engineering will be needed during implementation.	Compromises will be noticed by users, but there is a small risk of the compromise causing project failure.
75% - 80%	Must be done or significant process re-engineering will be needed during implementation.	Compromises will be noticed by users and occasionally get in the way of them properly doing their jobs. There is a moderate risk of the compromises causing some degree of project failure.
70% - 75%	Must be done or significant process re-engineering will be needed during implementation.	Compromises will prevent users from properly doing their jobs. There is a considerable risk of the compromise causing some degree of project failure.
Less than 70%	Must be done or significant process re-engineering will be needed during implementation.	Compromises will prevent users from properly doing their jobs. There is a very high risk of compromises causing project failure.

How does adjusting the requirements scope reduce process re-engineering during implementation? Returning to the CTMS example above, if the client had been expecting the new software to handle document management compliant with governmental rules and discovered during the implementation it did not, they would be scrambling to decide what to do.

This type of implementation hiccup would have caused a major delay with the rollout of the new software. However, because the client knew about the limit before implementation started, they had developed plans to accommodate it and it did not cause any implementation delays.

Use a heat map to manage requirements scope

The requirements scope is verified and, if necessary, reduced, using a heat map. Reducing requirements scope is best illustrated by means of the example below. The columns are as follows:

Column 1   The name of each group of requirements.

Column 2   The weight assigned to each group of requirements.

Column 3   The number of requirements in each group.

Column 4   The average actual score for each group. This column is used to verify the requirements scope.

Columns 5-10   The heatmap of the top six products on this evaluation.

Requirements Group Name	Group Weight	Reqmnts Count	Average Rating	Product: Fit Score:	OCT 88%	SBL 80%	CCE 78%	IPT 77%	BSI 71%	OPT 68%
Reports	1.0	6	75%		50%	83%	100%	100%	17%	100%
Reports \Create & Edit	1.0	8	84%		99%	99%	80%	94%	82%	48%
Reports \Defaults	1.0	21	97%		100%	100%	97%	99%	87%	96%
Reports \Defaults \Security	1.0	8	84%		98%	100%	77%	81%	79%	68%
Reports \Destinations	1.0	8	72%		100%	71%	53%	98%	47%	62%
Reports \Library	1.0	6	82%		100%	98%	75%	100%	62%	59%
Reports \Management	1.0	8	64%		100%	100%	100%	17%	0%	67%
Reports \Running	1.0	4	74%		100%	100%	78%	76%	35%	56%
Reports \Types \Charts	1.0	18	95%		100%	100%	89%	100%	100%	79%
Reports \Dashboards	1.0	12	0%		0%	0%	0%	0%	0%	0%
Reports \Dashboards \Management	1.0	8	0%		0%	0%	0%	0%	0%	0%
Reports \Tabular	1.0	15	80%		100%	100%	83%	65%	72%	57%
Reports \Usability	1.0	5	93%		100%	92%	100%	100%	100%	67%
Security	1.0	9	87%		99%	88%	63%	85%	97%	92%
Security \Access Control	1.0	5	64%		93%	29%	51%	78%	65%	66%
Security \Attacks	1.0	7	90%		99%	100%	72%	91%	91%	88%
Security \Audits	1.0	3	94%		98%	88%	100%	98%	100%	82%

Figure 11: Evaluation heatmap

In the heatmap above the shade of a cell indicates how well the requirements are met. White is a 100 percent score, while darker shades indicate lower scores. This shading allows the reader to visually compare products. The number in the cell is the actual score. Columns five to ten compare the top six products by requirements group. Column four is the average value of columns five to ten. Darker shades in column four indicate areas where the requirements are more than the market provides and scope adjustment may be needed.

As can be seen from the two rows circled above, no products support dashboard functionality. The choices are:

1. Find other products to evaluate (not always possible).

2. Reduce the scope of the requirements and use an add-on product to supply the needed dashboard functionality.

3. Re-engineer business processes to avoid the need for dashboards, e.g. use reports.

4. Develop custom dashboards with coding.

Since there are many dashboard products on the market, option two above would be the most practical solution. Thus, you would reduce the requirements scope to exclude dashboards.

Rather than deleting the dashboard requirements, you would reduce the weight to zero of the groups that contain those requirements. This prevents those groups from reducing fit scores, but preserves the information collected. You also avoid inadvertently deleting any requirements that are in more than one group.

Note

- This example has been slightly simplified to illustrate the scope reduction process.

- The actual score is used in the heatmap and not the fit score. The reason is that the fit score is only an estimate of the actual score, and would give a false heatmap picture when the percentage of requirements rated is too low.

When no products score well enough

The scope check is used to reduce the scope of the project so that requirements can be satisfied by products on the market. What happens, if after several passes at reducing scope, no potential software product has a high enough fit score?

When scope is reduced, the missing functionality is usually supplied with add-on products. An example is purchasing Coupa expense claims management to add to an otherwise very good ERP system that lacks that functionality.

A small number of add-on products are fine, especially if they have the right API interfaces. However, too many add-on products can cause problems, especially when there are inadequate APIs or problematic vendors.

Depending on what types of requirements must be satisfied, you may end up with a hodge-podge collection of add-on products and a weak core product. Under this circumstance, if the requirements not being satisfied have significant value to the business, you may want to consider building the software (See: Build or buy? on page 142).

Unsatisfied requirements

If a thorough job of reverse engineering requirements was done, you can know all significant requirements relevant to that particular problem domain have been captured (See: How to know when you have all requirements on page 185). What happens when there are valid requirements that no product being considered satisfies?

Enterprise software often has thousands of requirements, and there is always going to be some compromise. If you are proceeding with the purchase, those unmet requirements are not going to make any difference to the product selection.

However, unmet requirements may cause you to reconsider the decision to purchase. The existing software may not be that bad, and replacing it without satisfying those requirements may not deliver enough value to justify the project.

So, to answer that question, you need to estimate the ROI of the new software (See: Software ROI on page 98). You also want to avoid purchasing software that seems to do everything, but is not particularly good at anything. This happens when the best-fit software has a fit score of less than about 75 percent. To solve this problem the requirements scope must be reduced (see page 231).

Evaluating and comparing software

At the end of a selection project, only one software product will be purchased. While comparing products against requirements from many different angles can be interesting, there is always a danger of slowing the project down with endless debates about different perspectives.

In this section, we examine different ways to evaluate the result of the gap analysis. We start at the highest level of comparison, namely the fit score and then show some examples of more detailed comparisons and evaluations. Screenshots are from the Wayferry app, but the principles will apply to any tool used for software selection.

At the fit score level

The screenshot below shows several ERP and accounting products compared against the needs of a specific software buyer. Products are ranked by fit score, with NetSuite at the top. In this case, NetSuite represented the best fit with the buyer's requirements, and offered the smallest compromise. The client selected NetSuite, and they went live on schedule, as planned.

Product	Vendor	Rated	Fit Score
Netsuite ▾	Oracle	99%	92.74%
Acumatica Cloud ERP ▾	Acumatica	99%	92.2%
Multiview ▾	Multiview	99%	89.03%
Dynamics GP ▾	Microsoft	99%	88.03%
Intacct ▾	Intacct	99%	87.52%
Dynamics NAV ▾	Microsoft	99%	87.21%

New product | Export to Excel | Clear all filters

|◄ ◄ 1 ▾ ► ►| 100 ▾ products per page ↻

Figure 12: Gap analysis showing software ranked by fit score

At the heat map level

For a deeper look at the relative strengths and weaknesses of individual products, use a heat map. The idea behind the heatmap is to use color to identify the weak areas of products relative to each other, and the heat map is a very effective way of doing this. For a detailed explanation of how to use heat maps, see page 234.

At requirement group level

Before committing to purchasing software, you may want to examine the strengths and weaknesses of the selected product. For example, using the Wayferry app, the product ratings by group can be viewed on the *product ratings by group* page:

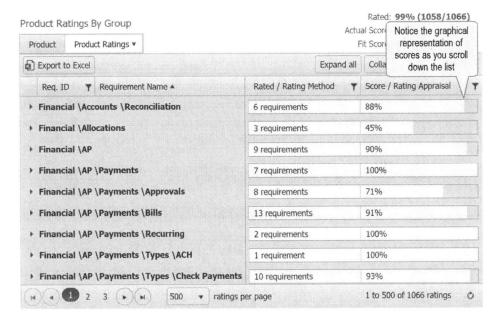

Figure 13: Screenshot of product ratings by requirements groups

- Scroll down the groups of requirements and view a graphic representation of how well the requirements are met. See the screenshot above.

- Using filters, you can examine the product from the perspective of showstopper requirements only, or from both critical and showstopper requirements. You will then see the same graphic representation of how well the requirements are met, but only for those returned by the filter.

- You can expand any group and see how the product rates for individual requirements in that group.

Requirement level product comparisons

The lowest or most detailed level of product comparison is where product ratings are compared at the individual requirement level. This is done for selected showstopper requirements only, requirements of lesser importance do not matter enough. See screenshot of Wayferry app below.

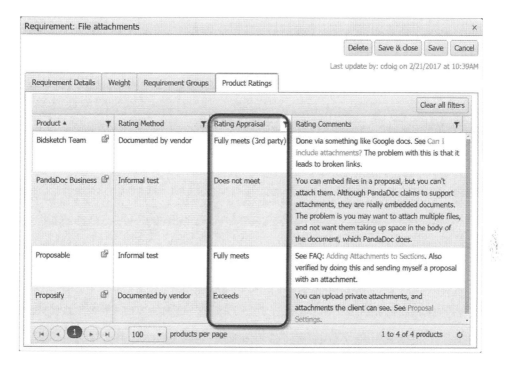

Figure 14: Comparing software products at the requirement level

When top products have similar fit scores

Assuming the top scoring products have fit scores in the high 80s or more, you are spoiled for choice. There are two ways of deciding on the best products:

- Some groups or requirements are always more important than others, and you can adjust group weights to tease fit scores apart.

- Use the demo feedback to make the product selection.

You can use either or both methods. Having this choice will place you in a strong position when negotiating contracts with software vendors.

Evaluation wrap-up

The evaluation measures how well potential products meet the requirements and the entire analysis is distilled into the fit score for each product. Because only one software product will be purchased, there is no need to slice and dice the evaluation from dozens of different angles. All those different ways of looking at the analysis can cause analysis paralysis and slow the project down.

Potential products are ranked by fit score. Typically, the top three products would be shortlisted for the demo, which takes us to the selection and purchase phase covered in the next chapter.

Key lessons

- Like the requirement weights, the product ratings scores are part of the fit score calculation.

- Product scores are normalized and expressed as percentages, where 100 percent means that a product fully meets all requirements. Normalized scores are easily compared.

- The gap analysis measures how well the potential software products meet the requirements and rolls up into the fit score, which distills the entire evaluation into one number. The fits score is a measure of the amount of compromise that must be made if that software product is purchased.

- The scope check verifies the buyer's requirements are well matched to the software features the market can provide. If there is a mismatch, e.g. the buyer wants more than the market can provide, the scope of the requirements must be reduced to bring them into alignment with products that can be purchased.

Checklist

At this point in the evaluation and selection project, the following should have been completed:

- Everything from the checklist on page 207 at the end of the requirements chapter.

- Due diligence should be completed for all potential software and implementation vendors.

- RFIs should have been submitted to potential vendors.

- The vendors should have completed and returned those RFIs and the information should have been captured in the software selection tool.

- The software selection tool should have calculated the gap analysis and ranked products by fit score.

- You will have verified the scope of the requirements is matched by software features that the market can supply.

Chapter 11.   Selection and Purchase

At this point you will have moved into the third phase of the project, namely selecting and purchasing the software. This phase opens with selecting the products on the final shortlist and then holding the software demos. Once demo feedback from the teams has been collected, the provisional software selection can be made.

It is called a provisional software selection because the product selected must go through two final checks before purchase negotiations can start. The first of these checks is an audit that verifies the vendor was not "over optimistic" with their RFI response. If the vendor misrepresented their software this step will eliminate them. The audit is followed by reference checks, including references not supplied by the vendor. Once these are out of the way you are ready to purchase.

The purchase is the contract negotiation. The larger the purchase, the greater the negotiating advantage you have, and the greater the risk you take. Be aware that software and implementation vendors are skilled at taking control of an enterprise purchase, often without buyers even realizing it. If you want to stay in control of your purchasing process, you must put in the work of a thorough selection as described in this book.

No matter how good your procurement and legal teams are, vendors have an edge over you because they are selling all day, every day. For example, vendor legal teams have spent years refining contracts to their advantage. While a whole book could be written about software contract negotiations, this chapter lays the basic groundwork.

The shortlist

The shortlist is the final, pared down list of software products that will be demonstrated before making the provisional selection decision. It consists of the highest scoring products from the gap analysis, and the optimum size is three products. If there are more than three, people will experience demo fatigue, especially for big software products like ERP where each product demo can last several days.

Three products also provide an advantage when negotiating contracts with software vendors, and there are alternatives if the provisionally selected product fails the RFI audit or reference check. However, sometimes only one or two make it onto the shortlist because the fit scores of other products are too low.

Occasionally one of the top three products from the analysis may be dropped from the shortlist, because, for example, the vendor's licensing terms might be unacceptable or the price may be too high.

Software demos

The purpose of the gap analysis is to select the product that best meets the requirements. The purpose of the demo is to confirm that selection and verify the software performs as expected.

> *The gap analysis makes the software selection decision and the demo confirms that decision.*

The demo is the fourth and last place where the selection project touches users and plays an important part in nurturing user buy-in. If the top products have very similar fit scores, user feedback from the demo can break the tie and make the selection.

The demo script

Vendors naturally want to show off their software in the best light, but the traditional "dog and pony show" does not mean much when it comes to selecting software. Skilled and charismatic salespeople are famous for creating a "reality distortion field" that can persuade the unwilling to make a purchase they later regret.

Although some may protest, most vendors like having a demo script because it tells them what the demo must show, rather than leaving them to guess. Remember that the purpose of the demo is to verify the software will perform as you expect.

How to create the demo script

The demo script must communicate to the vendor what you want to see in the demo and the approximate order you want these requirements demonstrated. To create such a script, follow these steps:

1. Create a list of all showstopper requirements. This would be exported from the system that manages your requirements.

2. Decide on the scenarios (business processes, use cases) that will be demonstrated and use these to group the requirements. For each scenario, sort the requirements into a logical order so the demo flows smoothly. You may want to prioritize the list of scenarios so that if you run out of time in the demo the most important scenarios have been covered.

3. Examine critical and other requirements related to the showstoppers. For example, it may be worth including some critical and very important requirements because they will not add significant time to the demo.

4. Estimate how long it should take to demo the requirements. If the estimated time is longer than the time available, eliminate some requirements to reduce the time necessary.

5. Send a draft version of the demo script to the selected vendors, and ask for their feedback, especially of the requirement demo timings. Give them a date when the feedback must be submitted. Use this feedback to fine tune the demo, and then send them the final script. Give them at least a few days to a week to prepare for the demo. Remember, they have other customers beside you and need to fit things into their schedule.

Planning and conducting demos

For larger products like ERP there will be several demos, where each demo concentrates on specific areas of the software. ERP demos can be spread out over several days for each product. For smaller software products, one demo is usually sufficient.

When planning demos, allow the first 15 to 30 minutes for the vendor to introduce themselves, their team, and to mention any product highlights. Vendors will do this anyway, whether you allow them the time or not. However, you need to insist they cover all the items on your demo script. Let them know they will be rated on how closely they stick to the script. The demo script focuses on showstopper requirements. If vendors avoid covering any of these, you can conclude their product is weak in those areas.

Limit individual segments of the demo to a maximum of 90 minutes. If a 3-hour demo is needed, include a 15-minute break in the middle with refreshments. If there are six hours of demos in one day, lay on a catered lunch for the attendees and give them at least an hour break in the middle, in addition to 15-minute breaks between the 90-minute sessions. Do not exceed six hours of demos in any one day – it is just too much to ask of people.

Expectations management

We have all experienced buyer's remorse when a highly anticipated purchase turned out to be a major disappointment. The same thing can happen when buying enterprise software. While the selected product may excel in most areas, it will be weak in a few places. No system is a perfect fit, and if expectations are too high, end-users will experience buyer's remorse.

Best practice for managing expectations is to make those compromises known before the demo. Remind users the decision is driven by their requirements and weights, and that the products being demonstrated are the best compromise.

One way to do this is, before the demo, email attendees a copy of the heatmap for the products being demonstrated (See the heat map on page 234). If the heatmap is printed out and given to attendees before the meeting, you can be sure the vendor will manage to acquire a copy that was left lying around! This allows attendees to see the weak areas of each product and they can prepare questions on those areas. To preserve the negotiation advantage, remind attendees that this information is confidential and should not be communicated to the vendors.

When the project team signs off against the selected product gap analysis by purchasing the software, expectations are aligned with what the software delivers. Realistic expectations help with user buy-in because nobody is unpleasantly surprised during implementation and subsequent production. Users can always go back to the evaluation to see that the selected product was indeed the best-fit for the organization, even if it is weak in a few areas. Knowing these weaknesses before the purchase helps set realistic user expectations.

Conducting the demo

When conducting the demo, ensure all users have a copy of the demo script so they know what the vendor is focused on demonstrating. The attendee version of the script need only list the high-level requirements; it does not need to go into the level of detail supplied to the vendor.

Let the vendor know how long they have for each part of the demo, and do not let them exceed this. Some presenters love the sound of their own voices and can drone on for far too long. Ensure you have somebody who can oversee the meeting and can handle problems like vendors taking too long, getting bogged down by attendees who monopolize questions and so on.

Demo feedback

It is vital that attendee feedback is collected immediately after the demo, and not left for later. People forget their impressions very quickly, and if they watch a second demo before responding to the first, they will not be able to provide valid feedback on the first product.

By this stage, the products in the demo have been thoroughly evaluated, so there should be no need to examine specific software features. Instead, you are looking for the attendee's overall impression of the software, which means the questions are relatively high level. Attendee feedback can be collected with paper forms, see: Appendix B: Questions for Software Demo Feedback on page 291. The same feedback could be collected using a smartphone app.

Individual responses to questions can be tabulated for consideration. Feedback where attendees rated the vendor or product can be averaged. This information is then considered along with the analysis when making the provisional software selection.

Provisional software selection

The software selection decision is based on the gap analysis and confirmed with feedback from the product demonstration. Usually, the software selection decision-maker and supporting team will meet to discuss the demo feedback and then make their provisional software decision.

However, let the buyer beware. It is the buyer's responsibility to verify the software being purchased really does meet requirements as expected. To do this, vendor RFI responses must be audited and customer references checked. The audit is done first because it can prompt questions that can be answered by reference customers.

Audit and validate

Ask a group of people who have played a significant part in enterprise software purchases if they have ever encountered vendors misrepresenting their software. This query will always get chuckles and a few laughs. It is common for vendors to tell their customers what those customers want to hear. It is also common for customers to be disappointed when unstated requirements are not met.

At this stage in the project, you are relying on the vendor accurately responding to requirements in the RFI, but real-world experience shows some salespeople misrepresent their software in an effort to close the deal. In all cases of RFI inaccuracies, the buyer pays the price in many ways. There are two reasons why this happens:

- **Poorly written requirements**. Salespeople always interpret unclear or ambiguous requirements in a way most favorable to their product. This is entirely reasonable; if the buyer does not make the effort to write good requirements, how can they expect salespeople to know what they really need?

- **Misrepresentation**. Some salespeople are simply too "optimistic" or aggressive when responding to RFIs.

The first problem can be remedied by writing better requirements (See: How to write good requirements on page 187).

The second problem is more insidious, and usually reveals itself when implementation dates start to slip. When requirements that can't be implemented as claimed are discovered, unplanned workarounds must be developed. The time needed to develop these workarounds causes project schedules to slip.

Alternatively, problems are discovered during user acceptance tests. Either way, by this time it is too late to do anything about the software because the purchase has been made. While you can build some protections into the purchase contract, it is far, far better to avoid the problem in the first place.

When aggressive salespeople misrepresent their software on the RFI, the audit exposes what appeared to be the best-fit software for what it really is. The audit has caught the problem *before* the purchase was made, and the organization has avoided a potential software disaster. The true best-fit software can then be selected.

> *On one ERP selection project we had sent out RFIs to potential vendors. One vendor rated almost every requirement on the RFI as "fully meets", and had a fit score of 99.8%. The request for a quote included a line that said "The purchasing decision will be based on responses to the RFI. Please describe what compensation would be offered if you claimed to fully meet a requirement in the RFI but during implementation it was discovered that this requirement was not fully met." The vendor's answer was "The RFI is our best effort to respond to the documentation the way it was presented to us, but we don't warrant any of that."*
>
> *This was such a blatant example of a vendor being "over-optimistic" with their RFI response that there was no need to even do the audit! Needless to say, that vendor did not get the business. If that RFI response was their "best effort", one shudders to think what would happen during the implementation!*

How to audit an RFI

When a software product is evaluated against a requirement, the rating method is captured (i.e. how that rating was done, see: The rating method list on page 210). Since the product has been provisionally selected for purchase, the accuracy of the product appraisal ratings must be verified to ensure the software was not misrepresented.

Select a sample of product appraisal ratings

Select all requirements weighted as "showstopper" or "critical," and that are appraised as "fully meets." Note that using the scoring system described in this book, this sample will have an actual score of 100 percent (because all requirements in the sample have been rated, the fit score is also 100 percent). The sample size should be at least 10 percent of all requirements.

Verify the product appraisal ratings

To verify the product appraisal ratings in the sample, for each requirement in turn, ask the vendor for evidence that their software does indeed meet that requirement. Use one of the three auditing methods below:

1. **Documentation audit method:** Examine user or admin documentation that describes the feature and verify that the requirement will be adequately met by the feature as described.

2. **Video audit method:** Examine demo or training videos that show how to use features and verify that the requirement will be adequately met by the feature as described.

3. **Sandbox audit method:** Use an online sandbox account to login and test the feature to verify that the requirement will be adequately met by that feature.

Using the scoring system described in this book, the sample of requirements will start with a fit score of 100 percent. For each requirement in the sample, examine the evidence to verify the software adequately meets it. If a requirement is inadequately met, reduce the rating appraisal from "fully meets" to something lower, for example "partly meets" or "does not meet."

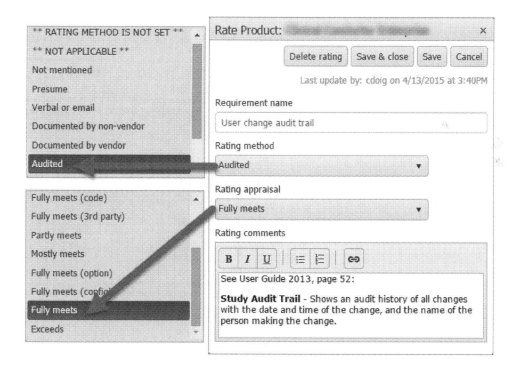

Figure 15: Screenshot of a requirement audit

After auditing the requirement, update the product rating method to "audited" as in the screenshot above. Add supporting evidence in the rating comments, for example, include a quote and a link to the source documentation. If the feature was audited using a sandbox account, include a description of the audit and the results.

The unused features problem

Sometimes vendors add features to their product to match the competition and make it easier to close a sale. While these are real features, they may never have been used by real customers and they may contain bugs or deficiencies. To detect this problem, ensure at least one third of the requirements sample is audited using the sandbox method. View the release history of the product and select recently released features for sandbox audits because they are most likely to suffer from this problem.

Adjust the product fit score

The last step of the audit is to adjust the fit score to reflect the audit findings. To do this, filter out everything except the audited product appraisal ratings. Recall that the actual score for the requirements in the audit sample was 100 percent because all requirements were fully met. The amount the actual score drops by for the sample of audited ratings is called the audit adjustment, and that adjustment is applied to the fit score of that product (See: Actual and fit scores defined on page 214).

The audit adjustment is the amount the score drops by for the sample of audited ratings.

For example, if the actual score of the audited sample was 93 percent, the audit adjustment is 7 percent. We assume that the fit score of all ratings for that product will drop by the same amount. If the product in question had a fit score of 85 percent and the audit adjustment was 7 percent, the audited fit score would drop to 78 percent.

Using the audited fit score may cause product rankings to change, particularly if the audit adjustment is more than 1 or 2 percent. If the audited fit score causes the provisionally selected product to drop several places in the ranking, that product is considered to have failed the audit. The original No. 2 product now becomes the new No. 1, and goes through the same audit process. If the audit adjustment of the original provisionally selected product was large, like 10 percent or 20 percent, you will have avoided a software failure.

> *We were helping one client select enterprise software. The gap analysis was complete and the client had shortlisted the top three vendors. This client had certain financial functionality needs that truly were showstoppers. Without those needs being satisfied there was little point in proceeding with the software purchase.*
>
> *The top two vendors both claimed to meet these requirements on their RFI responses, yet when it came to verifying, they could not show this functionality. They were immediately dropped from consideration. I asked one of the salespersons afterwards why they had claimed to meet those requirements when they did not, and he said they just wanted to get in front of the client and demo their product. This behavior was from one of the largest, top tier U.S. software companies, who are known for their aggressive selling.*

If the audit adjustment of the top product was in the 5 percent range and it caused that product to drop to second place, you may find the new No. 1 product will fare similarly after its audit, and go back to second place. You may decide to audit both products more thoroughly, or you may base your decision on demo feedback. Either way, when the audit adjustment is more than 1 or 2 percent, be prepared for an implementation that will take longer than expected.

Check references

The reference check is the last step before negotiating the purchase. It is done after the audit because occasionally an audit will raise questions that can be answered by references. The purpose of the reference check is to find out if things are not what they seem, for example:

- Confirm your selection. Is the reference's experience with the software in line with what you expect?

- Did the reference have any unexpected surprises with the implementation or early production? These are usually not things you want.

- Advance warnings of implementation problems that might be encountered so they can be factored into the plan.

- Recurring problems. For example, if every reference says that:

  o Module X is useless, if that module is important to you, you may need to examine your use of it more closely.

  o Implementation took twice as long as planned; you need to factor this into your implementation.

After each conversation with a reference you should be left feeling they are credible, their experience is relevant to your project, and that you have made the right choice with the software. Make sure you document answers to your reference questions because you will return to them.

Reference selection

When you have a choice of references, pick those that are like your organization, for example in your industry, have a similar customer base and geography (e.g. if you are multi-national, you don't want a reference that is only in your state). You also want somebody who installed the software at least six months ago and preferably not more than three years ago.

References should have a similar level of IT support to that of your organization. For example, if your IT department is about 60 people and the reference's IT department has about fifteen employees with the rest of the work outsourced, they might not be a useful reference.

You should also ask for references that no longer use the software. Why they are no longer a client can provide insight, and they will tend to be more forthcoming about their relationship with the vendor. There can be several reasons for the vendor refusing to do this, and they are all red flags.

- The vendor may not have any past clients, in which case the software may be a lot newer than expected, which can mean a lot more bugs.

- Most previous client relationships with the vendor have ended badly, and the vendor does not want you to find this out.

There are legitimate reasons for replacing software, for example an organization may have outgrown the software. Alternatively, one organization may have merged with another, there were duplicate systems, and this system was the one discarded. Whatever the reason, past clients can provide unique insights.

How to find independent references

Vendors will always supply some references, but the problem is that they have been cherry picked. They may also have been primed on how to answer your questions or even offered incentives to paint the right picture. There are two techniques to find references not supplied by the vendor: search by person, search by job, and both involve using LinkedIn.

Search by person

Search LinkedIn for people who mention the software in their profile. Verify the following:

- The person's employer is like your organization in terms of size, industry, customer base and geography.

- Examine their work history and verify they are real customers, and not former employees of the vendor.

- Verify they are at the appropriate level in the organization. For example, you probably don't want to speak to a sponsoring executive with no hands-on experience with the software, nor would you want to speak to a junior person who didn't have any project responsibility.

Then reach out to these people and ask them if they would be prepared to share their experience of the product with you. You will usually find some people who are willing to talk. You can use LinkedIn's InMail or email to contact them, or even call them up. If you need help with contacting references, speak to any competent sales person who will know how to find email addresses and phone numbers.

Search by job

Search the major job boards (including LinkedIn jobs) for companies advertising jobs for people with experience with that software. A little research using LinkedIn can uncover users at the organization, and you can try to speak with them.

Since you are considering a major software purchase, you should find some people who have used that product other than references supplied by the vendor. Too few users suggest that the vendor does not yet have enough real customers.

If the vendor left you with the impression that there are many customers and yet this research uncovered very few, the vendor was not being honest about their product. If this software is mission critical, an inadequate number of reference users could be a very good reason for avoiding that product.

Reference check setup

For larger software purchases you want to talk to several people in the organization at various levels. To ensure you are going to speak with the right people, before setting up a call verify they have appropriate titles and departments. For example, you might want to speak to:

- Somebody who is high enough in the organization for an overview.

- The project manager who oversaw the implementation.

- Users with experience in specific areas of the software.

Be respectful of the reference's time. Don't call them cold, schedule time on their calendar for the call. You have a very limited time with the reference, an hour if you are lucky. Structure the order of your questions to maximize the value of the information received from the reference.

Reference credibility

When speaking with references, do not mistake thoughtfulness for evasion. People usually take time to answer probing questions. If answers are too fast and with little thought, that is a red flag that the reference may not be credible.

Ask a few questions where you expect the answer to be critical of the software, the vendor, or the implementer. If the reference will not say anything non-trivial that is negative about them, that is another credibility red flag. If you ask a reference how implementation could have gone better and they have nothing to offer, you should be concerned. No major software implementation ever goes perfectly and there are always lessons to be learned.

Use the concept of cross questions to verify credibility: ask the same question in two (or more) different ways, and see if the answers are consistent. For example, if you asked, "Do you like X?" and they said yes, and later you asked, "Would you buy X again?" and they said no, those two answers conflict with each other, and that reduces the credibility of the reference.

For some sample reference questions see Appendix C: Questions for Software References on page 294.

Purchasing software

Once a software product has reached this stage, you are ready to purchase. The evaluation of the selected product documents and defines your expectations, and the limits and compromises of that software are known and understood by your team. You are now ready to negotiate the vendor's purchase contract. Assuming best-fit software was selected, the primary aim of negotiating a software contract is to maximize the ROI. This is achieved as follows:

- Getting a good price on license fees.

- Maintaining discounts and prices for future licensing needs, e.g. additional user licenses.

- Capping future increases in license fees.

- Removing limits designed to enhance the vendor's future revenue.

For software that will be purchased:

- Maintenance fees should be based on what was paid for the software, and not the list price.

- The purchase price should include the first year of maintenance.

- The software warranty should only start after the go-live date.

- Maintenance fees should only start after the warranty period ends.

While vendors that demonstrated their software know they are on the shortlist, you cannot let them know any more because it weakens your negotiation position. In addition, it is preferable to have a backup vendor because you can play them off against each other. Note that you only have a negotiation advantage before signing the contract. Once the contract is signed, it is the vendor who has the advantage over you.

Software contract risks

Software purchase contracts are designed to maximize extracting revenue from the customer. Software vendors have spent years perfecting them, and every time they saw an opportunity or were caught doing something unacceptable, they amended their contracts in their favor.

In a large procurement department, software purchases are but one of many items bought. The buyer's procurement and legal teams simply can't match the vendor's experience when negotiating software contracts and that puts them at a significant disadvantage.

For larger contracts involving millions of dollars, use a consultant who specializes in negotiating software license contracts. That consultant will save you much more than they will cost you.

However, if you are making a smaller enterprise purchase, there are strategies you can employ to stack the deck more in your favor. The smaller the deal and the bigger the vendor, the less negotiating advantage you have.

Typically, the vendor strategies for maximizing revenue revolve around imposing limits on the software, with the expectation that some event will cause the purchaser to exceed those limits.

Software negotiating and licensing is a huge topic, what is written here is just a small sample. The list is constantly being expanded by the vendor's creative legal and sales teams. These examples have been prompted by real situations where the vendor has used an event as an opportunity to extract more revenue from a customer.

> *Phil Downe of IT Negotiations.com shared a story about a software deal that stemmed from a divestiture. The contract allowed for re-assignment of the software to another party with the vendor's written permission, and that permission would not be unreasonably withheld. Phil was facing the vendor's VP of sales who said that he was giving written permission. But then he stated that he had never said there would not be a transfer fee, and proceeded to demand almost a million dollars! Ever since that incident Phil has required contracts to include the words "at no additional cost" even though they may appear to be redundant.*
>
> *(See: Lost clauses: What to look for in IT agreements by Phil Downe published on purchasingb2b.ca)*

1. Contractual ambiguity

Some vendors intentionally place ambiguity in their contract and then use it to increase revenue extracted during a software audit. To prevent this, the contract should contain a clause that states ambiguous terms will be resolved in the buyer's favor. After all, the vendor was the one who drafted the contract.

2. Right to business profits

Some contracts are structured to give vendors rights to business profits. The idea is that when times are tough license fees go down; when times improve they go up. Consider a variety of scenarios before agreeing to this kind of structure. The problem is that the downside is limited to the vendor, but there is no upside limit. If you do agree to it, it is wise to include caps to limit the amount of money the vendor would get.

3. Vendor entity changes

Ensure the contract protects you if the vendor is acquired by, or merges with, another vendor. Under these circumstances, the contract should allow early termination at no penalty. The contract should also have the option of continuing in its existing form for at least 24 months after the merger or acquisition so you can terminate at your convenience.

4. License transfers between entities

Some vendors force the acquiring company to re-purchase the software used by the acquired company in full. The contract should specifically state that if the company is acquired, the ownership of software licenses may be transferred to the acquiring company at no additional cost.

Along the same lines, if the company changes its name or legal structure, the contract should specifically state that software licenses may be transferred to the new entity at no additional cost. Likewise, if the company splits into two entities or spins off a division, the appropriate licenses and software can be transferred to the new entity at no additional cost.

A company in the food business acquired another food manufacturer who uses a cloud ERP system. Shortly after the acquisition closed the cloud ERP contract came up for renewal. The vendor claims that previous discounts no longer apply, and wants the new contract to be based on the combined entity, which results in much higher prices. The acquiring company is in a bind because this is cloud software, and if a deal is not negotiated, the vendor disables the ERP and production stops. This scenario is currently playing out, and it will be interesting to see if the acquiring company can find an acceptable way to move forward, or if the cloud vendor will "milk them dry."

5. Transferring licenses between users

If the licenses are specified by named users, to account for changes in staff, ensure the contract allows you to transfer licenses to new users as frequently as is needed at no additional cost. Also ensure that if you have external people like consultants or contract employees who would use the software you can transfer licenses to and from them, and that the contract does not restrict you to employees only. Note that user licenses are sometimes called "seats."

6. Parking licenses

Parking is the right to temporarily suspend support and/or maintenance of unused licenses or modules to reduce costs. The logic is that you should not have to pay for support or maintenance for licenses or software modules that are not being used.

Parking may be needed when you purchase extra licenses up front but only anticipate using them at some point in the future. Alternatively, parking may be needed when a company experiences a downturn and reduces the number of employees.

The contract should provide the right to later re-instate those parked licenses or modules. Re-activation fees should be reasonable and specified in the contract. For example, the contract should not require all the skipped support or maintenance to be paid. After all, the vendor expended no effort on those licenses or modules while they were parked.

7. Abandoning licenses

The contract should allow maintenance costs to be reduced when licenses, software modules or products are abandoned. There should be no penalty for abandoning purchased items.

Consider the case where too many user licenses were purchased at a discount on the initial contract. The contract should allow surplus licenses to be abandoned to reduce maintenance costs without triggering a maintenance increase on the licenses that remain.

The contract should not contain clauses that state that if licenses are abandoned, maintenance on the licenses that remain would be increased, for example, by being based on the list price rather than the discounted purchase price.

8. Indirect access

Indirect access to a software system occurs when somebody manipulates or views data in the system through a third-party interface. While some may argue such users are not true users of the software, there are vendors who feel differently and charge for this access. Examples of indirect access are:

- Mobile users viewing or manipulating data in the system via third-party software like an app.

- Salespeople using a CRM like Salesforce to view or edit customer master data in an ERP system.

- Customers interfacing with the system from a web front end to place and track orders.

> *SAP is an example of a vendor whose contracts may require fees for indirect access. British beverage and alcohol company, Diageo, used Salesforce to give customers and salespeople indirect access to data on their SAP ERP system. Diageo felt they were within their rights, especially because they had paid SAP a license fee to use the SAP PI integrator program, and it was their data. However, SAP felt differently and took them to court for license infringement. In a 2017 judgment, they were forced to pay almost $70 million for this indirect access.*

Indirect access is a significant area of risk exposure to software buyers. If a vendor insists on including indirect access clauses in their contract, this can dramatically increase the cost of that software. If fit scores are close enough, this clause may prompt the choice of an alternative software product.

9. Third-party access

Ensure the contract allows third-party access to the software. For example, at some point you may want to use a third-party vendor for maintenance.

Micromatic, a manufacturer of rotary actuators and automation systems located in Berne, Indiana had been using Infor's ERP software for almost 20 years. After an audit, Infor suddenly claimed that Micromatic owed them $131,000 in additional license fees for access to its software by two third-party support providers although these vendors only maintained Micromatic's computer systems, and did not use Infor's software.

In a Federal lawsuit, Micromatic asked the court for a declaratory judgment exonerating them from Infor's claims. The suit claimed that Infor's actions appeared to be part of a pattern designed to extract extra revenue from customers.

Infor then filed a lawsuit against Micromatic claiming wrongful third-party use. Also, the Infor suit argued that their software had been copied illegally and that Micromatic had allowed a contractor access to Infor's support system although this was not authorized. Infor gave their 20-year customer 15 days to resolve the problem. If the problem was not resolved Infor would terminate Micromatic's license and demand the return of the software.

(See: Infor, customer head to court over third-party system support by Chris Kanaracus, computerworld.com/article/2491689)

10. Premium support

Premium support is often needed when software starts being used, but once initial problems have been resolved and the team has become comfortable with it, support levels can be reduced. With gross margins as high as 90 percent for support, it is no wonder vendors fight tooth and nail to lock you in to pricey support contracts for as long as possible.

When support is purchased at a discount on an order, you want the right to reduce or cancel support for any product on that order without losing the discount for any other products on that same order. Beware of clauses that remove support discounts or trigger other increases when support is reduced.

Your contract should allow you to have various levels of support for various products from the same vendor. Avoid contract clauses that specify that all products from that vendor must have the same level of support. If you need premium support on one product, do you want to be forced to pay for it on all products?

11. Future terms

Some vendor contracts reference a 'Terms and Conditions' page on their website. Occasionally vendors update these pages and the changes invariably lower their risk and increase their revenue. The changes always seem to benefit the vendor and never the customer. When you are negotiating with a vendor, it is wise to avoid contracts that allow retroactive changes to the terms and conditions during the life of the contract.

> *Phil Downe of IT Negotiations.com shared a story where a vendor initially required a license for every user of the software. The purchase contract referenced the terms and conditions page on the vendor's website. Sometime later, the vendor amended the terms and conditions page to state that a license was required for every employee that could use the product. A few years into the contract, the customer wanted 100 more time and labor licenses, and was shocked to discover that to comply with the new terms they now needed to purchase another 900 licenses.*
>
> *(See: Lost clauses: What to look for in IT agreements by Phil Downe published on purchasingb2b.ca)*

12. Contract termination

All business relationships end at some time. Best practice is to ensure the contract includes reasonable clauses that govern the termination.

Say you spent several years on a cloud accounting system only to outgrow it, rather than moving historical transactions from the old system to the new, you may prefer to keep the software in an archived mode for several years without having to pay full price. It would be in your best interest to have the vendor offer an archived mode at a reasonable cost, or they could provide a standalone version of their software with your data. This issue needs to be resolved while the contract is being negotiated, and not left for the end of the contract when you have no leverage.

13. Auto renewals

Cloud contracts need to be renewed, or access to the system and data will be lost. Most vendors include a clause that automatically renews the contract for the *same term as the original term.*

A customer might have outgrown the software or want to end the relationship for another reason, and they might not notice the auto-renewal until it is too late. If your contract auto renews, you are stuck with that software for another term.

It is best practice to auto renew for no more than one year and ensure that the contract renews on the same terms.

Issues specific to software purchase contracts

14. Software maintenance

During the implementation, the organization is not getting any value from the software nor taking advantage of any new features or functionality. Software maintenance should only start when the software goes live in production, not when the software is purchased.

15. Physical location of software

Make certain the contract allows you to specify the physical location of the software, and lets you change it at no additional cost. If your organization is international, ensure the contract allows you to locate and use the software outside the U.S.

16. Software compliance audits

As software migrates to the cloud, the need for audits is reduced because vendors can see exactly what their customers are doing. However, for software in the data center or in a private cloud, software audits are an important part of the strategies and tactics vendors have developed to extract revenue from customers after the initial sale. Defense against audits starts with negotiating software contracts to mitigate future risk.

Pay attention to the vendor's rights to verify the software in use, particularly with providing them access to your systems. For example, if they can see their products they can see what other products you use, and that is information they are not entitled to have. To avoid this, the contract should specify the vendor can guide your team and provide them with input on scripts, but they may not have direct access to your systems.

The contract should have clauses that limit the vendor to collecting data about the products being audited and nothing else. These clauses should also specify the maximum duration of an audit, and how soon another audit for the same product may be conducted. Without these limits, audits can drag on until the vendor reaches their revenue extraction targets.

The complexity of software license contracts makes compliance especially challenging. Where there are conflicts between the license contracts you sign and the supporting documents the vendor considers part of the contract, the contract should include a clause that states wherever such conflicts are found, the interpretation that favors the buyer will apply.

Beware of vague license terms because vendors use them to claim you are out of compliance. Remove any vague terms from the license before you sign.

> *Oracle audited the Mars candy company. In an attempt to satisfy Oracle's demands, they provided 233,089 pages of documentation, but that was not sufficient. Eventually Mars had to file a lawsuit petitioning the court to order Oracle to scale back their audit efforts.*
>
> *The Mars complaint stated that Oracle demanded information to which it was not contractually entitled regarding servers that did not run Oracle software, and Mars personnel who did not use Oracle software. They went on to say that Oracle had falsely claimed that non-use of software nonetheless somehow constituted licensable use of software for which Mars owed Oracle. The case was settled out of court. One observer noted that if Oracle had contractual merit behind their claims, long ago they would have used a court case to send a message to their customers that they were serious about protecting their intellectual property.*
>
> *(See: What does an Oracle audit look like? This one certainly wasn't pretty on CIO.com by Katherine Noyes on cio.com/article/3024853)*

17. Unlimited backups

Ensure the contract allows you to make unlimited backup copies of the software. You do not want to have to purge backup archives just to keep under some arbitrary count.

Issues specific to cloud contracts

18. Adjusting user license counts

This problem occurs with cloud products. Most cloud vendors allow you to increase the number of user licenses at any time since they get more revenue. However, they don't offer that same flexibility if you want to reduce the number of licenses, presumably because it reduces their revenue.

- Ensure the contract allows you to increase the number of seats under the same terms as the original contract.

- Ensure the contract allows you to decrease the number of seats at the end of any month without penalty, and not force you to wait until the end of the year or contract renewal.

Some years ago, I was exploring adjusting user licenses with a sales rep from Box.com. They were quite happy to allow the number of users to go up at any time, but if I wanted to reduce the number of licenses I had to wait a year or two until the end of the current contract. The problem was this: If the company hired many temporary workers for a project that would last only a few months, they would be stuck with paying for those Box licenses until the end of the contract, even though they were not being used. That problem persuaded us not to go ahead with the purchase.

19. Physical location of data

If the physical location of your data matters, ensure the contract specifies the country or location, and that the data will not be moved without your written approval.

20. Data ownership

Make certain the contract specifies that you, and not the cloud vendor owns your data. Ensure that if the vendor is sold or files for bankruptcy, the data remains yours and may not be sold, or used in any other way.

21. Purging of old data

Make certain the contract does not allow the vendor to purge your old data without your written authorization.

Implementation contracts

Implementation contracts should be written based on business outcomes, not on milestones. Milestones could be installing an invoice module, configuring that module, passing the user acceptance testing etc. However, the desired business outcome is the ability to create a customer invoice within X minutes. It is entirely possible for a vendor to meet the milestones without achieving the desired business outcome.

> *Pet food maker Sunshine Mills of Red Bay, Alabama, purchased ERP software from Ross Systems. The company expected substantial savings from their new system, but instead had to hire additional people and deal with problems like system lockups and an inability to print invoices. Other promised functionality like a CEO dashboard that provided real-time plant data was not operational. Sunshine Mills sued Ross and won.*

Implementation scope

Fixed-price implementation contracts have the project scope tightly determined. When something new is found during the implementation, the project scope is modified with a change order. These change orders are a major source of revenue for implementation vendors and can cause costs to rise substantially.

New requirements found during the implementation are the primary cause of change orders. If a thorough requirement analysis using reverse engineering was done up front, the risk of finding significant new functional requirements during the implementation is minimized.

A technique to further reduce risk is to specify what is in and out of scope. First, list everything that is in scope on Appendix A, then list everything that is out of scope on Appendix B, and have the vendor sign off on that list as part of the contract.

The contract must specify that anything new found, which is not covered by Appendix B, is automatically assumed to be part of Appendix A and thus in scope.

License ownership

Sometimes implementation vendors do not purchase the software in the client's name, but rather in their own name. If the vendor is going to purchase licenses, specify in the contract that those licenses will be bought in your name, and verify that this is the case.

> *The U.S. Department of Labor (DOL) awarded Global Computer Enterprises Inc. (GCE) a 10-year, $50.4 million contract for Oracle Financials. Four years later GCE filed for bankruptcy. It appeared that GCE purchased the Oracle licenses for the DOL's financial systems in GCE's name. Since Oracle typically limits license transfers, it is very likely that the DOL will be forced to buy new licenses to continue operating its financial systems.*
>
> *(See: Lessons to be learned from a project nightmare by Bart Perkins: cio.com/article/2895025)*

Purchase optimization

There are several factors to take into consideration when purchasing software:

- **Purchasing too much**. The vendor made it seem that purchasing those extra licenses up front was such a good deal. After using the software for a while, you concluded this supposed cost saving was an extra expense and a waste of money because those licenses remain unused. To make it worse, you must continue paying maintenance on those licenses or lose them.

- **Purchasing too little**. Major software purchases should last 5 to 10 years or more, but you negotiated a short-term contract in case the software did not work as expected. You must repeat negotiations at the end of the initial contract, but because you are now an existing customer, you do not have your original negotiating advantage. You also left yourself vulnerable because you did not negotiate a cap on price increases for both extra licenses and extending the term of the contract.

- **Purchase timing**. To get the deal and improve their sales numbers software vendors will give their greatest concessions immediately before quarter or year-end periods close. To take advantage of these discounts you need to plan your purchasing strategy and timing. These discounts can significantly reduce software costs when taken over five years. Bear in mind that if you miss the window, you have lost the timing advantage.

For example, if your company requires the CEO sign the contract and he is out of town at that time, you have lost the concession.

- **Duplicating functionality**. When a company grows rapidly and time is much more of a constraint than money, different departments may purchase similar software products resulting in significant functional overlaps and duplicated data silos. This can be a very expensive mistake.

A while ago, I spoke to the CFO of a very successful medical device company in San Diego who assured me they did not need help with software evaluations. At a social event about three months later, I happened to be chatting informally with somebody in IT management from that same company. He described a recent spending frenzy when different departments had rushed in and bought different software products with overlapping functionality. It was now his problem to help rationalize that software and normalize the data collected. He was very frustrated with how much money the company had wasted in the process.

Why inviting software bids fails

Inviting vendors to submit their bid for a software purchase contract is popular, especially with government departments. However, the abysmal record of government software acquisitions shows this process is severely flawed. While bidding may be effective for commodity products, enterprise software is anything but a commodity.

To find best-fit software requires a lot of work for the purchasing organization, but for some strange reason many purchasers, especially in the government, either think they don't need to do that work or they don't know how to do it.

When purchasers ask vendors for bids they are assuming they will get lower prices, but invariably get lower value because they do not select the software that best meets their needs (See: Chapter 5: Select Software for Value, Not Price on page 81). Invariably there is an inadequate requirements analysis which means new requirements are found during implementation causing schedules to slip, cost to rise and business disruption when going live.

At this stage, if you've followed the process outlined in this book you will know which software product best meets requirements, has the greatest ROI and the greatest value to your organization. If you substitute bidding for the evaluation process, you are gambling with your organization's money, your job and your career.

Key lessons

- When it comes to software selection, the gap analysis makes the software selection decision, and the demo confirms that decision.

- Auditing vendor RFI responses is a powerful technique for discovering vendors that have misrepresented their software before purchase contracts are signed.

- When checking references, find references not supplied by the vendor.

- Before making reference calls, prepare a list of questions to ask. Each question should have an explanation of what that question is supposed to discover (See: Appendix C: Questions for Software References on page 294).

- Pay attention to software contract terms and clauses. Once the contract is signed all negotiating leverage is lost.

- Time your purchase to maximize negotiating leverage and get the best prices.

- Software is not a commodity product. Asking vendors to bid on a contract is one of the worst ways to purchase software and guarantees some degree of failure.

Checklist

At this point in the evaluation and selection project the following should have been completed:

- Everything from the checklist on page 240 at the end of the chapter on evaluation.

- The final shortlist will have been created. Typically, this is no more than three products.

- Demo scripts will have been created, the shortlist products demonstrated, and the feedback from those demos collated and summarized.

- One software product will have been provisionally selected. The RFI for that product will have been audited to verify the vendor did not misrepresent the software's capabilities. References will have been checked.

- If you are spending a substantial amount of money on software, you will have hired a consultant who specializes in software contract negotiation. Failing that, you will have developed a negotiation strategy.

- Finally, you would have signed the deal and purchased the software.

Chapter 12.   Post Purchase

Once the software is purchased, the project moves into Phase 4 of the evaluation and selection. This is where the information collected in the first three phases is used to prime the implementation so that the new software goes live on time, within budget and with a minimum of business disruption.

Prime implementations for success

Whether it is in the cloud or the data center, more than 90 percent of enterprise software purchases take longer to implement and cost more than planned. The same problems that caused the delays cause business disruption when going live.

Most implementation problems can be traced back to several issues that all have the same root cause. This section examines these issues and describes how to avoid them so your new software goes live on time, within budget, with minimal business disruption and meets expectations.

1. Unknown requirements

New requirements are discovered during implementation that should have been found during the analysis. When these new requirements are found, they take time to resolve.

2. Requirements that can't be implemented

A problem is caused by requirements that are not written to be implementable. Usually, this means the requirement was written at too high a level and without enough detail.

Suppose one feature desired from the new software was the ability for users to complete and sign a form on a tablet. The requirement was written as "has mobile app." When work started on that part of the implementation, it was discovered that while the software had a mobile app, that app did not include the ability to complete and sign a form. That meant new and unplanned work to resolve the problem.

3. Selecting a square peg for a round hole

All enterprise software purchases involve some degree of compromise. The goal of any evaluation is to find the software that minimizes compromise and fits the specific needs of the organization.

An inadequate requirements analysis usually means that the software selected is not the best fit for the particular needs. Making the wrong software fit, i.e. squeezing a square peg into a round hole, adds unnecessary delays to the implementation. In addition, the software will fail to meet expectations.

4. Not collecting information for implementation

While purchasing software is the obvious output of a selection project, there is another equally important but overlooked output, namely that of capturing the information needed to implement that software.

A major cause of delays during implementation is caused by consultants waiting for answers to implementation questions. When well written requirements include this information, those delays are minimized.

Root cause

These issues result in unplanned work, delays and increased implementation costs. As schedules start to slip, things get left for Phase 2 of the implementation, which causes business disruptions when going live.

The root cause of the problem in each case is an inadequate requirements analysis. Many organizations view the requirements analysis as unavoidable, but have no idea of its importance. As a result they do an inadequate job, and that leads to substantial overruns of the implementation budget.

ERP is usually the largest software purchase made by an organization. It is very rare for ERP implementations to take less than 25 percent longer than planned and schedules often slip by 50 percent or more. Some ERP implementations slip by several years. No matter what the cause of an inadequate requirements analysis, the result in all cases is the same -- the implementation takes much longer than expected. Cutting costs on the requirements analysis is a false economy.

The solution

- Requirements not found in the analysis are found during the implementation or when going live. The later in the process that they are discovered the more it will cost to satisfy them (See: Selection project costs on page 140). As part of the requirements analysis, use the process of reverse engineering (page 177) to discover all requirements, even unknown ones.

- Write requirements so they are implementable (page 197). Remember, you are not writing requirements to develop software, but you do need to write them in enough detail so the purchased software can be properly implemented.

- When weighting requirements for importance to the organization, take the opportunity to gather the information needed for implementation.

- Use a gap analysis to measure how well the software meets your requirements, and then select the software that best fits your needs. Audit the RFI of the selected software to verify the vendor did not misrepresent their product.

- If external consultants are hired to do the selection, ensure they have no financial interest in the software being selected. Best practice is to avoid using consultants who implement software because they can only recommend what they know. Rather, hire consultants who have a data-driven software selection process, e.g. ask them to show an example of their gap analysis work. If their gap analysis sample (page 218) is at too high a level (i.e. full of un-implementable requirements), do not hire them.

Implementation handover

The evaluation and selection process should have been designed to collect information that will be used by the implementation project. One of the characteristics of an adequate requirements analysis is that no significant new requirements will be found during the implementation. This means the evaluation contains a list of all significant requirements, and these requirements are written so they can be implemented.

In addition, each requirement has a rating appraisal that describes how well the selected software meets that requirement. This information is used to plan and execute the software implementation.

Planning the implementation schedule

All the information discovered and collected during the software selection is captured in the evaluation of the selected software. This information is given to the implementation project manager, who uses it to develop comprehensive and accurate project estimates. The estimation process is as follows:

1. The "fully meets" groups of requirements

    a. The project manager extracts all requirements appraised as "fully meets" and then estimates the configuration time needed to satisfy these requirements.

    b. The project manager extracts all requirements appraised as "fully meets (code)." In this case, small scripts need to be developed to meet each requirement. The project manager then estimates the time needed to develop that code for each of these individual requirements in turn.

    c. The same process is followed with "fully meets (add-on)" to identify any other modules or 3rd party software that must be bought.

2. The above process is followed with the other groups of requirement appraisals: "mostly meets," "partly meets," "slightly meets" and "does not meet." In each case the project manager repeats the "fully meets" process, and allows time for process re-engineering that will take place to accommodate the fact that the new software does not fully meet these requirements.

3. Once all time requirements have been estimated for all individual requirements, these times are factored into the implementation estimate.

While it is necessary to add estimated time for meetings, business process improvement, contingencies for unforeseen circumstances and so on, since all significant requirements should be in the evaluation, there should be no new requirements to cause delays. Also, note that the appraisal list does not include "customize" because cloud products cannot be customized; they are configured.

Even where source code could be customized, that is best avoided wherever possible because it makes upgrading that software difficult and risky.

Answering implementation consultant questions

Questions always arise during implementation. Many requirements have the reason why they are wanted and how important they are, and that should answer most questions a consultant might have about implementing that requirement.

However, if more information is needed, say, the requirement is weighted as a "showstopper" and the consultant wanted to be certain about how to configure it, the requirement has the names of the people who want it. The consultant can reach out directly to those people for an answer. Having this information readily available helps consultants to complete implementation tasks on time and within budget.

User acceptance testing

A comprehensive list of well-written requirements is the basis for creating user acceptance testing scripts. However, since user acceptance testing is firmly in the implementation domain and beyond the scope of this book, we will only touch on it briefly

Acceptance test failures

If things go wrong with a software implementation, an adequate set of requirements puts the customer in a much stronger position when trying to resolve problems with the vendor. Occasionally, software failures end up in court where the basis of the lawsuit is that the software did not meet the requirements.

To recap, an organization will develop a requirements profile, and vendors will respond to this via an RFI. The software is selected based on the RFI, but before the purchase the vendor's RFI response is audited to verify the software was not misrepresented (See: Audit and validate on page 247). The software is then purchased and implemented. One of the final steps before going live is user acceptance testing.

The user acceptance tests verify that the implemented software meets the requirements as specified in the requirements profile and as claimed in the vendor's RFI response. This means if the RFI claims "fully meets" for a requirement, the software must indeed fully meet that requirement. However, if the RFI says "does not meet" for a requirement the vendor is not expected to meet that requirement.

- If the software passes user acceptance testing against requirements and still cannot be used in production, then the requirements were at fault and the software purchaser must pay to fix the problem. They are at the vendor's mercy, and things get very expensive. The only way to avoid this problem is to develop adequate requirements in the first place.

- If the software fails user acceptance testing against requirements, the software or implementation vendor is at fault, and they must remedy the situation at their cost.

It is wise to do everything possible to avoid taking the vendor to court because no one really wins at this point. Larger vendors have extensive experience writing their contracts to defend themselves against these types of cases. Customers have little to no experience with suing software vendors, and the odds are heavily stacked against them. But if you do end up in court, an adequate requirements profile will immensely help your case.

Training

The goal of any software selection is to purchase best-fit software, and go live on time, on budget and with minimal business disruption. Although it is part of the implementation and not the selection, adequate end-user training is critical to a successful software launch.

Some years ago, Idec Pharmaceuticals (now Biogen) used Lotus Notes for email and collaboration. Although it was very popular in the life science industry at the time, most users hated Notes. It was so bad that at a company meeting in front of about 1,000 employees the CEO, Bill Rastetter, would joke about how atrocious Notes was. And it was not limited to just one joke!

At the time, I was responsible for the Lotus Notes development and admin teams. On the occasion of the next software upgrade to the latest version, there was an opportunity to ensure all employees were properly trained. We were fortunate to have the services of some very talented corporate trainers, and they managed to train 90 percent of the users.

One particularly vociferous German VP really hated Notes. After being trained, he said to the CFO that he finally understood its value. With this comment and the subsidence of user complaints, the CFO expressed the opinion that "hell has finally frozen over."

The aim of telling the above story is to emphasize how important training is to a successful software launch. There is little point in having a "perfect" software selection and implementation and then having the new software fail because of inadequate end-user training.

Key lessons

- A well-written and comprehensive set of requirements forms the basis of a software implementation that is on time, within budget, that causes minimal disruption of the business when going live and, above all, meets expectations.

- The information collected in evaluating the software against the requirements is used as a basis for estimating the duration of the implementation project. That same information is used to answer questions consultants will have during the implementation.

- Well-written requirements are the basis for user acceptance tests. They are also the basis for defending yourself if the implementation fails and you end up in court with the vendor.

- While it is really part of the implementation, adequate end-user training is essential to a successful software launch.

Chapter 13.   Selection Summary

This chapter summarizes the process steps needed to select the software that is the best fit for the particular needs. The process is also designed to collect information needed by the implementation team, and that minimizes implementation risks.

Project initiation

Before starting a software selection project, verify that it aligns with the organizational vision and business needs (See: The power of vision on page 106). Since enterprise software purchases are sizable investments, check that there is an adequate ROI (See: Software ROI on page 98).

If you are going to outsource the selection project, see Appendix A: Selecting Software Selection Consultants on page 283. If you are going to do the project yourself, you will need a tool to manage the thousands of requirements found in most enterprise software selections. See: Software selection tools on page 157.

Phase 1: Requirements analysis

1.   Meet with users

Start the project with a kickoff meeting where all users are invited. Explain the evaluation and selection process that will be used, and how their input will drive the selection. Let them know their contribution is valued, and answer any questions they might have (See: Project kick-off meeting on page 125).

2.   Interview users

Interview process owners and stakeholders to gather their requirements, and any software products they want considered. Remember that while users know requirements related to their pain points, few of them know much beyond that. Use these interviews to build rapport with the user community and other stakeholders (See: Asking users on page 175).

3. Software research

Research potential software products (See: How to find software products on page 163). When in doubt, rather include a potential product because it may be a useful source of information when reverse engineering requirements.

4. Develop requirements

Develop a comprehensive list of requirements (See: Sources of requirements on page 174). In particular, use the reverse engineering technique to discover all significant requirements, including unknowns (See: Reverse engineering on page 177).

Capture requirements in enough detail so that no significant new requirements will be found during the implementation (See: How many requirements are needed? on page 181 and How to know when you have all requirements on page 185). Ensure "obvious" requirements are included, because this information will be used by the implementation team (See: Obvious requirements on page 184).

Ensure requirements are well written (page 187), complete and verifiable (page 196), and implementable (page 197). Also, ensure that you have included software vendor due diligence requirements (page 228).

5. Weight requirements

Interview user teams to weight requirements for importance, which creates the *requirements profile*, your unique standard against which software products will be evaluated (See: How to weight requirements for importance on page 203).

For each requirement, capture who wants it, why they want it and how important it is to them. Also take the opportunity to capture any other relevant information about the requirement that would be used by implementation consultants, e.g. the requirement should be implemented in a particular way because the new system will interface to another system.

When users see their details written on requirements this nurtures buy-in and ownership of the new software (See: Creating and nurturing user buy-in on page 122). Keeping users focused on weighting requirements provides them with a framework for expressing their needs, and it also minimizes scope creep (See: Manage scope creep on page 202 and How to minimize requirements scope creep on page 186).

Phase 2: Software evaluation

6. Vendor due diligence

If third party implementation vendors will be used, perform due diligence on those vendors before sending them the RFI. You want the implementation vendor to be the one that responds to your RFI (See: Implementation vendor due diligence on page 222).

7. Solicit vendor RFI input

Use the *requirements profile* to create RFIs which are sent to vendors (See: Soliciting vendor input on page 223). Capture vendor responses to the RFI and use this information for the gap analysis (See: The gap analysis on page 218). Use the scores to rank the software by fit against your requirements.

8. Scope check

Use the scope check technique to verify that your requirements are well matched to the features of potential software products. That is how you avoid purchasing software that appears to do everything, but is not particularly good at anything (See: Scope check on page 231).

Phase 3: Selection & purchase

9. Select the final shortlist

Select up to three software products for demonstration (See: The shortlist on page 242). Usually, but not always, these are the top three ranking software products from the gap analysis.

10. Demos

Develop demo scripts based on showstopper requirements (See: The demo script on page 243). Plan and conduct the demos (see page 244). Then, capture feedback from users immediately after each demo (See: Demo feedback on page 246, and also see: Appendix B: Questions for Software Demo Feedback on page 291).

11. Provisional selection

Remember the gap analysis makes your software selection decision, and the demo confirms that decision. Based on the gap analysis and demo feedback, make your selection (See: Provisional software selection on page 246).

12. Audit and validate

Vendors can be "over-optimistic" when responding to RFIs, and salespeople sometimes even intentionally misrepresent their software's functionality in an effort to close the sale. Audit the RFI of the provisionally selected software to ensure it accurately reflects the capabilities of that software (See: How to audit an RFI on page 248).

13. Check references

References let you know how easy it was to work with the vendor and the software, and also if their expectations were met. Verify the references supplied by the vendor are in your industry and are companies of similar size to yours (See: Reference check setup on page 254).

Depending on the software, you can sometimes find independent references (See: How to find independent references on page 253) and if their answers are similar to those from the vendor supplied references, you can expect those answers to be reasonably accurate.

For sample reference questions, see: Appendix C: Questions for Software References on page 294.

14. Purchase

If the product passes the audit and reference checks, the provisional software selection decision is confirmed (See: Purchasing software on page 255). Your expectations are defined by the evaluation of the selected software, and you can proceed with the purchase knowing exactly how well your particular needs will be met.

However, you still need to negotiate the purchase. Bear in mind that when it comes to contracts, software vendors have far, far more experience than anybody on your team, and those contracts are designed to maximize their revenue (See: Software contract risks on page 255). Also see: Implementation contracts on page 265.

Phase 4: Post-purchase

15. Prime for success: the evaluation export

Once the contracts are signed, the final step of the selection project is to prime the implementation for success. The evaluation of the winning product is exported, and contains all the relevant information discovered and collected during the selection project.

The implementation project manager uses this data to prepare realistic project estimates and schedules (See: Planning the implementation schedule on page 273). In addition, well written requirements have the detail needed so implementation consultants can complete their work on schedule (See: Answering implementation consultant questions on page 274).

16. Implementation project management

For larger implementation projects, you might want a project manager to represent your interest on the implementation team (as opposed to the implementation company's project manager). At this stage of the software acquisition the software selection consultant will have an intimate knowledge of the requirements, and could be well placed to take on that role.

Conclusion

Enterprise software is very expensive. When considering the TCO over periods of 5 to 10 years, those investments are substantial fractions of annual revenue. With this amount of money at stake, failures are hideously expensive. Although organizations have been purchasing enterprise software for decades, success where that new software fully meets expectations remains surprisingly rare.

This book is designed to help solve the software purchasing problem, and boils down to this: The key to a successful software acquisition is a mature selection process. That selection process has only two goals:

1. To select the software that fits the needs like a "glove fits your hand."

2. To reduce implementation risks so the new software can go live on schedule, within budget, and with a minimum of business disruption.

If the new software meets these two goals, you have hit the ball out of the park!

To achieve this success you cannot wing it, you need a comprehensive process to evaluate and select software. This selection process must also be designed to collect critical information to reduce implementation risks.

Most organizations completely underestimate the importance of software selection, which is why success is so rare. Considering the amount of money at stake, why this happens remains a mystery (For some ideas see: Why Selecting Software is so Difficult on page 19).

However, by following the process outlined in this book you can reduce project risks and increase the probability of a successful software acquisition.

Appendix A: Selecting Software Selection Consultants

Vertical or horizontal consultants

There are two types of consulting companies that specialize in software selection:

- Vertical consultants specialize in one or a few related industry verticals. They start with a selection project, sell and implement the software and then support it going forward.

- Horizontal consultants specialize exclusively in software selection across many industries.

Which type of consultant is better for your software selection project and why?

Vertically oriented consultants

Consultants who specialize in an industry vertical tend to be a jack of all trades within that vertical. Software selection is only one part of their service offering, which may include software sales, implementation, support, and may even incorporate other services like staffing.

Because software selection is a small part of the service offering, their selection methodology tends to be immature. Instead of providing an objective data-driven analysis they tend to provide a subjective professional opinion. They usually use spreadsheets for the evaluation instead of more sophisticated tools. Their selection projects are not specifically designed to capture the critical information needed to minimize implementation risks.

Vertical consulting companies earn commissions on the software they help clients select. They have a conflict of interest between recommending the software that best meets your needs and recommending the software that earns them the most, which is why they only recommend software they sell, implement, or support.

If you select a vertical consultant you have effectively restricted your software selection to one of their products before you even start.

When it comes to the selection project itself, the interests of vertical consulting companies are not aligned with those of their customers. They tend to reduce the cost of selection projects, and treat them as a segue to lucrative implementation projects. Since a large part of their income is from implementing the software, they favor the products that are more difficult to implement because it increases their billable hours.

To see evidence of these conflicts of interest in action, query your professional network. You will find many ERP projects sold and implemented by vertically oriented consulting companies (industry specialists) but very few of the projects are completed as planned. Ask if expectations for the new software were met, and you will surely hear many tales of buyer's remorse.

Horizontally oriented consultants

Horizontal consulting companies specialize exclusively in software selection rather than in an industry vertical. Even though they work across many industries, since they focus only on the software selection, they have a much more mature selection process that delivers better results.

Horizontal consulting companies use subject matter experts familiar with your industry to ensure the nuances of your needs are captured in the selected software.

Horizontal consulting companies do not sell or implement software products so there is no conflict of interest with their recommendations. They will examine all products that could potentially meet your needs. If you select a horizontal consultant you have not restricted your software selection in any way.

Since horizontal consulting companies do not do implementations, there is no conflict of interest with finding the software that best matches your specific needs. Their methodology is designed to capture critical information that reduces implementation risks so the new software goes live as planned and meets expectations.

Consulting company size

You can hire the larger generalist consulting companies or the smaller boutique specialists. Some people feel the larger company is the safer choice because of a greater depth of experience. However, that greener grass they're sure only a big brand will deliver could be just beautifully-packaged AstroTurf. So, which is better and why?

Larger consulting companies

Larger consulting companies do much more than just software selection projects, which are one of their smaller revenue streams. As mentioned above, selection projects are often a segue to more lucrative implementation projects. Larger companies tend to be less attentive to any one customer because they have so many customers and projects.

A significant risk when dealing with large consulting firms that focus on specific industries is that proprietary information can inadvertently leak to competitors in that industry.

Although larger companies hold out the promise of more experience, often you tend to get more junior employees, especially if your company is not a large customer for them. Even large customers can get shoddy treatment (check out how IBM treated Bridgestone Tires in the example on page 135).

When you engage a larger firm you usually work with analysts, consultants, managers, or perhaps a vice president or junior partner. All of those people report to a manager who determines their career and financial rewards. Those people are more interested in making their manager happy than making you, the client, happy.

Larger consulting companies tend to be generalists, and their processes are never the best. They are slower at adopting innovative ideas and best practices than boutique consultancies, and they certainly aren't a hotbed of innovation.

Thought leaders regularly leave larger firms to form their own groups, for example Tom Peters. Other thinkers who have shaped the business environment never joined large firms in the first place, for example Peter Drucker and Stephen Covey.

Like chain restaurants, big firms may not deliver the tastiest fare, but clients think they can count on a consistent product. The real problem is that with fewer than 10 percent of enterprise software acquisitions fully meeting expectations, large firms lack new thinking and seldom deliver as expected.

Boutique consulting companies

Boutique consulting companies are more responsive because of the Avis principle: they must try harder (see page 55). Responsiveness is easy to test, just witness how responsive the company is to your requests during the sales process.

With their exclusive focus on software selection, boutique consulting companies are not distracted by other projects. When you hire a boutique consulting company you are generally working with the principal or a partner. Your opinion is the sole determinant of the project's success, and your referral is like gold to that company.

Rather than being generalists in an industry vertical, boutique consultants specialize in software selection, so they are better at it, and they have more sophisticated tools and methodologies.

Boutique consultants replace traditional thinking about software selections with exciting new perspectives that actually work. They publish their thought leadership in books, write for industry publications and speak at conferences.

It is easier to do business with boutique consulting companies. Their proposals and contracts are focused on solving your software selection problem. Contracts with larger companies have pages of dense legalese designed to protect them when things go wrong. And when issues arise, boutique consultants will not avoid or ignore you, but will work with you to resolve them.

Sometimes "good enough" consulting is all you need, but not when it comes to major enterprise software selections. It can pay handsome dividends to work with a consultant who is a software selection thought leader and who has the processes and tools to provide best in class service. Far too many companies do not appreciate the risk of mediocrity, and this shows in their mediocre bottom lines.

Pricing structure

With software selection projects you can pay consultants by the hour or go with a fixed fee for the project. Which pricing structure is better and why?

Hourly billing

Hourly fees do not align the two parties in the selection project contract. To keep costs down, the software buyer wants the selection project to finish as fast as possible. However, the consulting company wants to maximize their billable hours and have the project take as long as possible.

With hourly billing, it is more profitable for the consulting company to use its most inexperienced consultants because they pay them less per hour. Those junior consultants also take longer to do the work, meaning more billable hours.

When quoting hourly rates, consultants tend to understate costs to win the project. This makes them look cheaper, but there is absolutely no risk to them because when the project takes longer they score more billable hours. And, of course, it is you paying for those hours.

Fixed fees

Fixed-fee projects align the consulting company with the client because both parties want the project completed as fast as possible. To complete the work sooner, the consulting company will use the most experienced consultants available, rather than the junior consultants that would be used on an hourly project. In addition, more experienced consultant save the client money by steering them away from wrong decisions.

Fixed-fee quotes are higher than hourly quotes because the consulting company is taking all the risk of projects exceeding the planned schedule. However, if the project takes longer than expected, there is no impact on your budget.

Questions for software selection consultants

Do you sell, implement, or support any software products?

When considering software selection consultants, you want to avoid those with a stake in the software purchase. Specifically, this means avoiding consultants who sell, implement, or support software because they will invariably recommend one of their products. If you choose such a consultant, without realizing it, you have limited yourself to one of their products.

Will you please explain each step of your evaluation process, how it works and how each step contributes to selecting the best software for my needs?

They need to explain each step in their process, along with how and why it works, and how it contributes to a successful selection outcome. You are looking for processes that contain un-actionable steps, those steps where there is no way to tell if you have completed them properly. For example, if they have a step like "choose the selection committee wisely," ask how you can know if you have done this step properly. If you find such un-actionable steps, that is a red flag and their entire process is questionable.

Do you have a web page that describes your selection process, and can you send me a link to it?

When you read this page, it should articulate how your needs will be identified and how the software will be selected. You will be surprised at how often the page is written at such an elevated level that it tells you very little about the process, and that is a red flag.

Software evaluations can contain thousands of requirements. How do you manage these requirements?

You want to avoid consultants who use spreadsheets because those spreadsheets cannot scale up to handle the number of requirements found in enterprise software evaluations. They need to use a tool designed to manage requirements and do the gap analysis (See: Software selection tools on page 157).

How do you weight requirements for importance?

If they don't weight requirements, don't use this company to select your enterprise software (See: The use of requirement weights on page 202). Find out if they use a 2- or 3-point scale, or is the scale more comprehensive? A more comprehensive scale is better, up to about 7 points (because this information is used by the implementation consultants). Find out if they capture who wants each requirement, and if so, why they want it and how important it is to them (See: Answering implementation consultant questions on page 274). If they are not capturing this information, they will not be able to prime the implementation team for success.

Appendix A: Selecting Software Selection Consultants

How do you find unknown requirements?

They need some process like reverse engineering (see page 177) that will identify requirements the client does not know they have.

How do you verify the scope of the proposed software project?

It is all too easy to make the scope of new software too broad and select something that does many things but doesn't do anything well. The consultant should use a gap analysis to verify requirements are well matched with the software on the market. If the scope is too broad, they should advise the client to reduce it (See: Scope check on page 231). If the consultant does not do scope checks, they have an immature software selection process.

How do you prevent scope creep?

The primary way of preventing scope creep is to have a comprehensive list of requirements, and keep users focused on weighting those requirements for importance to them (See: How to minimize requirements scope creep on page 186). Do they do this or something similar?

Do you have libraries of requirements?

Libraries of requirements substantially reduce the time needed for requirements development. A software selection consultant should have two types of libraries:

- Functional requirements, for example, what the ERP, CRM etc. software needs to do.

- Nonfunctional requirements, e.g. covering things like security, usability, legal, license, compliance, support etc. These typically apply to any enterprise software purchase.

If the consultant does not have libraries, it suggests they have an immature selection process or they have not been in the business that long.

How do you use the selection process to minimize implementation risks?

The risks to be minimized are taking too long to implement the requirements, and that the requirements are not properly satisfied. During requirement weighting interviews the selection consultants need to capture who wants the requirement, why they want it and how important it is to them. This is used to answer questions that arise during the implementation (See: Answering implementation consultant questions on page 274).

How do you create and nurture user buy-in?

> Buy-in needs to be created by involving users in the software selection project. They need to feel their input was part of the software selection. If creating buy-in is left to the implementation, it is way too late (See: Creating and nurturing user buy-in on page 122).

When vendors respond to RFIs, how do you verify they have not misrepresented their software?

> The only way to verify an RFI does not misrepresent the software is to audit that RFI (See: How to audit an RFI on page 248). They may use another name for the audit, but the concept remains the same.

Once the software has been selected, what information do you give to the implementation team?

> The selection project should be designed to collect information that will be used for the implementation (See: Implementation handover on page 272). The more information that is handed over to the implementation team, the less the risk there is of delays, cost overruns and business disruption when going live.

Appendix B: Questions for Software Demo Feedback

As mentioned on page 243, the purpose of the gap analysis is to use an objective, data-driven approach that identifies the software product that best meets requirements. The purpose of the demo is to confirm that selection and verify the software performs as expected in the eyes of employees. It is critical to gather that attendee feedback immediately after the demo.

When it comes to the demo, you are looking for the overall feedback, and thus the questions asked are at a very high level. This appendix lists the questions we have found most effective.

Feedback metadata

Capture the following information from attendees about each demo:

- Attendee names (so you can, if necessary, ask for more detail about a response).

- Name of the software product being demonstrated.

- Functional area being demonstrated (used for things like ERP demos, which may have several demo sessions spread over a few days).

- Date and time of demo.

Open-ended questions

Responses to the open-ended questions listed below provide general feedback when making the provisional product selection. They can be used as tiebreakers if two software products are evenly matched.

Likes

What did you like about [product name]?

What did you like about [implementation vendor]?

Concerns

What concerns do you have about [product name]?

What concerns do you have about [implementation vendor]?

Other comments

Do you have any other comments?

> This is an opportunity for the demo attendee to add anything else that they want to say about the product or implementation vendor.

Rating questions

The answers to the rating questions are averaged across all attendees, and provide the overall demo feedback on each product. This feedback and the gap analysis are used to make the provisional software selection.

How well did the vendor stick to the script during the demo? (Attendee selects a value from a scale – see below)

> If the vendor did not stick to the demo script this can indicate two things:
>
> - The software is not very good at handling those areas that the script covered, and the vendor did not want to highlight this weaker functionality.
>
> - If the vendor did not stick to the script, this suggests you may have trouble working with them during the implementation.
>
> A low rating for the demo script may suggest that this is not the software/implementation vendor you want to proceed with.

Based on today's presentation, would you like to see [product name] selected? (Attendee selects a value from a scale – see below)

> This rating reflects the demo attendee's subjective rating for the product that was demonstrated.

Based on today's presentation, do you feel comfortable that [implementation vendor] could handle implementing the proposed software? (Attendee selects a value from a scale – see below)

> This rating reflects the demo attendee's subjective rating for the vendor that demonstrated the product.

Rating scale

For each rating question above, ask demo attendees to respond by selecting a value from a rating scale, like the example below.

Based on today's presentation, would you like to see [product name] selected? Select a numerical value from the scale below:							
No	0	1	2	3	4	5	Yes

Collecting demo feedback

Remember that it is vital to collect feedback from attendees while the demo is fresh in their mind.

Attendees can respond to paper based surveys that should be collected before they leave the demo venue. Alternatively, surveys can be done using an online survey product like surveymonkey.com. Online surveys make collecting and tabulating results much faster and easier than using paper. They also allow you to set a deadline for responses to be submitted by.

Summarizing demo feedback

Individual responses to open-ended questions are tabulated for consideration. Feedback where attendees rated the vendor or product is averaged. If the feedback was on paper forms, this is usually done in a spreadsheet. However, if an online survey product like surveymonkey.com is used, you will find it contains tools to analyze survey responses. Once the survey information has been collected and analyzed, this information is then considered along with the analysis when making the provisional software selection.

Appendix C: Questions for Software References

Below is a partial list of questions you can ask references. You can use them as a starting point and template for forming your own questions. Basically, it's good practice to follow the question with the reason why you are asking it and what you are trying to discover from that question. You will use this as a guide when probing deeper on any answers.

Most reference questions should be open ended requiring more than a yes or no answer. For example, instead of asking the reference if they are satisfied with the implementation, ask them to describe how the implementation went for them.

You don't have to ask all the questions on this list. Depending on who you are speaking to, some questions will not be relevant to that reference. In addition, when answering one question, a reference may provide answers to several others.

It is best practice to have the list of questions visible while speaking to the reference, and to capture the reference's answers. You can do this on-screen or you can print the list. If printing, add white space between questions so you have space to write the responses. You can also record the conversation, which helps you get through the list faster.

1. Vendor relationship questions

Did the vendor offer or give you, or your company, anything in return for being a reference?

> You are looking for conflict of interest, things that could cause the reference to give biased answers. Typically, this takes the form of gifts given to the reference personally, e.g. meals, vacations, charitable contributions made in the name of the reference, event tickets, money etc. Gifts could also be given to the reference's organization, e.g. things like reduced or eliminated maintenance fees.

How often do you get reference requests for this software?

> If they get many calls to be a reference, this could indicate that they are one of a very small number of customers who are willing to serve as references, and this may not be a good sign.

2. Purchasing questions

What other software did you consider before making the purchase, and why did you select this product?

> You want to know if they made a considered purchase decision or not. If the software was bought based on previous experience at another company without considering the fit at the new company, or if the decision-maker was "sold" on the new software, satisfaction is likely to be lower.

When did you purchase the software, and when did you go live with it?

> You do not want the purchase to be so recent there is little experience with using the software, vendor support etc. But you do not want the purchase to have occurred so long ago that they cannot recall anything useful about the implementation. Ideally, the purchase should have occurred between one and three years ago, and they should have been using the software for at least six months.

3. Implementation questions

What was your involvement with the implementation of the software?

> You want to speak to somebody who was intimately involved with the implementation and who has real experience, for example the customer's project manager. You do not want to speak to somebody with little hands on experience with the implementation, e.g. an executive sponsor.

What went well during the implementation?

> Things that went well for references are likely to go well for you. You probably do not need to devote substantial effort to these areas of the implementation project. Rather, you want to focus planning effort and resources on areas that did not go so well for references because you may have similar problems.

Appendix C: Questions for Software References

What would you do differently if you did the implementation again?

You are looking for insight that could help with your implementation.

What did you learn from the implementation that you wished you had known before starting the project?

You want to know about things that could help make your implementation better.

What was user buy-in like when the software when live? How could you have done a better job in selling the new software to the users and building buy-in?

You want to know how well the new software was received by the users, and if they took ownership of it. You also want any ideas of how you can sell the software internally to your users.

What was the implementation budget, and what was actually spent? Are there any outstanding implementation expenses you have not yet incurred?

This ratio could apply to you, or it could be worse because references chosen are likely the 'best of' examples regarding budget. For example, most ERPs are usually at least 25 percent more than budgeted.

How long did you plan for the implementation, and how long did it actually take to complete?

This is another way of asking the above question. You are really looking for an idea of how much your implementation might exceed the plan.

How much business disruption was there when you went live? Can you describe that disruption?

You want an idea of what type of disruption to expect so you can avoid it, or at least prepare for it.

How was the implementation project managed from your side as opposed to being done by the vendor's project manager?

Larger projects often need the services of a project manager to represent the client's interests on the implementation project. You also want to know what this person did, and how effective they were.

Did the implementation meet your expectations? Did anything go wrong?

Was it on time and on budget? Was there a minimum of business disruption when the new software went live? You are looking for hints that implementation plans are not realistic. You are also looking for issues that could be minimized or avoided with advanced planning.

Were you able to implement everything in the initial project, or did you have to leave some things for Phase 2 of the implementation or later?

When things slip to later, it suggests the software is more difficult to implement than expected. In addition, things left for later are a major cause of disruption when the software goes live.

What difficulties did you have with the implementation where things did not go as expected?

You are looking for issues that need to be factored into your implementation planning. For example, did interfacing to other systems take much longer than planned?

Did you do a "big bang" rollout, a phased rollout or start with a pilot project? Why did you do it this way, and what were the results? Would you do anything differently if you repeated the project?

You are looking to learn from their implementation, and you may use this to adjust your implementation. Perhaps they did a big bang rollout, and in retrospect think that a phased rollout would have been better. That insight might encourage you to do a phased rollout. Alternatively, they could say they did a pilot project, but in hindsight found it really wasn't necessary.

4. Professional services

Who was your implementation vendor, and what were they like? Would you use them again?

If there were problems with their implementation vendor, this might cause you to research your proposed implementation vendor in more depth. It is also useful to have other potential vendors that could be called on in the event of your implementation going awry.

How big was the implementation team, and what types of people were on it?

Did the implementation team include consultants, analysts, developers and project managers? Answers can help you develop the implementation plan from your perspective. If all the references give similar implementation teams sizes, and your current implementation vendor is proposing a substantially smaller team, this could suggest that the vendor is being too optimistic.

What training was provided, and what did you think of it? How much ongoing training was required?

You want to know if the training was adequate, or if it will need supplementing. You also want an idea of what will be needed in terms of ongoing training so you can ensure you have the necessary resources.

Was any customization of the software required (i.e. changes to the source code)? If so, please describe it.

You would be expecting to configure the software, but find it really needs customization to meet your requirements. If this was the case, that could cause you to reassess your purchase decision. Note:

- Customizations are best avoided because they must be redone every time the software is upgraded.

- Customization only applies where source code can be changed, as opposed to the system being configured. Multi-tenant cloud products cannot be customized because there is no access to the source code.

5. Software questions

Do you use the software yourself? What do you do with it?

You want to know if the reference's experience is firsthand or not. Firsthand experience is usually more valuable.

Did the software meet all expectations? If not, where did it fall short?

All software purchases involve some degree of compromise. You want to know what compromises they had to make, so you can assess how they might affect your organization.

What limitations have you found with the software?

No software is perfect. You want to know what limitations they found when using the software because those same limitations might affect you.

Are there parts of your process workflow where the software is inadequate? What manual processes and workarounds are followed when using the software?

This is another way of asking about limitations of the software that have been experienced in production. If any of these problems are ones that could affect you, you may want to develop workarounds.

What surprised you (either positive or negative) about the software?

Positive surprises can confirm your purchasing decision. Significant negative surprises can cause you to reassess that decision.

What lessons did you learn from implementing the software?

You are looking for information that could help your organization do a better job of the implementation. Specifically, you are looking for issues that could be avoided by better planning.

What other systems does the software interface with, and how easily were those integrations set up?

You are looking for integration difficulties so these can be factored into your implementation planning.

6. Production questions

Are you using the software in full production across your organization, is it in partial production as in a phased rollout, or is it in pilot production?

If all references are "pilot project" users, then nobody is using the software in a production environment. Do you really want the risks associated with being the first?

How many users do you have and what departments are they in?

You want to verify the reference's user base is like yours. For example, are they using the software around the world across the enterprise, in only one country, in only a few departments or are they only using it for a pilot?

How many employees are needed to manage and support the software, and what are their roles?

You want an idea of the ongoing effort your organization needs to undertake to make the best use of the software.

This applies more to larger products, e.g. where the buyer has their own software developers supporting the product. These could be help desk people, system admins, developers, managers and so on.

What new processes did you have to create to support the software in your production environment?

You want an idea of the effect the new software will have on your production environment so that you can plan for this work. For example, what needed to be done to create backups of your data in the new system?

When do you see this software being replaced?

You are not really interested in when it might be replaced, but rather you are fishing to see if the software is actually meeting the needs it was intended for, or if it failed to be what they hoped for.

7. Support questions

How good was the vendor support during implementation, and how much support did you need?

You want an idea of the quality of support provided by the software vendor, and you want to estimate how much support you might need.

How do you get technical support?

Can you submit a ticket, phone tech support, initiate a chat session with support, or send an email?

When you had a support issue, how long did it take the vendor to respond to and close the issue?

You want an idea of the quality of the vendor's support team. When there was an urgent problem, did they respond quickly? Were smaller issues ever overlooked?

What was the attitude of tech support? Was it friendly and helpful or cold and condescending? Could the support people relate to your users, or were there frequent misunderstandings caused by cultural issues?

You want to know what it will be like for your team to deal with the vendor's support team. Some foreign cultures are loath to say "no" and this can cause problems when dealing with users who expect direct answers. Tech support people whose native language is other than your own may cause further support problems.

If you report a problem by phone or email, do they create a ticket and email you a summary?

If they don't do this, there is no way to track issues submitted by your users.

Who resolves your support issues when they are beyond the scope of first-level support? Is it the vendor's software developers, consultants, or anybody else?

When you encounter difficult issues or bugs, you want to know that you have access to the developers in order to learn what is really going on and when you might expect a resolution. In addition, if the reference's team needed constant access to the developers, this suggests the software has a problem with bugs.

Can you log in to the software vendor's system and see all the support tickets your organization currently has open?

If you cannot see your open tickets, it is very difficult to manage the support being provided. Specifically, some issues will be forgotten and other issues will be submitted multiple times.

For cloud software: How often does the vendor push changes into production? Do they give you enough notice of these changes, and enough information about them?

For cloud software three or four updates per year is about right. More frequent updates can be too distracting. Much less than that, and the changes tend to be bigger and more disruptive.

If there is not enough notice of changes, and the changes themselves are not documented well enough, those changes can also be disruptive to users.

8. Concluding questions

If you moved to a new company with similar needs, would you make the same purchase again? Would you use the same implementation vendor?

While references may not want to criticize the software or the vendor, this question may reveal that things did not go as well as claimed.

Appendix C: Questions for Software References

What kind of ROI were you looking for? How does the actual ROI compare to what you expected?

Even if they did not do an ROI estimate, they may have an idea of the value they are getting from using the software. You want to know how long it took to reach breakeven. For example, did the software pay for itself in six months, or will it take six years? Was the actual ROI so low that they would not make the purchase again?

Overall, how well did the software meet expectations from your organization? If expectations weren't met, where did the software fail to meet them?

If expectations were not met it could be that those expectations were not managed, or there could be real shortcomings in the software.

Is there anything we should know about the software and software vendor before we make a purchasing decision? Is there anything you wished you had known about them before starting the project?

The answer may not be direct, but you are looking for hints of potential problems.

Can you supply the names of other users of this software outside your organization who could answer our questions?

This is another way to find reference customers not supplied by the vendor.

Author Profile

Chris graduated from the University of Cape Town, South Africa with a Bachelor of Electrical Engineering degree. While at university, he founded Cirrus Technology to supply information technology products to the corporate market. The focus at Cirrus was helping companies buy the best IT products for their particular needs. Cirrus also developed custom software for companies like the local 7-Eleven franchise holder and Metal Box, a British manufacturer of food cans that serviced the local fruit industry.

In the mid-90s, Chris immigrated to the U.S. with his family. He worked at a number of companies in technical, system admin and IT management roles: Seagate, Biogen, Netflix, Boeing, Bechtel SAIC, Discovery Communications and several startups. At all of these companies, he saw the same problem occurring repeatedly: major software purchases were made with an inadequate selection process. After going into production, that software often failed to meet expectations. Having faced this same problem while in IT management roles himself, Chris realized there was a gap in the market, which led him to found Wayferry.

Initially, Wayferry was focused on creating a SaaS tool to help select software. However, after realizing that the market wanted a solution to the software purchase problem more than it wanted a tool, Chris pivoted Wayferry into a consulting company designed to help clients make successful enterprise software acquisitions. This book was written to share what he has learned over years of helping clients make successful software purchases.

You can contact Chris at cdoig@wayferry.com

One Last Thing...

If you found this book useful I'd be very grateful if you would post a short review on Amazon, especially if you can share a successful enterprise software acquisition. Your support really does make a difference. I read all reviews personally and will include the feedback in my writing.

Glossary of Terms

3PL   Third-party Logistics

Acceptance Testing   Also called, Customer Acceptance Testing. See: User Acceptance Testing (UAT).

Actual score   A number that measures how well software meets requirements. Like the fit score, the value of the actual score *is reduced by unrated requirements*. This number is normalized so that 100 percent would mean that the software fully met every requirement.

AI   Artificial Intelligence

ALM   Application Lifecycle Management

API   Application Program Interface
A way for one application to communicate with another application. Common with cloud applications.

APM   Application Performance Management

APM   Application Portfolio Management

App   Short for "software application"

ATS   Applicant Tracking System

Avis principle   Smaller companies challenging their bigger competitors try harder because they must (see page 55).

BCM   Business Continuity Management

Best-fit   Best-fit software is the product that a gap analysis shows meets the needs of the purchasing organization better than any other potential products being considered.

Glossary of Terms

BI	Business Intelligence
BPM	Business Process Management
CAD	Computer Aided Design
CAD	Computer-Assisted Dispatch Used by cities to dispatch emergency services like police, fire etc.
Change order	A change to the project scope that increases costs to the software purchaser. Usually takes the form of a change to the implementation contract.
CLM	Customer Lifecycle Management
CLM	Contract Lifecycle Management
CMMI	Capability Maturity Model Integration
CMMS	Computerized Maintenance Management System
CMS	Content Management System
Configuration	The practice of setting initial values and parameters in software so that it can be used. This ranges from things like setting up charts of accounts in an ERP system down to placing a company logo on invoices. Note that configuration settings usually survive upgrades to new versions of the software.
COTS	Commercial Off-The-Shelf software Standard software that is sold by a vendor to multiple customers without any customization.
CPM	Corporate Performance Management
CPQ	Configure, Price, Quote

Glossary of Terms

CRM	Customer Relationship Management
	Software designed to help salespeople manage the relationship with their customers, for example scheduling follow up calls etc.
CSS	Cascading Style Sheets
	A type of code used to control the layout of a web page in a browser.
CTMS	Clinical Trials Management System
CTSM	Customer Ticket Service Management
Customization	The practice of editing the source code of a software product to make it conform to the needs of the organization. Customization requires access to the source code, which is why it is limited to COTS or open-source software. The chief problem with customizing software is that those changes must be redone if the software is upgraded to the latest version.
DBMS	Database Management System
Denormalized data	The same data existing in more than one place, for example the same customer data in the CRM and accounts payable systems.
Decision latency	The time needed for a decision to be made
DMS	Document Management System (Also EDMS)
DOM	Distributed Order Management
EAM	Enterprise Asset Management
ECM	Enterprise Content Management
EDC	Electronic Data Capture
EDI	Electronic Data Interchange
EDM	Enterprise Data Management

Glossary of Terms

EDMS	Electronic Document Management System (Also DMS)
EFSS	Enterprise File Synchronization and Sharing services
EHR	Electronic Health Records
EHS	Environmental Health and Safety
EMM	Enterprise Mobile Management
EMR	Electronic Medical Records
EMS	Emergency Management System
EMS	Emergency Medical System
EMS	Energy Management System
EPM	Enterprise Performance Management
EPM	Enterprise Portfolio Management
ERM	Enterprise Risk Management
ERP	Enterprise Resource Planning
	Software designed to manage all aspects of a business. Originally, ERP started in manufacturing where it managed the product orders to delivery cycle and the financial side of the business. ERP has grown to include things like HRIS, CRM and time tracking. Today ERP is used by many industries other than manufacturing.
ETL	Extract, Transform, Load
eTMF	Electronic Trial Master File
Fit score	A number that measures how well a software product meets the requirements. Unlike the actual score, the value of the fit score is NOT reduced by unrated requirements. The fit score is an estimate of what the actual score would be, and the accuracy increases as the number of rated requirements increases. If all requirements have been rated, the actual score and the fit score

	are identical. This number is normalized so that 100 percent would mean that a product fully met every requirement.
Gap analysis	The process of measuring how well potential software products meet a specific set of requirements.
HCM	Human Capital Management
HRIS	Human Resources Information System
HRMS	Human Resources Management System
HTML	A form of code used to create web pages in browsers.
IAM	Identity and Access Management
IP	Intellectual Property For example, copyrights, patents etc.
ITSM	Information Technology Service Management
Legacy software	Software that has been on the market for many years, is outdated, uses old methods or technology, and may need replacement.
LIMS	Laboratory Information Management System
LMS	Learning Management System
MDM	Master Data Management
MMIS	Medicaid Management Information System
MRP	Materials Requirements Planning
NDA	Non-Disclosure Agreement
NPD	New Product Development
NPV	Net Present Value
Operational life	The time that the software is used in production after implementation and before retirement. For software like

	ERP you expect an operational life of at least 10 years. For other major software purchases you expect at least 5 years.
OS	Operating system For example iOS, Android, or Windows.
Out-of-the-box	An out-of-the-box feature or functionality (also called OOTB or off the shelf) is a feature or functionality of a software product that works immediately after installation without the need for any configuration or modification.
PaaS	Platform-as-a-Service
PIM	Product Information Management
PLM	Product Lifecycle Management
PMS	Patient Management Software
PMS	Project Management Software
POS	Point of Sale
PPM	Project Portfolio Management
Product appraisal rating	A measure of how well a software product meets a requirement, e.g. "fully meets" or "partly meets" etc. Sometimes abbreviated to "product rating."
PSA	Professional Services Automation
QMS	Quality Management System
Reality distortion field	The ability of a charismatic salesperson to influence a potential client (See: "Reality distortion field" in Wikipedia).
Reverse engineering	The process of examining the features of multiple potential software products and writing them as requirements.

Glossary of Terms

Requirements profile	A comprehensive list of requirements that have been weighted for importance to the organization.
RFB	Request For Bid
RFI	Request For Information Typically used to assess how well a software product meets requirements.
RFI response	An RFI where a vendor has evaluated how well their software meets the requirements on that RFI.
RFP	Request For Proposal
RFQ	Request For Quote
RFx	Request For something: information, proposal, quote, bid etc.
ROA	Return On Assets
ROI	Return On Investment
RTIM	Real-Time Interaction Management
SaaS	Software-as-a-Service Another name for software in the cloud.
SAM	Software Asset Management
SCM	Supply Chain Management
Sandbox account	A user account set up to allow a potential customer to examine a software product in detail. This is quite common with cloud software products.
Seat	A software license for one person
SFA	Sales Force Automation
SIEM	Security Information and Event Management

Glossary of Terms

SME	Subject Matter Expert A person well versed with the type of software being considered, and the business domain in which that software operates. Typically, this person will have been through several implementations of different software products that involve their area of expertise. A key role for the subject matter expert is to help the organization think through scenarios they might not otherwise consider when weighting requirements.
Software agreement	The same as a software contract. To be consistent, this book uses the term software contract for all software agreements.
Software application	Another name for a software product. May be abbreviated to "app"
SOP	Standard Operating Procedure
SRM	Supplier Relationship Management
SSMS	Software Selection Maturity Scale A measure of software evaluation and selection process maturity.
TAMS	Track Access Management System
TCO	Total Cost of Ownership
Technical debt	Updating software takes time and money. When many updates to a software product are skipped, the costs of doing an upgrade to the latest version of that product will be substantially higher. That extra cost is called the technical debt.
TMS	Transportation Management System
Traceability matrix	A document that can trace all requirements back to who wants them, why they are wanted and how important they are to those people.

Glossary of Terms

UI	User Interface
UAT	User acceptance testing
	UAT is the last set of tests before going live with the software. Here the people who will use the software verify that it can handle the required tasks they need to do in their jobs. Sometimes called Customer Acceptance Testing.
VM	Virtual Machine
VMS	Vendor Management System
	An application (usually on the web) used to manage and procure staffing services like temps, contingent labor and outside contractors.
VNA	Vendor Neutral Archive
VoIP	Voice-over-IP
	A form of telephony that uses the internet instead of dedicated phone circuits.
WCM	Web Content Management
WCS	Warehouse Control System
WEM	Workforce Engagement Management
WMS	Warehouse Management System

References

Enterprise Software Selection by Shaun Snapp.

Enterprise Software TCO by Shaun Snapp.

The Executive's Guide to Consultants: How to Find, Hire and Get Great Results from Outside Experts by David Fields.

Wikipedia: Sometimes Wikipedia articles summarized terms or concepts well, and that text was used. Those summaries have been credited to Wikipedia.

Table of Figures

Index

C

D

Index

E

F

Index

G

H

I

J

P

Index

S

T

U

V

W

Y